Famous Fairways

Peter Allen

Famous Fairways

A look at the world of championship courses

 Stanley Paul, London

Stanley Paul & Co Ltd,
178–202 Great Portland Street, London W.1
An imprint of the Hutchinson Group
London Melbourne Sydney Auckland
Bombay Toronto Johannesburg New York
First published 1968 © Peter Christopher Allen
This book has been set in Garamond,
printed in Great Britain on Twin-wire offset paper by Anchor Press,
and bound by Wm. Brendon, both of Tiptree, Essex

Contents

1	*Introductory*	*page* 1
2	*The championship links of Scotland*	
	Prestwick	10
	St Andrews	12
	Musselburgh	20
	Muirfield	22
	Troon	25
	Carnoustie	27
	Turnberry	28
3	*Other Scottish courses*	
	North Inch	30
	Dornoch	31
	Western Gailes	34
	Gullane	34
	North Berwick	35
	Gleneagles	37
	Southerness-on-Solway	38
4	*Channel Coast*	
	Prince's	39
	Sandwich	40
	Deal	44
	Littlestone	49

Contents

Rye	49
Hayling Island	51
Channel Islands *La Moye, Gorey, Guernsey*	53
Bembridge	57

5 The West and Wales

Lelant	58
St Enodoc	59
Westward Ho!	60
Burnham and Berrow	63
Porthcawl	63
Aberdovey	65
Harlech	66

6 Golf in Ireland

Killarney	68
Portrush	68
Dollymount	69
The Island	70
Portmarnock	71
Newcastle	73

7 North by West

Hoylake	77
Formby	81
Wallasey	82
Birkdale	82
Southport and Ainsdale	85
Blundellsands	85
Lytham and St Annes	85
Ganton	88

8 Others in England

Felixstowe	91
Hunstanton	93
Brancaster	95
Worlington and Newmarket	97
Walton Heath	99

	Sunningdale	102
	Liphook	104
9	*Golf in America – South and West*	
	Mid Ocean	108
	Augusta National	109
	Peach Tree	113
	Sea Island	113
	Pinehurst	114
	Pacific Grove	116
	Pebble Beach	117
	Cypress Point	119
	Spyglass Hill	121
	San Francisco Golf Club	123
	Olympic Club	124
	Capilano	125
	Oak Bay	127
	Banff and Jasper Park	128
10	*Golf in America – the East*	
	Royal Montreal	130
	Kanawaki	131
	Pine Valley	132
	National Golf Links of America	137
	Shinnecock Hills	140
	Links Club	140
	The Country Club	140
	Merion	143
	Garden City	145
	Ekwanok	146
	Baltusrol	147
	Olympia Fields	148
	Country Club of Detroit	148
	Oakland Hills	149
11	*Other foreign parts*	
	Scandinavia	151
	Switzerland	152
	France	152
	Spain	153

Contents

South America	155
Pacific	157
Australia	157
Acknowledgements	159
Bibliography	163

Illustrations

Between pages 12 and 13

The 18th green at St Andrews
St Andrews Bay and the estuary of the River Eden
The 6th green at Sandwich
Bobby Jones at St Andrews
A group of champions at the Open at Muirfield in 1929
Admiral Maitland Dougall, who won the Gold Medal at St Andrews in 1860
The 15th hole at Swinley Forest near Ascot
Part of the course at Harlech in North Wales

Between pages 28 and 29

The Ailsa Course at Turnberry
The famous 'Postage Stamp' hole at Troon
The 17th green at Prestwick, 'the Alps'
A. H. Padgham, a champion of pre-war days, putting at Muirfield
The step-green of the 5th hole at Carnoustie
The green of what is now the 4th hole at Musselburgh
Hell bunker on the long 14th hole at St Andrews
Playing out of the Road bunker at the 17th hole at St Andrews
Peter Thomson at St Andrews

Between pages 44 and 45

On the King's Course at Gleneagles
Going down Gullane Hill
The author on the 16th green of the North Inch Course at Perth

Illustrations

Royal Dornoch from the air
The 13th hole at North Berwick
The 7th hole at Rye
The view from the top of 'the Maiden' at Sandwich

Between pages 60 and 61

Putting on the 3rd green at Deal
Peter Alliss driving from the 9th tee on the La Moye links in Jersey
The 3rd hole at Burnham and Berrow
The famous Himalayas bunker at the 6th hole at St Enodoc in Cornwall
The Harlech links showing the 16th hole
The 3rd hole at Aberdovey
The 14th green on the Royal Porthcawl links
The great Cape bunker at Westward Ho!

Between pages 68 and 69

Two views on the links of the Royal County Down Golf Club of Newcastle
The 4th green at Portrush
On the links of the Royal Dublin Golf Club at Dollymount
On the 3rd green at Killarney
The last green at Royal Lytham and St Annes
The short 9th at Royal Lytham and St Annes
The short 7th hole at the Royal Birkdale Golf Club
The 9th green at Hoylake
The sleepered face of the bunkers at 'Gumbleys', at Southport and Ainsdale
Formby where the sea-woods are a prominent feature
The second shot to the 345-yard 10th hole at Liphook
Ganton and the famous dog-legged 12th seen from the tee
At the 16th on the Old Course at Walton Heath
Felixstowe, one of the oldest courses in England

Between pages 92 and 93

A famous view on the Old Course at Sunningdale
Hunstanton with a plateau green among the sandhills at the 7th hole
Royal Worlington and Newmarket Club
The green of the short 15th hole at Spyglass Hill
The short 16th at Cypress Point

Illustrations

A much photographed hole at the Mid Ocean Club in Bermuda
The 7th green at Pebble Beach
The green at the 13th hole at Augusta National

Between pages 108 and 109

The view from the picture-window of the men's locker room at Capilano
A beautiful Canadian mountain course, at Jasper Park
Banff Springs high up in the Canadian Rockies
The green of the short 3rd hole on the new Spyglass Hill Golf Course
The green on the short 15th at Cypress Point, California
Sam Snead playing the 8th hole at the Peach Tree Club, Atlanta
The short 17th hole on the famous No. 2 Course at Pinehurst, North Carolina

Between pages 124 and 125

Aerial view of the Baltusrol Golf Club in New Jersey
On the National Golf Links of America
The Oakland Hills Golf Club near Detroit
The 17th hole at the Country Club at Brookline near Boston
The second shot, a pitch, to the 8th hole, at Pine Valley as it is today
The same shot as it was in the early 1920s
The beautifully moulded green of the short 10th hole at Pine Valley
The 10th green on the Red Course of the Jockey Club in Buenos Aires

Between pages 140 and 141

Golf in the shadow of the Rock of Gavea near Rio de Janeiro
Golf at Crans-sur-Sierre in Switzerland
Playing amongst the dunes and pines at Le Touquet
The seaside course at Shek-O on Hong Kong Island
The second green on the West Course of the Royal Melbourne Club
A new layout in the south of Spain at Sotogrande
Golf at Pau on the French slopes of the Pyrenees

Colour plates

	facing page
St Andrews, showing the approach to the famous Road Hole	36
The plateau green of the 16th hole at Deal	64
The shot to the beautiful curving 14th hole at Portmarnock	64
The splendid 18th hole at Pebble Beach in California	100
The 3rd hole at Pine Valley	132

To golf widows the world over

1 Introductory

The famous ground where championship golf has been played is historic turf indeed, particularly the seaside links of Britain, where, as Henry Longhurst has so often and so aptly said, 'we in the British Isles have the luck to possess in our small islands the golfing treasure house of the world. This is largely an accident of geography for which we can take no credit but which has left us with an unparalleled variety of golf on heather and moors, on the Downs and in ancestral parks, complete with deer, and above all on those otherwise useless stretches of "links-land" left by the receding of the sea anything up to fifteen million years ago.'

This is a plain man's look at these famous places, by one who, with no more than a moderate skill at it, has spent forty-five years in fierce enjoyment of the game, by far the best *pastime* yet devised by man. As Lord Balfour put it, 'The wit of man has never invented a pastime equal to golf for its healthful recreation, its pleasurable excitement and its never-ending source of amusement'—and I would add its test of character and ability to separate the men from the boys. My zest for the game has been coupled with the desire to see as many famous links and courses as possible in a normal lifetime, and to play all the championship and historic circuits in the British Isles—and to have succeeded in this latter as late as 1966—and as many others as possible abroad—all during the course of nearly a million miles of travel.

My qualification for writing about golf courses is, therefore, only that I have been playing on them lovingly for over forty years and have now sampled about 400 of them all over the world from Yellowknife to Mar del Plata and from Musselburgh to Melbourne. I write from the standpoint of the single-figure handicap player, though now, alas, in the upper levels of that category, and the descriptions of shots and holes are from this

Introductory

stance, i.e. a good drive which goes 220–5 yards, a four-iron shot of 160–5 yards and a nine-iron of about 110 yards, in still air. I also write from the standpoint of no longer consenting to play off the back tees; playing off the ordinary tees after the age of fifty-five enables one still to play the holes more or less as they were intended, whereas 'two woods and a wedge' from the back tee of a long par four is no fun at all. For the younger player who still has length what I write may have some relevance if he plays from the back tees and I from the regular ones.

I am one of those who admire most of all the seaside golf courses laid out on links-land. Here in the British Isles there is a rich variety of golf links originating as places for play from the Scottish game lost in the mists of history. Links-land, or at any rate links-land suitable for golf, is quite common on the coasts of Britain and Ireland and quite uncommon elsewhere, especially in hotter climates. The combination of dune country, sandy soil, thin crisp turf near the sea for both fairways and greens, coarse sea grass for the rough, natural plateaux and dells, uneven rolling terrain is only easily found where there is a sufficient rainfall to nurture the grass on such light soil, where the climate is also cool enough to prevent the whole thing being burnt up in summer. The coasts of Scotland abound in this admirable combination and so too do enough places in England, Ireland and Wales to make a wonderful collection.

Links-land, of course, exists on the Continent, at Le Touquet and Biarritz, for example, and in great profusion just north of The Hague. America is not so lucky. Some eight holes at Cypress Point on the Californian coast are on true links-land, so are the first five holes at Spyglass Hill next door and nine holes on the public course nearby at Pacific Grove; there are also a few links holes at the Monterey Country Club. On the other hand, the inland holes at Cypress Point and Spyglass and those at Pebble Beach next door, though fine and wonderfully scenic golf near the ocean, are not golf links at all. Nor, I fear, is the National Golf Links of America on Long Island on real links-land, which is a great pity, as several of the holes there are designed to resemble famous holes on links in England and Scotland; without the turf, the climate, the atmosphere and the surroundings, the holes in fact come out as something quite different. In the autumn of 1966 I heard, with the utmost dismay, a rumour in St Andrews that some misguided persons in the United States had commissioned Laurie Auchterlonie, the Honorary Professional of the Royal and Ancient, to construct for them *an exact replica* of the Old Course in Pennsylvania down to the finest details that surveying and bulldozing could produce. However, this turned out to be incorrect, though a course is being constructed to use some of the features of the Old Course such as the vast double green which serves the fifth and thirteenth holes and a 'Road Hole'. This shows good sense, for the other plan would have been a waste of time and money, as there isn't the slightest hope that such a construction would give rise to anything in any way resembling the original.

Great variations of terrain occur on links-land, towering high sandhills at Sandwich, Birkdale and Newcastle, County Down, flat but rippling fairways at St Andrews and Carnoustie, a wonderful series of natural plateaux, just made for greens, at Dornoch, treeless windswept turf at Deal and Troon, and black, mysterious, impenetrable sea-woods at Muirfield and Formby.

The rough, too, has its varieties, though on all links the harsh dune grass is found. Westward Ho! has some fierce spiky rushes which can impale a ball and do grievous bodily harm to the golfer; on the Cheshire and Lancashire coasts there is wild-rose scrub in the rough, and devilish it can be to get out of; St Andrews still has some heather and quite a lot of gorse; Newcastle has abundant heather on its landward nine, while parts of the Hayling Island links are covered with tree-lupins. On the links holes at Cypress Point, mesembryanthemum or Ice Plant, which the Australians so charmingly call Pig Face, makes almost the toughest rough of all.

By no means all the great American players share my love of links-land, notably Sam Snead, whose first reaction to the Old Course was that it looked 'the sort of real estate you couldn't give away', but then his other reactions to Britain in 1946 were equally ungenerous and inept. So it was with pleased surprise that I read this in Walter Hagen's autobiography:

'For the second time the British links had defeated me. Here in America we have developed the finest of man-made courses in the world, but the real test of a golfer is a seaside links in the British Isles. Situated close beside the ocean, beset with rolling sand-dunes and winds that whip off the channel and the seas, conditions change with the tide. The hazards are far greater than meet the eye. At Deal I had played shots where the wind picked the ball up and almost slapped it back in my face. At St Andrews I learned that distance was secondary to placing the ball accurately. I learned, also, that in order to be at the top in the golf profession, I must be able to play any course in the world in par.

'During the year between Deal and St Andrews I had tried to gain skill for the British and Scottish links by playing some of our own seaside courses, such as the National on Long Island, Pebble Beach and Cypress Point in California. But there was all the difference in the world between these courses and the rugged windswept links of Sandwich, Hoylake, Carnoustie, Prestwick, Troon and Lytham St Anne's.

'I knew the fault lay not with the links but with my game. With the opportunity to play continuously over them Harry Vardon, J. H. Taylor,

Introductory

James Braid and Alex Herd became masters of the skill required to conquer them. Instead of trying for distance they worked on a low ball which would travel hard and sharp against the wind—a ball which they could control. They were experts with the pitch and run shot. They needed to be, for the wind would grab a ball and carry it in any direction.

'In the United States we developed the wedge, and it's a fine club where the turf conditions are excellent and the wind is light. We could hit the ball up with action on it. But that same shot on the British seaside links was disastrous. I know because I tried it and once the ball was up in a strong wind the action disappeared and the ball, minus control, would land on a high green and roll over into a trap.

'After 1921 I worked on a ball hit quail-high—a ball hit hard enough to resist the pull of that fierce wind and yet not too fast to roll over a lightning-fast green. I tried for short approach shots, keeping contact between me and the ball—giving it enough action to cover the uneven approach surface but not enough to let the wind get under it.

'I've repeatedly insisted that I liked competition. Well, I had it from the links in the British Isles. And far from upsetting me, it challenged my skill as a championship golfer so greatly that I was more and more determined to win that British Open Cup.'

So far the British Open Championship has been played on golf links only, and on only thirteen at that. When the Open Championship first began it was always played at Prestwick, where the meeting was held from 1860 to 1870 until the Belt was won outright by young Tom Morris, the greatest player of his generation. At that time Prestwick was a cat's cradle of a twelve-hole course inside the wall and three rounds in one day constituted the Championship. In the circumstances of those times—rough unkempt fairways and greens, by modern standards, and with stony gutta balls and the uncouth implements of the day—young Tommy's score of 149 for thirty-six holes in 1870 is surely one of the greatest day's golf in the entire history of the game.

After a blank year in 1871 the Championship was resumed, with thirty-six holes played on a three-links rota, Prestwick, which had twelve holes, St Andrews, with eighteen, and Musselburgh, which was a nine-hole, course. This rota continued until 1892, when the tournament was extended to seventy-two holes and Muirfield came in as a championship course in place of Musselburgh, where the Championship was last held in 1889.

Sandwich was the first English links to join the Open Championship rota, coming in in 1894, followed by Hoylake in 1897. The only other links to join this exclusive 'club' up to World War I was Deal, which held the Championship in 1909.

Introductory

Between the wars Troon was included in the rota in 1923—but had to wait twenty-seven years before another Open Championship was held there—Lytham and St Annes came in in 1926 and history was made there that year by Bobby Jones. Carnoustie was added in 1931 and Prince's at Sandwich made its only appearance in 1932, the year Gene Sarazen won. Since World War II the only newcomers have been Portrush in Northern Ireland, where the Championship was held in 1951 and gave Britain its last winner, and Birkdale in Lancashire, which was added to the list in 1954.

All these thirteen links survive, though Prince's has been completely remade and it takes some imagination to picture Musselburgh as a serious golfing ground. Except for Musselburgh, however, the other twelve are thriving, though the great upsurge in the popularity of golf looks like ruling out any championship future for Prestwick, Deal, the two Sandwich courses and Portrush, and more's the pity. Deal indeed hasn't been used for the Open since 1920, being unfit for play in 1949 owing to the effects of the war, and the shambles of an uncontrollable crowd put paid to Prestwick, the original home of the Championship, in 1925. These days, the course must be accessible, as huge crowds now have to be handled, large centres of population tapped and ample accommodation must be available. So not only do five of the championship links look like dropping out, but other splendid links like Dornoch, Westward Ho! and Newcastle seem unlikely ever to come in, though 'possibles' are Turnberry and Portmarnock near Dublin, if the Open ever followed the Amateur Championship to Eire.

For the British Amateur Championship requirements for crowds and accommodation are far less exacting and a rather wider range of seaside courses has been used, but only once, in 1963, when the Amateur was held at Ganton near Scarborough, has it been held inland. Even here there was some excuse, for Ganton is as near a links as one could find inland, a patch of sandy turf left by an earlier sea. All the thirteen links used for the Open have been used for the Amateur except Musselburgh and Prince's, Sandwich, with six others besides, to a total of seventeen.

The Amateur Championship originated at Hoylake in 1885, twenty-five years after the first Open, but like many such things it began unofficially and the first winner, Mr A. F. MacFie, a Scot, was only 'canonised' after the event. From 1886 on, the event was official and followed the circuit of St Andrews, Prestwick, Sandwich and Hoylake in a rota. Then from 1897 the list was extended to bring in Muirfield and these five links held all the Amateur Championships until Westward Ho! came in in 1912 when John Ball won his eighth and last title. Deal was added in 1923 and Lytham and St Annes in 1935, each of these coming in after the Open had been played there. Troon was used for the first time in that historic year 1938 when my old friend Charlie Yates of Atlanta, Georgia, who won the

Introductory

Championship, endeared himself to the crowd at St Andrews after Britain had won the Walker Cup for the first and only time by leading the singing of 'a wee doch an' doris' from the club-house steps.

After World War II the Amateur Championship broke more and more fresh ground, using Birkdale in 1946 ahead of the Open, and Carnoustie, which had held the Open in 1931 and 1937, in 1947. In 1949 a big breakaway occurred and the Championship moved to the Republic of Ireland to the magnificent links of Portmarnock near Dublin and a splendid Irish win from S. M. McCready ensued. This move has not been repeated and no more Amateur and no Open Championships have gone to Eire. Porthcawl in South Wales came on the Amateur rota in 1951, Formby on the Lancashire coast in 1957 and Portrush in Northern Ireland in 1960. Next year another new links was added, the reconstructed Ailsa course at Turnberry, which had been re-formed from a wartime airfield with conspicuous success. Then in 1964 the move to Ganton was made, the only island venue so far and, as a traditionalist, I hope for ever. (As we go to press we learn that Newcastle, in Northern Ireland, will house the Amateur in 1970.)

In the early days of competitive golf a hundred years ago and more the Scottish professionals were the most talented players and they commanded the Open Championship for thirty years. Then, when the great surge forward of popularity in golf came in the 1880's and 1890's and the game became suddenly popular in England, a formidable group of amateurs arose, reaching the peak of their influence and power in the 1890's—John Ball, Harold Hilton and Horace Hutchinson for England, Freddie Tait, J. E. Laidlay, Leslie Balfour Melville and, a little later, Robert Maxwell for Scotland. This rich flowering of the amateur game, which occurred in turn in the United States in the 1920's, was very like the golden age of cricket, with W.G., Ranji, MacLaren, F. S. Jackson, C. B. Fry, Spooner and Jessop as good as any of the pros of their day. Then as the games developed in the new century here, the professionals came forward again to rule the roost, with the great Triumvirate of golf—Vardon, Braid and J. H. Taylor—in command like their counterparts in cricket, Hobbs, Rhodes, Hirst and Woolley.

But in their golden era the great amateurs were great indeed, none more than John Ball of Hoylake, who was the first Englishman and the first amateur to win the Open, at Prestwick, of all places, in 1890 and he won the Amateur that year as well. Ball never won the Open again, but he won the Amateur no less than eight times in all, first in 1888 and last twenty-four years later. Altogether he played in the Amateur over a span of thirty-nine years, finishing his career in it in 1927. In 1921, in his sixtieth year, he got as far as the sixth round; as he said, 'if only a storm of wind and rain would sweep across the links from the Welsh hills I feel I could beat all of

Introductory

them once again'. He first played in the Open in 1876 when he was fifteen, and for the last time as Walter Hagen's partner in 1924, so in all he had fifty years of championship golf. As Hagen says:

'I was sincerely pleased when the committee informed me that Mr John Ball was entering his last British Open and had requested that he be paired with me, Walter *High*gen. I went over immediately to assure him I'd be very honoured to play with him. "Uncle John" was a legend in British golf. He had competed in his first Open at the age of fifteen in 1876 and had finished sixth. Between 1888 and 1912 he won the British Amateur title eight times and in 1890 he became the first British amateur ever to win the British Open. Now at the age of sixty-three he was right there shooting for another win. He was playing in his last Championship on the very course where his father's hotel had been located when "Uncle John" began his golfing career. In fact, the course was laid out on the grounds where his father had originally raced fine horses.'

Harold Hilton won the Open twice and would have won it a third time if he had not had a frightful eight at the short fifth at Prestwick in 1898. He won the British Amateur four times and the U.S. Amateur once—in 1911—one of a minute band of three non-Americans to do so. 'There were wonderful giants of old, you know.'

And wonderful giants, of course, there are in the professional game which has come to dominate modern golf. With the prizes now available to professional players, the chances of the first-class amateur remaining in the game and winning any of the major events are becoming less and less likely. For a time the money power of the American 'circuit' made the British Open look less and less important to the great American golfers, but recently, and to a large extent thanks to Arnold Palmer, there has been a change and the need to win here on our links at least once has now become a required part of an international professional's progress. Walter Hagen's book puts it in these words:

'In spite of all the new fields to conquer offered our present-day golfers, I still hold that no golfer is a true champion until he has played and won the great British Open cup . . . until he conquers those windswept seaside links. Before Ben Hogan won the National Open at Oakmont Country Club in 1953 I got on the telephone to urge him to try for the British Open. He did . . . and by winning added tremendously to his stature as a top golfer of all time.'

This is not a history of golf, far from it, but some reference to the earliest foundations of the game is necessary to get any sort of sense of history, without which much of the story of the great links is absent.

Introductory

Golf started a long time ago in Scotland. Indeed, it was so well established in 1457, whatever its form, that it had to be 'utterly cryed down and not to be used' and again by statute in 1491 lest it interfere with the defence of the Realm. Then after peace broke out with the auld foe in 1502 the brakes were off and golf got going again. From then on members of the Royal House, who were great golf addicts, could indulge their pleasure. As Robert Browning quotes, Catherine of Aragon, the first wife of Henry VIII, wrote to Cardinal Wolsey: 'And all his subjects be very glad, Master Almoner, I thank God, to be busy with golf, for they take it for pastime' —they do indeed and to this day.

The first great Royal Golfer was without doubt King James IV, who died at Flodden Field in 1513; his son, James V, was a noted player, and his daughter Mary, Queen of Scots, was also; indeed she got into trouble for playing so soon after her husband Darnley was murdered. Then when the thrones were united under James VI of Scotland and James I of England, golf came over the border. At this stage it is reported that a golf club was organised at Blackheath in 1608, though there is no evidence for this, which is not to say that golf wasn't played there.

Without doubt, golf on Blackheath led to the first international match, for it is said a dispute arose about the origins of the game between two of the English gentry, who claimed it for South Britain—obviously without the slightest knowledge of golfing history—and King Charles II's brother, James, Duke of York, who in 1681 and 1682 was Commissioner from his brother to the Scottish Parliament. To settle this absurd argument a match was fixed on Leith links between the two English fops and the Duke and his Scottish partner. The Duke with great good sense selected the cobbler James Patersone as his partner and they won handsomely. The shoemaker got his share of the stake, or all of it, some versions say, and with it built himself a house in the Canongate in Edinburgh called the Golfer's Land, which, alas, has just recently been pulled down, notwithstanding the escutcheon fixed on it by the grateful Duke, bearing the newly organised arms of the Patersone family with the crest of a hand grasping a golf club and the motto 'Far and Sure'.

Now with this talk of the early days of golf in Scotland, where was it played and on what sort of ground? I imagine the whole game began with an impromptu set-up, hitting to holes in the ground rather to exercise or display virtuosity than make a match. Then in the late eighteenth and early nineteenth centuries came a prescribed course, but with widely different ideas as to how many holes there should be and what they should be like. In these days, when to match American orthodoxy you must have two nines of roughly equal length, each ending at the club-house, with two par threes and two par fives on each nine, the golf course of 200 years ago

Introductory

seems wildly anarchic. Eighteen holes was certainly not standard and can be attributed to the layout of St Andrews and the influence of the Royal and Ancient Club, but it in turn started its life with twenty-two holes. Leith links, its origins lost in the mists of time, had only five holes in its heyday, varying between 414 and 496 yards in length, and, dear God, what effort the Duke and James Patersone must have applied to do even one of them in five! While Leith links had only five holes, subsequently enlarged to seven, and St Andrews had a round of twenty-two, though only in fact twelve actual holes in the turf, Montrose had no less than twenty-five. Blackheath, which survived in the old primitive form until the end of World War I, had seven holes and—bearing in mind the powers of the feathery and the later gutty ball—they must have been a sore trial, measuring 170, 335, 380, 540, 500, 230 and 410 yards; it is small wonder that the course record in 1910 with the rubber-cored ball was 95, or eleven over fours for twenty-one holes, at a time when few course records were not well below an average of fours.

Well, Leith links has gone as a golf course, though I hit two surreptitious shots there last year just to say I'd done it, but with the ground surrounded by houses, street lamps and hard roads and the grass criss-crossed by tarmac paths, with tennis courts and rugby posts at one end it is a far cry and a long stretch of the imagination to picture the Duke and James Patersone playing their big money game there. Bruntsfield links in the centre of Edinburgh is also historic turf, but it is equally confined and you can't easily picture James IV and Mary, Queen of Scots, playing on this rather flaccid grass, but of course they did. But at least golf, of a sort, the dismallest pitch and putt sort, is still played here and here for old times' sake I too have played; but today it is not really a golf course, nor really is Musselburgh but as a home of the Championship it will rate a further description later. Then, of course, St Andrews, the Championship links *par excellence*, comes through unscathed from all this early ball-flogging on rough common land. Also in the category of a surviving golf course in the true sense from medieval times is the course at Perth on the North Inch, where golf has been played certainly for 375 years and very probably for more than 500, and this too we will describe in due course.

The history and origin of golf clubs, as opposed to the places where golf has been played from time immemorial, is another fascinating topic, but not for this book. The layout of this book can be said to be semi-geographical and all the courses described I have played on myself, though my knowledge of them differs widely in extent; some of them also I have not played on for some years. So we will start with the famous links of Scotland and with the home of the first Open Championship in 1860.

2 The championship links of Scotland

Prestwick

Prestwick has had its day they say, no longer suitable for a championship, impossible for crowd control, too short for the big guns—though playing it in half a gale of bitter wind from the north-west after a soaking March you'd hardly think so. But I suppose it's true, and certain it is that the Open hasn't been here since that disastrous afternoon in 1925 when Macdonald Smith, five strokes ahead of the field with one round to go, was destroyed by the mob who wanted to see him win, and the Amateur has not been here since 1952.

And yet and yet . . . It is to me much more than a museum of what golf was like sixty years ago; I find it still a wonderfully subtle and exacting links. True, there are a lot of old-fashioned features, like wooden sleepers in the faces of some of the bunkers, blind shots and tiny greens with protecting humps and hillocks which may kick your ball away, often unfairly, which can't appeal to the lordly professionals of today, whose appetite for money, provided by you and me, makes ever-increasing demands that the tailoring of the game and the courses should suit them rather than their patrons, lest they should have to learn to adapt their play to the conditions.

You start with a tough hole, a tough short par four which is a rare thing, but the shot up the narrowing fairway with an out-of-bounds wall on your right is no fun at all with any wind across your line off the sea. Bernard Darwin recalls seeing a friend who was feeling a little brittle hit his first shot on to the railway from which it kicked back on to the fairway; he then hit his second on to the line and it kicked back on to the green and ran into the hole. The second is an ordinary short hole of no great terrors and then comes 'the Cardinal', a 500-yard par five with a minute tiny green—which all par fives should have—amid the humps by the Pow burn and on the way the vast sleepered Cardinal bunker lying right across the fairway to be carried by the second shot.

The fourth is a wonderfully good par four of 376 yards, with a tight drive between the Pow Burn on the right and bunkers on the left; the green is, as it were, in a crook of the arm of the burn and catastrophe is never far off, as J. H. Taylor found in his disastrous last round in the Open Championship with Harry Vardon in 1914, Vardon's sixth Open, and the end of an era in more ways than one.

The fifth is—or are—the 'Himalayas', a big blind thump of 200 yards over a huge sandhill; very old-fashioned, of course, but not easy, with the green heavily bunkered and none too big.

Four holes follow to the turn, good tough exacting holes, but somehow they don't seem part of the old links—and indeed they are not—being out in the fields by the railway; nevertheless if we can leave these fields with two fives and two fours we can be well satisfied; I'd settle for that, anyway.

The tenth is 474 yards and called par four, but as it goes straight out into the prevailing wind, five is much more reasonable. The hole is not much of a favourite of mine but the green is on an upper level and has to be 'fetched' by a proper shot.

Eleven is a beautiful short hole, comparatively new, with a bunker short on the left-hand edge of the green which gathers any ill-hit rubbish. Twelve takes two big plain hits down a plain flat fairway and then a nice pitch to a small green set among humps and mounds; it was once protected by a wall in front in the old days when Prestwick was a criss-cross of twelve holes inside the wall.

The thirteenth, 'Sea Hedrig', at 461 yards is reachable in two but no longer by me, alas; the little shot to the green is beset by heavily folded humpy ground, and the green, on a little plateau, must be one of the smallest on any first-class course, not only small but set across the line of play so that the target area is minute, but what a superb hole at which to do a four, at which to play a cunning run-up to scuttle across the folded ground up the final slope and lie close to the hole; to me a jewel of a hole.

At the fourteenth you drive across the 'Goose Dubs', reedy marshy ground and a carry not to be despised off the back tee with any wind against you; then you pitch to a generously big green in front of the clubhouse windows.

You finish with the Loop and if you think that holes of 321, 288, 376 and 287 yards and sixteen strokes to do them in are a piece of cake you can think again. The fifteenth has the narrowest fairway I know. I hit a good shot there a year or so ago, about 230 yards I suppose, and at that point my ball lay in the middle of the fairway eight yards from the rough on the right and nine yards from the rough on the left—and the rough is rough. The green is small and tightly bunkered. The sixteenth, 'the Cardinal's Back', has a less exacting tee shot, but a tiny green which runs away from you perched above the end of the great Cardinal bunker. The seventeenth is the 'Alps', where if you hit a good drive you can hit a blind second shot over a great sandhill. You scramble to the top hoping you are on the small green, but instead find you are in the historic sleepered bunker in front of it from which Freddie Tait played his famous shot out of water in the final of the Amateur in 1899 and John Ball followed that with as good a shot off hard wet sand. Not a good hole by today's standards, I suppose, but I hope they never change it.

Only at the last do you fancy your chances of a three, for it's not at all long and not at all difficult if you get your drive away. Well, that's the round; I think you'll find that somehow a good score has eluded you, but these small keen greens and the humps and hollows round them don't help, and the rough, as I say, is rough. The bunkers too are deep and uncompromising and numerous. *And* there is the wind, the almost incessant wind.

Perhaps from among innumerable championship results here one might select an odd one, the Amateur of 1928 which was won by a distinguished and underrated British player, Phil Perkins. Odd because that same year he also got into the final of the U.S. Amateur losing to Bobby Jones, the like of which we have not seen since, and only once before when Harold Hilton won both, in 1911. Perkins stayed in America and turned pro and was joint runner-up to Sarazen in the U.S. Open of 1932. Few British players have done as well as Phil Perkins in America.

So to the club-house, a splendid Victorian survival with a labyrinth of locker rooms in which you can easily get lost, and an old-fashioned atmosphere of furnishings and style but a warm and friendly welcome from the members and good food and drink in generous measure.

St Andrews

As Patric Dickinson says in his enjoyable book, 'There is nothing new to say about St Andrews, just as there is nothing new to say about Shakespeare.' Indeed I had thought of writing the whole of this section in quotations.

After all, who could describe the first hole better than Bernard Darwin:

'With this preliminary observation, we may tee up our ball in front of the Royal and Ancient Club-house for one of the least alarming tee-shots in existence. In front of us stretches a vast flat plain, and unless we slice the ball outrageously on to the sea beach, no harm can befall us. At the same

Golf's headquarters. The 18th green at St Andrews with the club-house of the Royal and Ancient Club behind. The depression on the left of the green is the Valley of Sin (*G. M. Cowie*)

ABOVE St Andrews Bay and the estuary of the River Eden, showing all the golf courses from the Eden Course on the left of the railway, with the Old Course next, then the New Course and the Jubilee Course on the right. The Swilcan burn can be seen clearly crossing the 18th and 1st fairways of the Old (*The Central Press Photos Ltd*)

BELOW Links-land. The 6th green at Sandwich and the famous sandhill, 'the Maiden', on the left (*H. W. Neale*)

ABOVE The greatest player of all time—Bobby Jones at St Andrews in 1936 (*G. M. Cowie*)

BELOW LEFT A group of champions at the Open at Muirfield in 1929. *Back row, left to right:* Harry Vardon, James Braid, Sandy Herd, Jack White Arnaud Massy. *Front row, left to right:* George Duncan, Walter Hagen, Jim Barnes, Ted Ray (*Keystone Press Agency Ltd*)

BELOW RIGHT Admiral Maitland Dougall, who won the Gold Medal at St Andrews in 1860 (*Scotscraig G.C.*)

ABOVE Golf in the heather and pine country of Berkshire. The 15th hole at Swinley Forest near Ascot (*The Sport & General Press Agency Ltd*)
BELOW Links-land. Part of the golf course at Harlech in North Wales showing the 16th hole (*Frank Gardner*)

time we had much better hit a good shot, because the Swilcan burn guards the green, and we want to carry it and get a four. It is an inglorious little stream enough: we could easily jump over it were we not afraid of looking foolish if we fell in, and yet it catches an amazing number of balls. It is now part of golfing history that when Mr Leslie Balfour Melville won the Amateur Championship (in 1895) he beat successively at the nineteenth hole Mr W. Greig, Mr Laurence Auchterlonie and Mr John Ball (in the final), and all three of these redoubtable persons plumped the ball into this apparently paltry little streamlet with their approach shots.'

Love at first sight is very rare at St Andrews, and many famous players, especially from abroad, have taken a dim view of the links on first acquaintance and then later came to love it. Perhaps the most famous of these is Bobby Jones, who writes:

'Beginning with the puzzled dislike I had felt for the Old Course when I first played in 1921, by 1930 I had come to love it. I thought that I appreciated its subtleties. I had taken great pains to learn the location of all the little pot bunkers and felt that I had a complete familiarity with all the devious little slopes and swales which could deflect well-intended shots in such exasperating ways. I may have been flattering myself, yet I felt very confident that I should encounter no opponent having an advantage over me on the score of local knowledge. Truly if I had had to select one course on which to play the match of my life, I should have selected the Old Course.'

Robert Trent Jones, the great American golf architect, sums it up very well:

'The first few rounds a golfer plays on the Old Course are not likely to alter his first estimate that it is vastly overrated. He will be puzzled to understand the rhapsodies that have been composed about the perfect strategic position of its trapping, the subtle undulations of its huge double greens, the endless tumbling of its fairways, which seldom give him a chance to play a shot from a level stance. Then, as he plays on, it begins to soak in through his pores that whenever he plays a fine shot, he is rewarded; whenever he doesn't play the right shot, he is penalised, in proportion; and whenever he thinks out his round hole by hole, he scores well. This is the essence of strategic architecture: to encourage initiative, reward a well-played, daring stroke more than a cautious stroke, and yet to insist that there must be planning and honest self-appraisal behind the daring.'

All this must be true, because so many and such different people are agreed on it, but alas I am still at the stage short of idolatry. While I have played a good many rounds on the Old Course I have not played enough to know it really intimately, nor seen enough of the different moods brought by the wind. I'm still in the state of ignorance which feels that it is rather too subtle and that there are too many unattractive holes, difficult though they may be, to offset the excellence of the others. While the eleventh, twelfth, thirteenth and fourteenth, for example, are as fine as they come, the eighth, ninth and tenth are poor stuff to my iconoclastic eye and I've not much time for the first and eighteenth, although I have visited both the Swilcan burn at the first and the Valley of Sin at the last, like many better players before me. But that having been said, I will be the first to admit that I enjoy and respect the Old Course in full measure, that it has some of the most delightful shots and holes you can find anywhere, that several of these qualify for what Henry Longhurst reminds us was the late Tom Simpson's test of greatness, that you start worrying about the hole before you get to it, while you know that almost to the last moment of any round you can meet disaster: as I once heard that renowned octogenarian handicap player Admiral Benson say on Medal Day, 'I was going well until I had an eleven at the seventeenth.' I would, however, allow myself to ask the impertinent question: cannot some of the blemishes in the Old Course be changed? After all, the course has been changed greatly in the last century, in spite of some transatlantic beliefs to the contrary; the course has been widened, the whins and heather cut back; the nature of the fairways and greens has been much softened; we no longer share the same hole at seven holes and double greens have been built to accommodate holes going out and coming in; the Road Hole green is comparatively recent and the famous black sheds at the seventeenth were also quite new and have now been replaced by a new Railway Hotel and 'gazebo', while the surface of the sixth green is no longer composed of 'earth, heather and shells' without a blade of grass. True, the Old Course, except for some back tees and a few bunkers, has been altered little since 1913, but it would be a pity to believe that nothing must ever be altered again. I suppose there was an uproar when the 'Kruger' and 'Mrs Kruger' bunkers were put in at the ninth at the turn of the century, but I think there might be a case for a little moulding to be applied to that tennis court of a green or even an 'Eisenhower' bunker added; possibly there might even be a case for replacing Halket's bunker to catch a sliced drive at the first hole or even 'Tam's Coo' between the 'Principal's Nose' and the railway.

However, let us return to the Old Course as it is, rather than as it was or might be. As so many have observed, the subtlety of the bunkering is a striking feature, though the irreverent might be tempted to think that at some holes where the bunkers are just where you want to go the subtlety is rather like that of a battle-axe. To me the slopes and contours of the greens are the most delightful features; many of the greens are on small plateaux like the second, twelfth, fourteenth and seventeenth and some on quite high ones, the two 'High' holes and the long fifth, for example. Moreover, the size and alignment of the greens usually match the shot admirably. Thus the twelfth hole, which needs only a short approach, offers you a narrow green on a little plateau set across the line which would be unfair for a longer shot; the green at the par-five fourteenth is also small and difficult, as it should be, likewise that at the seventeenth. A distinctive feature of the Old Course is what I might call the 'Protective Ridge', such as that which protects the entrance to the beautifully moulded plateau green at the second; similarly at the third a small ridge covers the run in to the green. At the long fifth it is very pronounced—ridge, swale, plateau green; the sixth has it too very conspicuously, also the tenth and the short eighth.

Another feature, as Bernard Darwin points out, is the fierce proximity of the bunkers to the greens, which often deters you from playing to the pin, so leaving you with a long and difficult putt. A wild shot indeed can sometimes give you a world-record putt; I believe one of ninety-five yards has been holed. The whole links is surprisingly flat and thereby easy on the feet, flat, that is, not level, for the fairways are full of small humps and hollows, undulations and waves. Then as Laurence Auchterlonie, the club's honorary professional, points out, the lie of the land draws a misdirected shot inexorably into certain bunkers even from a great distance away. He quotes a game he was playing with the late Willie Murray, the Walker Cup player. Laurie hit a shot to the sixteenth green which his opponent applauded, but the pro said, 'No, it's in the bunker', which Murray declined to believe: but it was.

Now, assuming that we have crossed the burn successfully at the first and got a four, we must address ourselves to a stiff run out to the northwest which will take us in a straight line, more or less, to the seventh green and the shores of the River Eden. These holes are immensely affected by the wind; with a breeze from the east they can seem surprisingly short, but with a 'Guardbridge wind' from the north-west they can seem brutally long. The second hole, the 'Dyke', shows this admirably, for your second shot can require an eight-iron or a spoon to cover its 403 yards; if you have a long shot the temptation to hit away to the right, away from the tightly bunkered left-hand side, is great, but then you may have a really difficult run-in to the holeside. This is a superb hole.

The third hole, the 'Cartgate Out', which shares a double green with the fifteenth, is dominated all the way from the tee by the deep Cartgate bunker which eats right into the left side of the green; again the 'Protective Ridge' keeps a clear view of the bottom of the pin from you. Next the

'Ginger Beer' hole at 424 yards demands a very tough drive over or to either side of a big bluff and is again protected by a large hillock in the centre of the fairway in front of the green. At this point if we have four fours on the book or three fours and a five if the wind is adverse we've done very well, for at the fifth the 'Hole o' Cross Out' at 522 yards we will assuredly need three hits to get up if we can avoid the sporadic crop of bunkers about 220 yards from the tee; we can then hit with fair confidence with our seconds and end with a pitch to the huge double green of about an acre which we share with the thirteenth, the 'Hole o' Cross In'.

The 370-yard sixth, the 'Heathery Hole Out', has heather and whins to the right, as its name says, and once more a pronounced protective ridge in front of the green; I have a fond memory of this not very memorable hole, for it yielded me a birdie in my first Medal when I badly needed some support from evil things past and for bad things to come.

The 'High Hole Out' shares a green with the short eleventh and the lines of play cross here; although the hole is only 354 yards long it has very tight drive with again a rough bluff in the centre of things and the high plateau green has some desperate slopes if you have a long putt. Next comes the short flat eighth hole over a ridge and small bunker to a huge green; I don't care for it. Nor do I care for the 310-yard ninth, in spite of 'Kruger' and 'Mrs Kruger'; the hole is totally flat and the green a flat continuation of the fairway. None the less drama occurred here in the first round of the Open in 1921, a championship charged with drama all the way. Jock Hutchison, the eventual winner—who now, a spry octogenarian, leads off the play in the Masters' Tournament at Augusta each year with Fred McLeod—holed the eighth in one stroke. At the ninth his drive, racing up the baked fairway, looked headed for the hole; a spectator rushed out of the crowd and pulled out the flag, whereupon the ball hit the hole and just stayed out; by that intemperate interference the rare achievement of two successive holes in one, and an unheard-of feat in a championship, might have been achieved. As it was, Hutchison was pretty well served by fate, for not only did two other iron shots hit the pin but by an unlucky and, let it be said, stupid accident, Roger Wethered backed and trod on to his ball at the fourteenth hole in the third round and lost a penalty stroke; in spite of this he had a 72 and was drawing up to the leaders. Here again I must quote Bernard Darwin, who says:

'It is always assumed as an incontestable and logical proposition that if he had not incurred this penalty stroke he would have beaten Hutchison by one stroke. This seems to me an unjustifiable assumption. If he had not incurred the penalty Mr Wethered might have beaten Hutchison by one stroke or by more than one stroke or he might not have tied with him.

To assume otherwise is to neglect one obvious fact, that every happening in a round of golf has some effect on the player's mind and the state of his mind has some effect on his stroke. It is such an assumption as we all make about our own rounds but it is founded on unsound premises. All we can say about this penalty stroke is that Mr Wethered did very unluckily lose a shot at a particular hole. What would have happened if he had not, no human being can tell.'

What did happen, however, was that in a splendid last round of 71 Wethered pitched short at the eighteenth into the Valley of Sin and took five, whereas if he had got his four he would have won outright; Bernardo's verdict was 'one can only grieve because a five at that last hole is not merely the loss of a stroke, it is a waste of a stroke'. As it was, Jock Hutchison had the formidable task of needing a 70 to tie and he got it, a splendid tough finish. Bobby Jones reports that Roger Wethered was only persuaded with some difficulty to stay for the play-off, as he had given his word that he'd go south for a village cricket match on the Saturday, but Wethered denies this. In the event he need not have stayed, for Hutchison murdered him.

After this long digression let us resume our round, with, I hope, a score of under 40 on the card after nine holes. The tenth, a 314-yarder, ought not to harm us, and just as well, for now we get down to brass tacks with the 163-yard eleventh, the 'High Hole In'. This hole has been described so often that I will not try to do it again at any length. It is dominated by the steep hostile slope of the green towards the tee, the evil little pot-bunker 'Strath' under the right-hand wing of the green, and a hideous pit, the 'Hill' bunker, about ten feet deep under the left-hand wing. You mustn't go over or you'll never stop the return shot out of the rough grass of the shore of the Eden, so you are often short from the tee or go into Scylla or Charybdis. Many famous cards have gone to the winds here. Bobby Jones, Arnaud Massy and your humble author have all come to grief in the Hill bunker. It is fair to say that with the softer condition of the course this is not as terrifying a hole as it used to be.

After this the twelfth, the 316-yard 'Heathery Hole In', must seem to come as a relief, especially as you can see from the tee nothing, nothing at all, to impede your straight run to the green. Well, that's too bad, for there are at least six bunkers strewn across the fairway, all hidden on the reverse slopes of undulations. It seems inconceivable that anyone could have designed such deliberately malicious bunkering as this and indeed they did not, for what we are playing is the fairway of the original High hole the wrong way round; when played in the opposite direction this fairway has no hidden bunkers and is perfectly fair and reasonable; the tee to the twelfth hole was then far over to the left of the present twelfth tee. However, the hidden bunkers are there now and you have to play either a tight tee shot down the extreme right edge of the fairway or away far to the left. The former gives you the easier pitch to the narrow plateau green, and very narrow it is with the slope of the green running away from you.

The thirteenth at 409 yards is a beautiful two-shotter; according to Henry Longhurst, Tom Simpson, the great golf architect and connoisseur of life in general, has stated that this is the best single hole in golf. On a straight line you mustn't drive too far or like my powerful friend Rush you run out of fairway where a ridge comes across; the long hitter has to go away over some bunkers far to the left. On my line, however, you have a fairly substantial second shot over broken humpy ground up to the big double green with two bunkers eating into its very edge; a three there the other evening with the aid of my five-wood in the closing stages of my golfing life was sweet indeed.

Fourteen is the 'Long Hole In', 513 yards off the Medal tee and 560 for the Championship. You can slice over the wall out-of-bounds easily enough or pull your tee shot into the 'Beardies', a nest of odious pot-bunkers; then as 'Hell' bunker is 410 yards from our tee you have an important decision. If you've hit a very fine drive you can go out and carry 'Hell', but if you are in doubt then play safe and away with you over to the left beyond the Elysian Fields, for 'Hell' is no place to enjoy yourself. In any case, you need a delicate third to get on, becuase the green is on a steep plateau of no great size which runs away from you. This hole is a rare thing, a first-rate par five of not excessive length.

To get the best shot to the fifteenth, 404 yards, you must drive over to the left, for a protective ridge comes in on the right of the fairway to hinder the approach if you are too far over on that side; but, of course, a drive to the left is beset by bunkers, including the large Cottage bunker.

The 351-yard sixteenth, the 'Corner of the Dyke', is a splendid hole. You have the choice of driving between the 'Principal's Nose' and the railway, a bare thirty-yard gap which gives a comparatively simple shot into the green, or away to the left and safety, but needing a longer and tougher shot to the green because then the 'Wig' bunker comes into the picture. Those who feel they can carry the 'Principal's Nose' have to watch or they'll be carrying it and finding themselves in 'Deacon Sime' just beyond.

Next comes the famous Road Hole, 466 yards long, with its narrow green right up against the hard gravelly path and then the road itself. The play of the hole is ruled by the small 'Road' bunker which eats into the left flank of the green. The mouldings of the plateau are such that any shot at all weakly hit to the green inevitably runs into the Road bunker.

Once in it you have to dunch the ball out on to the narrowest part of the green with the road beyond, an alarming shot. Before all this you have to drive over the black sheds of the 'Stationmaster's Garden' to get the best line, or you did at the moment of writing, but with the new hotel on this site all is now changed; then if you can make it you have a go for this small green. To get home here with two big hits gives supreme satisfaction, but your mind is never free from all the tales of disaster you have heard about it. In any competition the players can never relax until this hole is behind them. In the 1960 Centenary Championship Arnold Palmer never tamed this hole and so failed to beat Nagle. It played a significant part in Bobby Jones's winning of the 'Grand Slam' in 1930. In the first championship he won that year, the British Amateur, he had a desperate match with Cyril Tolley; Jones's second had gone past the 'Road' bunker and hit a spectator, but lay well, near the green; Tolley was close to the bunker and hit a beautiful little delicate chip over it to lie dead. Bob had to bottle an eight-foot putt to get a half, which he did, and then won at the nineteenth with the help of a stymie.

After the seventeenth the last hole is a let-down and a relief, the counterpart of the first across the plain. The Swilcan burn is no danger and the green is very large for a 356-yard hole; there are no bunkers and there is only the 'Valley of Sin', a depression in front of the left side of the green which catches a weakly-hit shot and from which you usually take three more to get down.

I like a story told about Guy Ellis, a man of some eccentricity, at the eighteenth. He came in at the very end of the field on Medal Day and some friends came out of the club-house to find out how he had done. His ball lay at the back of the green, a difficult downhill putt. After some figuring his friends said, 'Guy, if you hole that you'll tie for second place.' After a prolonged study of the putt from both sides he said, 'I can't hole it,' and picked his ball up and walked into the club-house.

The stories of St Andrews are innumerable, but best of all I enjoy this one from J. B. Salmond's history of the R. and A.:

'Captain later Admiral Maitland Dougall is remembered particularly in the annals of our Club because of his famous feat at the Autumn Meeting in 1860. An extraordinary tempest was raging on the Medal Day, and the rain was lashing down. A vessel was in distress in the bay, the lifeboat was launched at the mouth of the Swilcan, but there was difficulty in manning it. Maitland Dougall, who was to play in the Medal, took the stroke-oar. The lifeboat was five hours at sea. When it returned, Maitland Dougall went on to the tee to play his round, which he completed, and succeeded in winning the Club Gold Medal by returning 112 strokes. He had bored a hole in his ball and put in some buck-shot so that the ball would keep low in the heavy wind.'

The Admiral went on to more successes, as he won no fewer than fifteen medals in his time. Two portraits of him hang in the club-house of the Scotscraig Club nearby, a virile handsome figure with a bold jutting nose, an eagle eye and majestic whiskers like a more splendid Mr Gladstone. The first hole at Scotscraig links, where he was captain, is still called the 'Admiral' to this day.

Maitland Dougall has another claim to fame, as he was the only witness, from his home nearby, of the Tay Bridge disaster when in thick and wicked weather in December 1879 the bridge and a train on it were blown down in a raging gale with the loss of all on board.

Musselburgh

The Open Championship was played at Musselburgh six times between 1874 and 1889, but then the glory departed, the Honourable Company of Edinburgh Golfers taking themselves off to the new links at Muirfield and the Championship with them and leaving the nine holes of Musselburgh links to decay away to their present parlous condition.

The surroundings are bleak, a bit of scruffy common hemmed in by an undistinguished race course and a gasworks, some terrace houses, and a pub. The club-house is a locked shed on which is painted, in an amateur hand, 'Golf Charges, Adults 1s., Juveniles 6d'. The boys from Loretto School nearby play here sometimes. The course is a travesty, the bunkers are grown over, there are no flags or even flagsticks and no tee boxes or any other pilferable apparatus; the coarse thick turf and the rails of the race course make nonsense of the third and fourth holes, aided by iron fences running across the line of play. There are narrow fairways, appalling rough, tiny coarse greens with the holes gouged out by an uncouth crew of small urchins. And yet you somehow could just see a glimmer of the old glories, the second hole—originally the first—called the 'Graves', with the green in its dell, the next 'Linkfield', a tough two-shot hole spoiled by the race course, then the long fourth, 'Mrs Forman's', up to the end of the course to the pub which is still Forman's Inn. After that there is a long one-shot across the end of the links, the 'Sea Hole', followed by the present sixth, 'Pandy', once over a big bunker, now hidden under grass but still with the steeply banked step green, which Willie Park of Musselburgh, who laid out so many courses in the 'nineties, copied at the eighth at Worplesdon and the thirteenth (now the third) at Huntercombe. I must say that both the copies, or imitations, vastly improve on the original, though perhaps today, with the original green reduced in size and the hole idiotically cut on the very steepest part of the bank, one gets no real idea of the hole as it used to be played by golfers.

The round ends by a two-shot hole out towards the beach and then two drive-and-run-up holes back to the locked pavilion, the 'Hole Across', and suitably enough the 'Gas'. In its palmy days the round ended with the one-shot hole with which it now begins, a good clout on to a plateau green, a very tricky shot to gauge today to a hole with no flagstick, for you are then without sense of distance or direction.

Musselburgh is famous for the Park family, who have been associated with the town for 400 years. Old Willie Park won the Open Championship four times, his brother Mungo won it once and his son Willie Junior twice in 1887 and 1889. Young Willie Park's daughter has been Scottish Ladies Champion and played for Great Britain in recent times. In the words of the *Golfer's Handbook*:

'For twenty years old Willie Park had a standing challenge in "Bell's Life", London, to play any man in the world for £100 aside, and he was always ready to defend his challenge. Old Willie Park played numerous matches against Old Tom (Morris); no two professionals ever played so many big matches for stakes over different greens. The big matches took place in 1856, 1858, 1862, 1871 and 1882. The last match came to an abrupt finish at Musselburgh when Willie stood two up and six to play. Bob Chambers (the head of the Edinburgh house of publishers), the referee, stopped play because spectators were interfering with the balls. Chambers and Morris went into Forman's public house and Park, after waiting some time, sent a message that if Morris did not come out and finish the match, he would play the remaining holes alone and claim the stakes. This he did.'

The spectators at Musselburgh—'they damned miners', Andrew Kirkaldy called them—were notorious in protecting the interests of their own favourites and judicious kicks to the ball were frequent. J. H. Taylor suffered so badly from these attentions in his challenge match with young Willie Park in 1895 that Vardon in his great challenge match in 1899, also with young Willie, refused to play the Scottish half at Musselburgh and they played at North Berwick instead.

The Championship here in 1883 produced a dramatic finish, which robbed the local champion, Bob Ferguson, of four straight wins which would have matched the record of young Tom Morris of ten years before. Willie Fernie, in spite of a ten at one hole, scored 159 for the thirty-six holes, but the redoubtable champion forced a tie by finishing with three threes. In the play-off Ferguson was a stroke ahead and got his four, the regulation figure at the last. But Fernie, in the words of Robert Browning, 'not only drove the green but holed a long "steal" for a two and the Championship'.

The championship links of Scotland

All along the coast south and east of Edinburgh is a great and famous chain of golf links, as extensive and magnificent as a similar chain along the west coast of Scotland. Longniddry, New Luffness, Gullane, with three courses, Muirfield and North Berwick, renowned names these and renowned golf too. The turf along this length of coast is of particularly fine quality and the greens made from it are exceptional.

Muirfield

Of these links Muirfield is the most famous, though perhaps not the best known, for it is the private club of the Honourable Company of Edinburgh Golfers, a society founded in 1744, ten years before the Royal and Ancient and unlike the public links of St Andrews or Carnoustie has not been thrown open to all and sundry. Be that as it may, the club knows how to put on a modern championship, as those of us who saw the 1966 Open can assert, and the upkeep and grooming of the links are impeccable. The bunkers are famous with their walls of turf sods as neatly put together as an expertly made dry-wall.

Muirfield, which has had its ups and downs of public esteem, began later than nearly all the other famous Scottish links, being opened in 1891. It was first used for the Open Championship in 1892 when it came in for a lot of criticism. Confined inside a stone wall then it gave, not wholly unreasonably, the impression of being an inland course. As Bernard Darwin puts it:

'Andrew Kirkaldy had many years ago called Muirfield "an auld watermeadie" and there was just enough truth in the aphorism to make it unforgettable. Now the wall has been thrown down and some of the sandhills have become part of the course with a great gain in picturesqueness and probably of golfing quality also.'

Continuing with Bernard Darwin for a moment—for who can put it better:

'Muirfield still retains and always will retain a certain inland character. This proceeds from the fact that we are always or nearly always playing our shots between two lines of rough. I regard St Andrews and Rye as the most entirely seaside golf courses. There we are either on the course or we are in a bunker or a hazard. There is no fairway and no rough.[1] Muirfield is the exact converse; there is a very distinct fairway and very distinct rough. Sometimes the rough is more and sometimes less severe.'

Well, at the Open of 1966 the rough was, I should say, at its most severe and that knee-length grass bending before a stiff breeze on the last day was

[1] I must say I take leave to disagree with this statement as too sweeping.

a terrifying sight; it certainly destroyed a number of cards, notably Arnold Palmer's and Phil Rodgers's on that afternoon.

So not only does Muirfield differ in this respect from other great links but also in many other ways. For instance, it lacks the obscurities and subtlety of St Andrews, with its hidden bunkers and protective slopes, or the ancient complexities of Prestwick. It is not a straight-out-and-home links—for which much thanks. Indeed, it follows the almost required pattern of American courses of today, two loops of nine holes, the second loop being inside the first, and two par threes and two par fives in each nine. Moreover, for all the proud traditions of the Honourable Company, the course has never been a sacred cow to be preserved unmolested; major changes have been made—thus the course has been substantially altered twice—and minor changes in bunkering and other hazards frequently introduced, such as the removal of the black sleepers which walled many bunkers and their replacement by turf walls and the planting of trees on the right of the eighth hole to prevent any further use of Walter Hagen's bold short-cut to the green which served him so well in 1929 with two birdies on the last day's play.

Nonetheless, some admirable traditions are prized by the Honourable Company. After all, they drew up the first set of rules of golf, in 1744—ten years before those of the R. and A.—when they were housed at Leith links, and their first winner of the Silver Club, which made him 'Captain of the Golf', surgeon John Rattray got involved in 'the '45'. He was called out in the early hours of the morning to attend the wounded of Prince Charles Edward's army after the Battle of Prestonpans; he followed the White Cockade to Derby and retreated with it too, being taken at the stricken field of Culloden, though he was later released. And the pictures in the clubhouse are a notable collection, including Raeburn's full-length portrait of his fellow-member Alexander Keith, and the portrait, which adorned the cover of the 1966 Open Championship programme, of William St Clair of Roslin, four times captain of the club, who was the last descendant of an ancestor who came over with William the Norman in 1066 and may well have spent the night before the Battle of Hastings with the rest of William's army in my garden on Telham Hill.

So to the golf. The first thing to note about the play at Muirfield is that it's all above board; you can see what is demanded of you, the bunkers are all on view and like it or not the play is laid out before your eyes. Let us see this through the eyes of Herbert Warren Wind, that distinguished golf writer from the United States:

'Muirfield's great quality is its frankness—its honesty. There are no hidden bunkers, no recondite burns, no misleading and capricious terrain.

The championship links of Scotland

Every hazard is clearly visible. Chiefly for this reason, the course has always been extremely popular with foreign golfers and especially Americans; it has a sort of "inland" flavour that makes visitors feel much more at home on it than on any other British championship course. Moreover, Muirfield is perhaps the most beautifully conditioned course in Britain.'

Sam McKinlay, the well-known Scottish golf writer and a former player for Britain in the Walker Cup, says this:

'When I was younger and still enjoyed a modest competence in golf, I used to think that if I had to play a match for my life on a course of my choice I would plump for Muirfield. It is the best and fairest of courses—not, perhaps, the course where I would choose to play all my golf if my activities had to be restricted to one links, for it is a little too fierce, too long, too exposed to the winds that sweep down Gullane Hill or in from the North Sea. But a man who has command of his game and of himself will fare better at Muirfield than almost any other course I know. It rewards the good shot, penalises the bad one, and is so constructed that it is a complete examination of the player.'

Well, what's the snag, there must be one, or this would be the one great perfect course in all the world? So let's say it in a little quiet voice—it lacks charm. It is a fair, just examination just as Hoylake is. You respect it, you respect it tremendously, but you somehow don't quite get to love it.

You start out with three par fours, the second and third of no great length, and here the great players are hoping for birdies, then a well-bunkered par three, followed by a 516-yard hole where Nicklaus got up with a drive and an eight-iron downwind. The sixth is a tough dog-leg with bunkers at the elbow, and the seventh a tough par three into the prevailing wind. The eighth is a famous hole, 451 yards now, with a great cluster of bunkers on the right of the fairway where the drive reaches, and a cross-bunker in front of the green. Hagen used to take his own line far away to the right here, but this has now been bottled up. Along the left side of the fairway is Archerfield Wood, dark and sinister, which plays a part as Graden Sea Wood in Robert Louis Stevenson's story *The Pavilion on the Links*.

The ninth is a really tough hole with a narrow target area for the drive and then a very tight shot indeed up to the green with bunkers on the right and a wall and out-of-bounds on the left. It was here that we saw Doug Sanders hole a fifty-yard chip for an eagle in the last round of the 1966 Open, without which he would not have got a tie for second place. The second nine is rather easier than the first and some very low scores were done in 1966, including Phil Rodgers's 30. The tenth, 475 yards, with a west wind sweeping across at right angles, can give a lot of trouble, but the last two holes have been the most notable for separating the men from the boys. The seventeenth at 528 yards, although Roberto de Vincenzo did it in two in one championship, eluded all the contestants on the last day of the 1966 Open except Jack Nicklaus, although it was played with the help of a brisk breeze. It was here that Nicklaus showed his mettle, after barely surviving a terrible run of trouble in the middle of the last nine, by belting a five-iron shot right home to the green, to follow up his three-iron off the tee to get a birdie four when his pursuers couldn't better a par five. The last hole, a really tough 429-yarder with three bunkers on the left and one on the right waiting to grab your drive, bunkers in front of the green and on either side of it, showed Nicklaus's class for he played a dead straight one-iron off the tee followed by a beautiful cup-up number three-iron which held up into the wind and finished pin high to the right of the hole giving him an easy putt.

Troon

Troon is next door to Prestwick on the Ayrshire coast and came into the championship rota in 1923 when Arthur Havers won a welcome victory for Britain after two years of American success. Although it is so close to Prestwick—there is even a party-fence I believe—Troon is considerably different, less humpy, bumpy and hillocky, instead with bigger bolder sandhills, a more straight-forward layout, less charming, longer and I suppose for the modern ball tougher. Troon has been lengthened a number of times, most recently for the 1962 championship which Arnold Palmer so spectacularly won, and can now be stretched to over 7,000 yards. This I suppose is necessary—though I would prefer some limitation of the ball— and I suppose that if Arnold and Co. went to work on 6,500 yard Prestwick they might score in the very low sixties; I'd love to see them try. Palmer has described his championship here in his excellent book *My Game and Yours* but unfortunately his management organisation refused to allow a quotation to be made. I had liked particularly Palmer's resolve not to get 'locked into a life-and-death struggle with the course' and all that followed. So it is too bad that we are not allowed to quote. However, Palmer gave everybody a lesson of how to play a fast dry links at Troon that year, winning from Nagle by six shots and scoring three out of the six rounds in the entire tournament under 70, one of them a spreadeagling 67. In contrast Gary Player couldn't cope at all and failed to survive 'the cut' while Jack Nicklaus, not yet at his majestic peak, wallowed along twenty-nine shots behind Palmer in the aggregate.

Another famous victory here was that of Charlie Yates—a close friend of mine in his later years—from Atlanta, Georgia, who took our Amateur Championship the first time it was played at Troon in 1938, beating the Irishman Cecil Ewing in the final. This was the famous year in Walker Cup history when Britain won its only victory after we had been whitewashed at Pine Valley in 1936 and this description of Charlie and his friends by Henry Longhurst caught my fancy:

'Four of their side hailed from the south, and wickedly good players they were too: Ed White, from Texas, slim and dark with humorous film-star eyes; Walter Emery, of Oklahoma City, a big happy-go-lucky fellow of infinite zest; Reynolds Smith from Dallas, stocky, dark and determined; and Charlie Yates, a wise-cracking, happy-go-lucky young protégé of Bobby Jones down in Atlanta. So infectious, incidentally, were Yates's high spirits that two years later he accomplished the unprecedented feat of standing on the steps of the Royal and Ancient Club-house at St Andrews after the Walker Cup match and inducing the crowd to accompany him in "A wee doch an' doris".

'The voices of this quartet intrigued their British visitors, who had not heard the like except in the movies and hardly believed it then. Their average age was twenty-three, which in golfing maturity is equivalent perhaps to thirty over here. They chewed stubs of black cigars and let forth a barrage of wise-cracking good humour. Emery had a broad-brimmed hat and needed only a lasso hanging from his golf bag to complete the picture.'

Another famous win at Troon in the Amateur was that of John Beharrel, who took the championship of 1956 a few weeks after his eighteenth birthday, the youngest winner up to that time, and if this is by far his main distinction in first-class golf to date there is plenty of time yet.

Well, we had better go out and have a look at the links, which is one of the out-and-home variety. The first six holes run south along the shore, three moderate par fours each under 400 yards as a start, of gradually increasing difficulty, and we had better take not more than thirteen shots over them, for we get into the long-hitting area from then on, the 510–545-yard fourth with a long one-shotter next and then the 580-yard sixth (550 yards off my tee) with a great swale in front of the green, a big hole in every sense of the word.

We then turn away from the coast with a most attractive hole, a mild dog-leg, among the sandhills with many traps for the drive and a plateau green. After this we have the shortest hole in British championship golf, the 125-yard 'Postage Stamp', or more properly 'Ailsa', named for the hump behind the green which resembles Ailsa Craig in shape. Awful disasters have happened here, for the green is proportionately small and the protecting bunkers deep and grasping. In 1950 in the Open a German amateur scored fifteen here, having visited all three of the protecting bunkers and enjoying five strokes in one of them; he did well to complete the round in 92.

Leaving 'Ailsa' with a three, we hope, we turn into the sandhills with three difficult and testing holes, with a notably big carry off the tee at the tenth as we turn for home and a recently lengthened eleventh hole, which might be named for Arnold Palmer, up to the railway before the 'Fox', the twelfth, takes us back towards the sea. So a straight run-in via an immense sixteenth to the difficult seventeenth one-shotter, a 225-yard stroke to a plateau green and then a tightly bunkered 375-yard hole finishes the round.

Carnoustie

One of the pleasures of golf as opposed to, say, cricket or lawn tennis is that no two courses are alike, nor are they expected to be. While Bramall Lane may differ from the Worcester County ground in its surroundings, the playing surface can only vary to a minor degree, but at golf no part of any course need resemble any part of any other. Carnoustie is quite different from St Andrews, Prestwick, Muirfield or Troon, better in some respects, less good in others, but a splendid testing, difficult links in its own right. It is a public course, and the amenities, which are to be improved, often suggest that it's less trouble to change your shoes in the car park than to make more elaborate arrangements. Don't be put off by that, for you are in for a first-class exacting testing round of golf.

The feature of Carnoustie is the water hazards which, in the shape of two burns, the Barry burn and Jockie's burn, wind all over the place, usually where you would least like to encounter them. The links is flat, the fairways, while carrying a fair share of small undulations, are much less humpy than many; attractive sea-woods of fir break up the monotony; while you are not distracted by any view of the sea, there is, as on so many good golf courses, the railway along one flank.

You start out with a generous hole of 401 yards with a nice gathering green in a hollow to help you on your way. You then play a similar but rather longer and tighter hole in the same direction. The third is a beautiful drive and pitch back towards town to a small green with Jockie's burn to carry with the pitch. So far, so good. The fourth, out again along the other side of the sea-wood you skirted on the third, is a longer par four, but still not very long; somehow more fives get on the card here than should. The fifth is a beauty, dog-legged to a plateau green but still not too long for the ordinary player. The sixth, a par five, gives a lot of trouble to the pros who are looking for a four, while for us there are mid-fairway bunkers about 210 yards from the tee, and then Jockie's burn edging into the fairway about 200 yards further on. You follow with a par four along the out-of-bounds to the left, then an undistinguished short hole and then a two-shotter to the railway, just a bit longer and softer to the run of the ball than it looks.

The tenth hole is 'South America', a two-shot hole of 406 yards with the Barry burn just rather too close to the front apron of the green for comfort. The name of this hole is attributed to a farewell party for a citizen of the town who was off to seek his fortune; in the morning after the party he woke up there—and never went any farther. After this the eleventh back parallel is not too tough, nor is the twelfth, in spite of its protective ridge in front of the green, provided, and only provided, that we play it as a par five.

Thirteen is a short hole but tightly bunkered, so fours are too common. After that come the 'Spectacles', a fine slashing hole of 473 yards with its green backing on to that of the fourth. The hole gets its name from the two big bunkers in the face of the ridge across the fairway nearly 400 yards from the tee which blinds the view of the hole and traps the timid shot or the shot played after an indifferent drive. Fifteen is an absolute beauty, a two-shot hole of 423 yards to a green in a shallow dell, a wonderfully satisfying hole at which to get a four. The sixteenth is a terribly tough par three, of 235 yards, to a small plateau green.

At the seventeenth we have to cross the snake path of the Barry burn thrice, so there are three chances of getting into it, and then we have to hit a firm shot home to a small gathering green, quite hard to find at 428 yards. The eighteenth is 453 yards back to the kiosk, and here you may have to cross the burn twice, unimportantly from the tee and bitterly importantly with a long second or a short pitch, for it runs right across, bang in front of the green. For the tournament player this hole can demand a terrible decision: to go for it and fail or play short and miss a four.

To my taste this is one of the great links: without a wind not too harsh and not too rough on the man content with an 80. But if you want a 72 then you've got to play golf.

Carnoustie has come late into the championship rota and I suppose its greatest moments came in 1953 when Hogan came over to try to win the British Open to add to his U.S. title. His views of the links differ somewhat from ours, but they were interesting and refreshing and it is unfortunate that we are not free to quote them.

Turnberry

Turnberry, on the southern Ayrshire coast, is the last of the Scottish championship links, coming into the rota, so far for the Amateur only, in

The latest of the Scottish championship courses, the Ailsa Course at Turnberry, showing the 10th green and the rocky island of Ailsa Craig on the horizon
(*W. Ralston Ltd by permission of British Transport Hotels Ltd*)

ABOVE The famous 'Postage Stamp' hole at Troon. At 125 yards this is the shortest hole on any championship course in Britain (*H. W. Neale*)
BELOW The 17th green at Prestwick, 'the Alps'. The bunker is rather shallower and less formidable than it used to be and the sleepered face less evident. The second shot is played blind over a large sandhill (*S. H. Benson*)

ABOVE A. H. Padgham, a champion of pre-war days, putting on the short 13th green at Muirfield; the 12th green is behind (*The Sport & General Press Agency Ltd*)

BELOW LEFT The step-green of the 377/389-yard 5th hole at Carnoustie (*H. W. Neale*)

BELOW RIGHT The green of what is now the 4th hole at Musselburgh links known as 'Mrs Forman's'. Forman's Inn is still the dominant feature here (*Peter Allen*)

ABOVE Hell bunker on the long 14th hole at St Andrews with the town in the distance. The green is just beyond the third player from the right about 100 yards from the bunker (*G. M. Cowie*)
CENTRE Playing out of the Road bunker at the 17th hole at St Andrews, a most difficult shot with the green so narrow and the road beyond (*Sport & General Press Agency Ltd*)
BELOW Even Peter Thomson can get in the Swilcan Burn at the first hole at St Andrews (*Keystone Press Agency Ltd*)

1961. It was also used in the disastrous Walker Cup match in 1963, when after leading six to three on the first day Britain crashed to ruin on the second.

Turnberry is part of a British Rail holiday 'complex', with a large—and good—hotel on the cliff overlooking the links-land, with two courses, and the southern end of the Firth of Clyde with the granite dome of Ailsa Craig predominating out to sea, Arran further off, then the Mull of Kintyre and under extreme weather conditions the far coast of Antrim near Portrush. Of course, all these are only visible in exceptional circumstances and we had better recall the rather dour local pronouncement: 'If you can see Ailsa Craig it's going to rain and if you can't see it it's raining.'

Before Hitler's war there were two holiday courses here. Then an R.A.F. Coastal Command station flattened out the fairways and built concrete runways. At the end of the war it all looked a dead loss. But British Rail for once refused to accept defeat and the two courses were reconstructed by MacKenzie Ross, one still a holiday circuit and the other, the 'Ailsa', giving the full treatment. I must say that the only time I played it, off the back tees, on a windy autumn day I found it extremely long and tough, but there were some beautiful shots to recompense you. Thus after a modest up-and-down start on the flatter ground inland from the big sandhills you come to the 155-yard fourth cocked up in the dunes, with the coast in between you and the green which has that characteristic of all difficult holes—it looks much farther than it is. After a big par-five sixth there is another heavy one-shot into the hills of 235 yards or more, which I can't get on against the wind, but Billy Joe Patton unfortunately can. So up we go hitting to the seventh and eighth—half a mile between them—so that we can be ready to tackle the drive at the ninth to a 420-yard hole, from a rocky pinnacle out to sea, and hit our ball over the cliffs and surging in-running tide to a fairway and green by the lighthouse, the apotheosis of seaside golf. The tenth along the cliffs is another exhilarating two-shotter. From then on it is rather less exciting until the short fifteenth, a hole with a minute green perched up in the hills with nothing but it to shoot at, where I believe in the Walker Cup Charles Coe, an Augusta member, holed a horribly important chip to frustrate us. Then comes the attractive par-four sixteenth, 380 yards downhill but with a deep burn in front of the green into which Michael Bonallack's shot went in those fatal foursomes on the second day to turn the tide inexorably against us. A long seventeenth follows, another bad hole for Britain in this match, before a milder finishing hole. So ends a great links in a great setting—don't miss it.

3 Other Scottish courses

This chapter presents some problems, for there are so many great Scottish courses outside the championship list. Many of these, had they been more accessible, might well have housed the Open or the Amateur; Dornoch, Cruden Bay and Machrihanish at once come to mind and others perhaps are as good.

In the end it seems best to keep to a strictly personal line and only visit courses I know myself, which will lead, I fear, to some notable omissions: Montrose, Nairn, Lossiemouth, Machrihanish, Leven, Scotscraig, Cruden Bay, Rosemount, Balgownie and others. This chapter is rather a mixed bag then, but has provided many pleasant hours in collecting the information.

North Inch

The North Inch, in the city of Perth, like the South Inch, is public parkland lying along the bank of the River Tay. Golf has been played on this spot for centuries. It would be reasonable to suppose that 500 years ago, when golf was being suppressed in Scotland for interfering with archery, this was a golf course, but records are silent. However, the Kirk Session records pinpoint one tolerably early date:

'Nov. 19, 1599—John Gardiner, James Bowman, Laurence Chalmers and Laurence Cuthbert confessed that they were playing at the golf on the North Inch at the time of the preaching afternoon on the Sabbath. The Session rebuked them, and admonished them to resort to the hearing of the Word diligently on the Sabbath in time coming, which they promised to do.'

Today there are eighteen holes on the North Inch, together with football and hockey fields, with a total length for the course of 5,000-odd yards. There is nothing really to show that it is indeed historic turf. The ground is flat, there are a few trees; the river is on one side, with perhaps a man or two in waders trying for a salmon, and solid citizens' houses on the other. Various games are played, numerous golfers are on the move and dogs are being exercised; it looks rather like Clapham Common. The length of the course has varied; in very early days there were only six holes, then nine, and for quite a time ten; thirteen holes were the round for a time and finally eighteen; the holes have also moved away from the city, which would be easy enough with their simple layout.

The start of the round is dreary in the extreme, flat, featureless and without rough or hazards, three holes up and down the common. As the Rev. T. D. Miller wrote at the turn of the century, 'To a stranger, at the first glance, the Inch seems sadly lacking in hazards. In the park part there is ample scope for the wildest of drives. But it is when we leave the Inch and gain the peninsula that the real sport begins.' And that it so today, bunkers shrewdly placed, small greens and the proximity of the river, all make for good fun once out beyond the parkland. The holes at the end, the long one-shot fourteenth up to the river's edge, the 368-yard fifteenth all along it with the easy possibility of a hook into it, the short tricky little sixteenth right by the water, all these are excellent sport. So after a disappointing start and a dreary eighteenth we find we have enjoyed ourselves more than we expected, but, of course, we have not played the actual *holes* which King James VI played, but have played just on the *ground* where he and his predecessors played. The holes must have altered many times, but no matter, it is good to have visited such an historic spot. After all, the great players of a hundred years ago all competed here: Young Tom, Allan Robertson, Willie Park, and the most famous of the players in the town, Bob Andrews named 'The Rook'.

Dornoch

My friend Rush and I with our wives made a special pilgrimage to Dornoch in July 1966 and I am glad we did, for this introduced us to a most famous and all-too-rarely visited links. The reason for this is easy to understand—remoteness. For Dornoch is 220 miles from Edinburgh and even when you get to Inverness, and you think you ought to be very near, you still have over sixty miles of not very fast road to go.

The course is never crowded, hardly occupied sometimes, even in high summer. Herbert Warren Wind, the American writer, who is such a perceptive observer of golf and such a beautiful writer on the game, said this on his first visit:

'While no one expects the pro shop at a Scottish club to resemble our temples of merchandising, the shop at Dornoch, close by the first tee,

Other Scottish courses

turned out to be nothing but a glassed-in booth with a roof of corrugated tin painted brownish red. There was no one on duty when we arrived. We tried the club-house, a small two-storey building in which, except for a new bar, everything must be quite as it was in 1904, when the club celebrated the official opening of its extended eighteen holes. . . .

'I could not help thinking that on such a glorious morning—and Saturday too—the Old Course at St Andrews was probably overrun with golfers yet here at what one might call the St Andrews of the North, there was not a soul to be seen except a big gray cat with one blind eye. He is called Nelson, and prowls placidly round the first tee from morn to night—the reincarnation, unquestionably, of some old golfer who never got his fill. . . . However, this same remoteness explains the unique position that Dornoch has long held in golf; for over half a century it has been regarded as one of the outstanding courses in the world by men close to the heart of the game, yet very few of them have ever played it.'

One has heard so much of Dornoch that it would not be surprising if reality was a disappointment, but here for once it isn't so, a splendid magnificent natural links with some of the most beautiful sites for greens on natural plateaux that you could imagine. Moreover, it includes my 'dream hole'; over many years I had had a recurring dream of a golf hole going up and up, intensely green, with heather in the rough, up into a sky of driving wet clouds and fleeting sunlight as the mists blew across. Always in the dream it was the same. The sixteenth at Dornoch, the first time we played it, was just like that, except that we saw no heather in the rough, but like enough for me to say at once 'This is it'; there was an absolute sense of *déja vu*—and I've never had the dream again.

If you could pin a couple of defects on Dornoch it is that it is a straight out-and-home course and that it has four short holes of much the same length, for I have used a four-iron at each of them in one round. But this is very minor criticism for what otherwise earns lyrical praise.

The links lies along Dornoch Firth and from every hole there is a view of the sea, by no means a characteristic of seaside links, witness Birkdale, for example, Deal or St Andrews, where a sight of the sea is fleeting indeed. Dornoch links is on two levels, the upper holes on a ridge of sandhills and the lower holes down in among them close to the beach, so close in fact that at the short tenth a moderate pull will put you on the shore. A most ingenious feature of Dornoch is that in changing levels you play downhill three times—at the third, eighth and seventeenth—and only play uphill once, at the sixteenth; the other changes of level are made by walking up to the tee, vastly preferable to beating a golf ball uphill, the most tedious of all forms of the game.

You start out with a short par four of 350 yards where the ground runs kindly for you and a birdie is always a possibility; after that there is a stiff tough par three with a bunker at the left edge which embraces you all too readily. You then transfer to the lower level with an exhilarating drive downhill with a shot to the green at 410 yards which is not easy; the green doesn't gather the ball. The fourth is much the same length with the green on a plateau, a fine shot. The fifth, too, has a plateau green, a real beauty, so moulded that although the hole is only 335 yards it's a tough difficult four. The green lies well in from the front of the carry. This hole is called 'Hilton', no doubt after Harold of that ilk rather than Conrad, judging by the hotels in Dornoch. Six is a short hole among the sandhills, again the green is on its plateau. So then you walk uphill and play a rather mild uninteresting short par five along the top of the sandhills.

This is, however, taken care of by the lovely eighth, where you drive over a precipice towards the northern sea, then probably off a hanging lie, a stiff iron-shot down, down over a lot of humps and bumps and a little dead ground to a green in a little dell.

Then at the ninth you turn for home, and probably into the wind, for a mild and helpful par five. After that all mercy is done with and you have to play for your life against the prevailing wind. The tenth is a short hole, set among the bents and bunkers and the shore just off line.

Eleven is a very tough 445-yard par four out of my reach, only redeemed by twelve which is a shortish par five. Thirteen is another stiff iron shot into the wind, par three. Fourteen is 'Foxy', a famous double dog-leg or double-banana hole 450 yards, which needs a big drawn drive, followed by a big faded brassie along a shallow valley up to a plateau green, all without a single bunker. This hole is splendid for bigger golfers than I am, but too far for me as a four hole. The fifteenth is a short par four with a big sandy hill to carry and sixteen is long and uphill and in spite of being the 'dream hole' the dullest on the links. The seventeenth, though, is a gorgeous hole, a big drive downhill and downwind, with a firm iron shot over the protecting bunkers in the face of the ridge on which, fifty yards on, the green is moulded. After that the walk up to the eighteenth tee and the subsequent hole 455 yards along the top of the ridge, with the swale in front of the green are only moderately interesting. Altogether the 6,505-yard course is rated at 72, and if you can match that—gross or net—you have achieved something.

No great tournaments have been played at Dornoch—for, after all, it is about 58 degrees north of the Equator—but in its day, which goes back to 1616, some distinguished players have been moulded by it. Donald Ross, one of America's great golf architects, came from Dornoch. Sir Ernest Holderness, Amateur Champion of 1922 and 1924, developed his game there, and very good it was; Roger Wethered, who won the Amateur in 1923 and so nearly won the Open in 1921, was another pupil of Dornoch, and so was his sister Joyce Wethered, the greatest woman player of all time. After all, didn't Bobby Jones reply to the question put forty years ago, 'How does it feel to be the greatest player in the world?': 'I don't know, the greatest player in the world is a woman.' It is especially agreeable to find that Herbert Warren Wind at the end of his round was delighted by Dornoch. He says:

'... I played an exceedingly solid round, for me, and that was important to me. Dornoch was one course I wanted very much to like, and, say what you will, you cannot like a course unless you play it reasonably well. I should imagine that Dornoch usually elicits a golfer's best game. It doesn't overawe you with its length. It supplies plenty of gorseless "lebensraum" to err in. It keeps you on your toes by making it clear from the outset that it rewards only shots that have been well thought out and well executed. And it encourages you to hit decisive shots by providing vigorous, close-cropped turf, on which the ball sits up beautifully, and very true greens, which are a joy to putt. In a word, I found Dornoch all I had hoped it would be—a thoroughly modern old links with that rare equipoise of charm and character that only the great courses possess.'

Western Gailes

The links of the Western Club at Gailes on the Ayrshire coast lies between Troon and Irvine, hard by Glasgow Gailes, with which it is sometimes confused. It is one of the finest links in Scotland, though less renowned than some, for few major titles, other than the Scottish Amateur and Professional Championships, have been contested there.

The course runs in a big loop out from the club-house, first to the north, then with a long run to the south among the dunes close to the shore, and then a final turn back northwards for the last five holes to the finish. There is an abundance of fine sandhills, and several of the greens, like the first, are in delightful natural dells or saucers. There are only three short holes, but none of them easy; the seventh is a tough shot through a gap in the sandhills to an unwelcoming green, while the thirteenth has a burn to call to the aid of all its bunkers.

When on the pilgrimage to Troon, Prestwick and Turnberry try to spare time for a round at Western Gailes; you will be repaid.

Gullane

Moving now to the east coast of Scotland east of Edinburgh, we should if we can spend a week, for there is a rich profusion of beautiful links, of which after Muirfield the best is perhaps Gullane No. 1, though proponents of New Luffness, with its superlative greens, or historic North Berwick might not agree. However, I have to come down for Gullane No. 1 if only that I had a flashy lucky round there recently with three birdies in the first six holes. The No. 2 course is rather shorter than No. 1, which, after all, is used for Open Championship qualifying rounds, while No. 3 is distinctly shorter. They all have this in common, though, excellent turf and greens and a climb up Gullane Hill. This is well worth the effort, for the view from the top on a fine day is a wonderful sight: Muirfield links spread out like a map on the right, the Firth of Forth ahead, with distant hills beyond to the north, Aberlady Bay running away to the left towards Edinburgh, of which the main features and even the Forth Bridges can be seen in clear weather. And all around at your feet acres of fine turf, emerald greens with their flags and links merging with links for miles it seems.

The course is a good deal hillier than many seaside links because of the great hump of Gullane Hill, but apart from the second, fifth and sixth the climbing won't bother you too much and you have some enjoyable shots downhill to compensate, like those at the seventh and the seventeenth. There are four short holes, of which two stick in my memory, the 192-yard fourth, where I hit the stick with an outrageously overhit shot over the guarding cross-bunker and so got an underserved two, and the attractive plateau green of the 153-yard thirteenth, cocked up in the sandhills. Another memorable hole is the seventeenth, where you drive downhill and quite probably downwind and then find yourself confronted by three huge bunkers in a ridge guarding the green with no way round.

North Berwick

Moving along the coast past Muirfield we must pause for a round on the West Links at North Berwick, a public course like Carnoustie and St Andrews, but good and famous golf, for all that.

You start out with a tricky hole, 'Point Garry', for although it's only 330 yards long you can possibly drive too far and get into a hideously unattractive gully about 200 yards from the tee leading down to the shore, so be careful or you will spoil your pitch up to a high green, shared with the par-five seventeenth, 'Point Garry In'. The green is a malevolent one, sloping to the sea. The second hole, the 'Sea Hole', along the coast puts the fear of God into you, for if you go for a proper line to enable you to get home in two, and you slice it ever so little, there you are on the beach again. Then follows a short par five which necessitates hitting your second shot over a stone wall, a dull hole this.

The fourth is 'Carl Kemp', a stiff iron shot to a green amid bumps,

Other Scottish courses

humps, bunkers and even a few rocks. Then a moderate-length two-shotter bending to the right, followed by another short hole, the 'Quarry', over a great pit with bunkers in it. So to number seven, a difficult 360-yarder, for the green is guarded very close up by the Eil or Eel burn, for which the hole is named; don't underclub here—I did and paid for it.

With two rather moderate par fives, moderate in length and moderate in quality, we are out at the end of the links.

We turn for home with a tightly bunkered par three hitting down from a tee in the sandhills. Then a 500-yarder hugging the hills on the left-hand side of the fairway leading to a small plateau green. A dog-leg 360-yarder takes us back close to the shore and after that the fun begins. The thirteenth, the 'Pit', is 350 yards long, the second half of it flanked on the left by a stone wall about three feet high. The fairway is on one side of the stone wall and the long narrow green on the other. If you have driven cleverly up the left side of the fairway your pitch will be almost along the line of the wall and up the length of the green, very good. But if you drive right of centre, then you are pitching more or less across the line of the wall and across the line of the green, which is all too near the beach for comfort. Then you have to do something clever or else exceedingly skilful. I had beginner's luck here, for on hard ground my ball bounced over the wall and on to the green, which annoyed my friend Gibb exceedingly, as well it might.

The fourteenth is 'Perfection', a drive and iron hole of 382 yards. You drive on to a fairway, which cants to the right off the slopes of a big sandhill; if you hit a bad slice you may be among Carl Kemp's rocks. However, if you are on the fairway then you blaze away with a completely blind shot over a big hill running across your front, aiming at a tall marker on the very beach itself. The green looks perilously near the shore and no doubt people have been known to putt into the sea, certainly hit their approach shots into it.

The fifteenth is the most famous hole at North Berwick, the 'Redan', a big thump of 195 yards over a hill to a plateau green set rather across the line of play guarded by a huge deep bunker under the left-hand side of the escarpment of the green and lesser bunkers on the right. This hole has been copied, or rather imitated, innumerable times in the United States, notably at the National, at the Links Club and at Merion East, always with the feature of the green on the plateau and the deep encroaching bunker lying under its flank. Well, I don't know what's the matter with me or whether I played off the wrong tee, but I found the hole totally unsatisfactory, as it was masked by a great hump about 125 yards from the tee which spoiled the look of the hole as well as half blinding it. If the hump

St Andrews, known by name to golfers the world over.

Photo: Gerry Cranham

were bulldozed away the hole would be no easier and far better. Alas for one of the great disappointments of a golfing life!

The sixteenth is a curious hole, with its green close under the windows of the Marine Hotel. You drive over the wall and have to watch that you don't go into the ditch about 210 yards out; you then play over some bunkers with about a five-iron to a green which even Trent Jones would think was eccentric in shape: two little plateaux joined by a narrow neck formed by a deep gully but all mown putting surface; how you putt from one plateau to the other I wouldn't know.

Seventeen, 'Point Garry In', is a par five, uphill at the finish, of 470 yards; the hole has a reputation for terror, as the small green slopes sharply towards the sea and there is a big cross-bunker seventy yards short of the hole.

Finally we hit home to a plateau green 275 yards off and, of course, hope here for a three to finish; however, the slopes of the plateau tend to shrug you off, so you may be disappointed. There's a story here of a young pro in his first tournament saying to his caddie, 'I don't need a driver I'll go over the green if I hit it,' to which his caddie replied dourly, 'Ye'll no hit it'.

Among the charms of North Berwick is the scenery, the coastline being enhanced by the Bass Rock and several rocky islets and the Forth busy with shipping.

Gleneagles

We must not leave Scotland without a visit to Gleneagles if only that to the outside world it is better known and more visited than anywhere in the British Isles except St Andrews; every American golfer has heard of St Andrews and 99 per cent of them have heard of Gleneagles.

Well, there are many things in its favour, first of all a superb setting in a shallow valley between the Ochil Hills to the south and foothills leading up to the Grampians to the north. On a fine day in early autumn there is no more beautiful place in the world to play golf, none, not any. Then there is a splendid hotel—that is if you can afford it—with excellent food and service, shops and all the amenities, very unrailwaylike for all that it is owned by British Railways. Incidentally, you can sometimes stay at the Dormy House down by the courses at half the price.

But how about the golf, or should we say gowff? It is not difficult, but it is not meant to be, either on the King's or the Queen's course; the fairways are wide and smooth, the greens large and the bunkers do not intimidate. It is fairly long and the pull uphill on the King's from the second green to the sixth can be a weariness of the flesh if the wind is in

Other Scottish courses

your teeth. The *look* of both courses is excellent and they are beautifully kept; they flatter you delicately. Nevertheless, there are some highly picturesque and delightful holes, the exhilarating drive downhill at the second, the blind shot over the hill at the third, the short fifth like a dome amid bunkers and the drive and iron at the ninth. Coming in there's the big 285-yard belt over the hillocks and hazards to the green at the fourteenth and a big two-shotter immediately preceding it.

To end on a sour note I must declare that I find the nauseating Scottish ballyhoo with which Gleneagles is larded totally revolting. The holes have been elaborately named with such trash as the 'Heich o' Fash', the 'Warslin' Lea', the 'Wee Bogle', and others which you can't bring yourself to even try to pronounce.

Southerness-on-Solway

We will end this chapter with a brief reference to the links at Southerness-on-Solway on the coast to the south of Dumfries. Not only is this a beautiful place with views along the coast of Galloway and inland to the mountain of Criffel, and also across the Solway to the mountains of the Lake District, and on a clear day even to the Isle of Man, but it is also an attractive natural links. More distinctive, it is one of the few golf *links* to be built since World War II.

It has been laid out on a flat area of links-land with some heather and it gives the impression that not much money has been spent on it. It is all the better for that, for like the old links of the last century, use has had to be made of natural hollows and dells and plateaux and shelves for greens and tees and the bunkers are often scars and scrapes ocurring naturally in the thin turf. Wind-eroded bunkers are not uncommon and sometimes give you a very bad lie. But it is a delightful natural golf links with some absolutely charming holes, the two short holes early in the round, the two-shot eighth across the creek, the excellent two-shotters coming in at thirteen, fifteen and sixteen. Don't miss it if you are in the neighbourhood.

Near Southerness, indeed within less than a mile of the links, John Paul Jones, Admiral and sea rover, was born. He threw in his lot with the American revolutionaries in 1775 and during the ensuing war harassed British shipping off our own coasts as far afield as Lowestoft. Later he took service with Catherine the Great of Russia as Kontradmiral Pavel Ivanovitch Jones and eventually died in reduced circumstances in France.

He also gave his name to a dance which is practised to this day.

4 Channel Coast

Prince's

I wish I could like Prince's as much as my own true loves on this stretch of wonderful links-land, Sandwich and Deal, but alas I cannot. What's more, I fear that I can't feel that the new courses here are as attractive as the old one which was blasted out of existence in World War II.

Before the war this championship links, on which Sarazen won with a record total in 1932, had a great deal of charm with its shallow valleys and dog-leg holes and the range of sandhills, the Himalayas, at the far end near the coastguard cottages, over which you had to whack twice, once as a second shot to the eighth and once as a drive to the eleventh.

The war altered all this; first the needs of coastal defence, then the use of the area as a battle-training area, removed the landmarks and created a wilderness from which, with the best will in the world, the old links could not have been revived. So an entirely new layout of twenty-seven holes was ordained by the new patron of the links, the late Sir Aynsley Bridgland, an eighteen-hole course of championship calibre, the Blue, and the nine-hole circuit, the Red. The Red nine is not inferior in length and difficulty to the Blue and a combination of holes from each course is sometimes used, as in the Curtis Cup matches in 1956 against the ladies of America, which incidentally Britain won.

It is very hard to say why these great courses, and great they are all right, should fail to exercise the charm of Sandwich and Deal. The links-land, though lacking any large sandhills like those at Sandwich next door, is of the true quality, the shallow valleys are still there and full of folded and testing lies, the holes have been laid out with the greatest care to provide pleasure and pain depending on the needs of the day, by many alternative teeing grounds. There are many plateau greens of great charm and all the bunkers you need. True, the ground from the club-house looks uninspiring, but that's true in many another place; it's flat and somehow seems much flatter than it used to be; it is treeless, but Deal and Sandwich are treeless too. None the less, you do somehow get the impression that this is the less attractive end of the wonderful stretch of golfing country which runs for five miles from the outskirts of Deal town due north to Pegwell Bay and the mouth of the Stour. Pegwell Bay is its wonderful blue, the cliffs of Ramsgate are shining white and the larks rise singing from the rough, as Bernard Darwin has often reminded us, but a hideous power station defaces the northern horizon. I also take it rather hard that the first two holes on the Blue course add up to the distressing total of 1,048 yards, even if the first hole is indeed the famous seventeenth of the old links. There is some big hitting to be done coming home, with a huge tenth hole half into the prevailing wind, as are thirteen, fourteen, fifteen, seventeen and eighteen. The last two are as attractive a pair as you'll find anywhere, the seventeenth 410 yards long, horribly beset with bunkers round the green, including a real live cross-bunker in front and the 367-yard eighteenth without a bunker at all but a crown-green to throw off any but the straightest second shot.

Use has been made of old greens and fairways, often approached now from another direction. Thus the present seventeenth green was the old first green, the fourth and fifth were remade from the old sixth and seventh, and the eighteenth green is the original one, but a whole series of new holes has come into existence, several on a hitherto unused area near the beach, of which the short eleventh is notable, with a small island green perched in the sandhills above a wasteland valley and needing no bunkers to help or distract you.

The most famous son of Prince's—and this is literally true, for he was born in the club-house—is the Walker Cup player and captain, Wing Commander Laddie Lucas, who became a famous pilot in the Battle of Britain. Once when the fight was hottest and he was in dire trouble with a disabled plane he was able to make use of his local knowledge and land his damaged Spitfire at the far end of the course after first attempting to get down on the first fairway.

Sandwich

The links of the Royal St George's Golf Club at Sandwich differs markedly from that of Prince's, its neighbour to the north, and of the Royal Cinque Ports at Deal to the south. Sandwich has a lumpier hillier terrain than either neighbour, the sandhills are bigger, the valleys deeper and in places the waves in the fairways more pronounced.

Sandwich in its early days was known essentially as a driver's course and in truth it is so today, for the carries, especially off the back tees, and for me now from the ordinary tees, make you think. Long driving, if it be straight, pays everywhere and nowhere more than here.

There is a more than ordinary carry at the short third, a big brute of a sandhill at the fourth, something similar at seven and a good need to get well along from the ninth. The tee shots at the eleventh and twelfth each need to carry a substantial bunkered ridge and also at the 'Suez Canal' hole, the fourteenth. So if you are not hitting your drives or have a tendency to top or hit 'thin' you are in dire trouble, indeed you won't get round at all. But if you are driving well, then the game falls into place and the course is not monumentally long or harsh. True, some holes are very plentifully supplied with bunkers, notably the short holes other than number three, and in places the bunkering is very severe in its closeness to the greens.

Everybody remarks on the attractive solitude of Sandwich, where each hole seems to be cut off from all the others in its own valley or piece of empty links, so that however crowded the green may be, you are hardly ever aware of more than one game beside your own. There is a pleasant conservative air about the place; the course has hardly been altered in the last forty years, nor should it have been, and the club-house, save for the elimination of sand-boxes and earth closets, is equally unchanged. A relaxed peaceful leather-furnished smoking room persists and you can still get a tankard of ale from the wood. I have detected only one change for the worse: you now have to pay for matches. It used to impress me enormously as a young man in the 'twenties when the steward said, while ignoring the proffered penny, 'There is no charge for matches in this club, sir.'

You start with a mild enough drive from the first tee, but it should be well hit or you will end up in a hollow on the fairway called the 'Kitchen', from which it's a long shot to get home. Even with a good drive the shot to the green is tight because of a big bunker right in front and right up close, a tough shot for a hole of 429 yards from the medal tee.

The second is shorter, with attractive humps and hollows in front of the green on a little saddle of land with a fall on each side; nevertheless, this is one of the less difficult fours.

The 'Sahara' comes next, a full belt of 222 yards, or more from the back tee, over a big sandhill with two deep bunkers in it; once over the hill you have some bumps to clear, but then a big generous green. This is not a particular favourite of mine, but it has been a very famous hole in its early days and was imitated, but not copied, at the National Golf Links of America.

The fourth out to the end of the links is a beauty. You have an alarming drive over a huge sandhill with two deep gaping bunkers in it. As Ian

Fleming describes it in *Goldfinger*: 'You drive over one of the tallest and deepest bunkers in the United Kingdom.' If you surmount that you get a nice flat lie from which to play just about a full shot to a beautifully-sited green on a little plateau beyond some deep undulations of the fairway.

At the fifth you hit towards the sea and an invisible fairway with sandhills apparently everywhere, the great bulk of the tallest of all, the 'Maiden', away on the left. If your drive is to the right spot you can turn half left and hit a good stiff iron shot through a gap in the sandhills to a flat green beyond, out by the shore road. If your drive wasn't quite correct you will have to clear a sandhill, perhaps with a spoon or four-wood to make the green.

At number six you play a short hole to a green under the shadow of the 'Maiden' to which you once had to come over the mountain. Into the prevailing wind if it is not too strong it is about a four- or five-iron, I suppose, or even a six—not too exacting.

The seventh, out towards the sea again, needs a good carrying drive over the confronting hill, but then the play up a shallow valley offers no terrors if you are content with a par five. The short eighth, 'Hades', looks from the tee not unlike the sixth, save for the surrounding sandhills; the shot is twenty yards longer and the frontal bunker much bigger; the green, too, has a violent ridge across it.

The ninth, the 'Corsets'—named after a pair of constricting bunkers—is a beautiful hole. You play from a high tee down into a much folded valley; bunkers confuse the issue for you and then you have to play a high pitch, perhaps a six-iron, to a narrow but long plateau green protected by a hump and trap on the left and a sharp fall-off to the right.

By the end of the first half, as at Deal, you should have quite a good score if your driving has been sound; 36 or 37 is not too great a feat. The second half is a much tougher affair and for me anything under 40 is a real achievement.

You start with a splendid hole up a shallow valley and culminating with, say, a five- or six-iron shot to a small green the shape of a mushroom perched at the top of a sharp rise with cavernous bunkers guarding it on either hand. An insufficiently hit shot sometimes seems to run off cruelly and one hit 'thin' or too strong goes down a precipice at the back. The eleventh, after making the carry from the tee, is not a severe par four, as the plateau green has a protecting wall behind it and is not tightly bunkered. The twelfth, with its diagonal carry, is a great favourite of mine; it is a short par four of 325 yards, but the tee shot is most testing. If you bite off too much you don't make the fairway, too little and you have a hard shot to a green beset with deep bunkers right close to its edge. The thirteenth is a really excellent hole, 443 yards off the back tee and 430 off mine, with a diagonal carry from the tee of no great severity. The second shot is one of the great ones in golf, for three bunkers *en echelon* eat into the fairway sixty to ninety yards short of the green and dominate your thinking—I've been in all of them—and then there are wing bunkers at the front of the green and another for good measure further up on the left. The green is beautifully moulded, with a flanking hill to the right.

At fourteen you leave the big hills after the drive over the last range and get on to the flat and your drive had better be a good one or you'll have to think about the 'Suez Canal' 335 yards from the tee, if there's any wind. Otherwise as a par five the hole offers no particular terrors, though it ruined Sarazen's chances in the Open of 1928.

The fifteenth, though quite flat, is a great hole, 440 yards from the regular tee. Driving over some cross-bunkers which shouldn't bother you, you are confronted with the need to hit to a tiny humpy green with a deep cross-bunker only a yard or two short of it and another bunker to catch a shot ever so slightly hooked; even if you decide not to try for the carry the little pitch is no sitting duck; a four here is a joy, and to get home in two 'to carry the distant surf of the bunkers', as James Bond did against Goldfinger, is bliss.

Sixteen, 154 to 163 yards, has no less than twelve bunkers round it, so you're on the green or in one of them for sure; I take leave not to admire it.

The seventeenth back among the humps and bumps is a fine two-shotter with a plateau green well set up, but with an 'armchair' back all round it —save where bunkers eat into the edge of the green. Finally, there is another relatively flat raking two-shotter of 429–41 yards to end with, with the guarding bunkers rather too close to the prepared surface for comfort. All too often when a four has been needed to win or tie here a five has come on to the card, as happened to George Duncan in his great round in pursuit of Hagen in 1922.

Sandwich, like all great links, has some wonderful tales to tell. Possibly the most remarkable day's golf, at any rate in living memory, was in the Walker Cup match of 1930. J. A. Stout, 'the Bridlington Dentist', as the newspapers christened him, went round in the morning in 68 to be four up on Don Moe; what's more, he started 3.3.3 after lunch to be seven up. Well, he lost. Moe went round in 67, was all square after seventeen holes and piled Pelion upon Ossa with a three at the eighteenth.

Here the first foreigner took a British championship when Walter Travis, an Australian by birth and an American by nationality, won the Amateur Championship in 1904 and apparently got himself cordially disliked in the process; his uncanny skill with a centre-shafter putter resulted, with what I hope is uncharacteristic British unsportsmanship, in this instrument being banned for forty years.

Channel Coast

Harry Bradshaw's beer-bottle shot is also famous. In the second round of the Open of 1949, when leading the field, he found his ball in a broken bottle at the back of the fifth green. Electing to play it, which authorities now believe he need not have done, he smashed the bottle and released the ball but took six to the hole. In the end he only tied for the Championship and lost to Locke on the play-off.

As you may infer from the quotations, one of the best accounts of Sandwich is in *Goldfinger* in which the captain-elect of the Royal St George's club describes the famous match between James Bond and the villain for $10,000 which reaches a surprising climax. Unfortunately, as the narrative reads, Goldfinger surrendered a match which he really won; if he'd kept his head and known the rules, as he claimed, he could have maintained, quite rightly, that he'd holed out with the ball he'd driven from the tee and that was all he need have said.

Deal

If I had one more round of golf to play on earth I would choose Deal as the links on which to play it. Sometimes I have unfaithfully thought that Sandwich would be the place for this mournful event, but after forty-five years of golf all chopping and changing is past and I have decided undoubtedly now for Deal.

That this should be so arises partly from love and admiration for the golf but as much from a sentimental attachment for the links formed years ago, then left neglected for decades and only recently revived in my old age.

For the Royal Cinque Ports Golf Club at Deal was the first championship links I played on, coming down here in 1925 as a rather fresh young man who was just beginning to put a game together and capable on such circuits as Southfield and West Byfleet of scores in the low eighties. We put up at the Royal Hotel, with the sea washing and sighing on the shingle under the windows, as it still does today; we were young and eager, playing thirty-six holes a day and sometimes nine 'after tea'; we drank a good deal of beer and danced every evening at the hotel to the gramophone; the receptionist had very pretty legs but I was far too shy to tell her so. Halcyon days.

The golf was an eye-opener; the sandhills, the humpy fairways, the awkward stances, the fierce rough, the cavernous bunkers full of soft fine sand, the shots to dells or plateau greens, and, above all, the wind, the perpetual remorseless wind, combined to take all the starch out of this young man and leave a humiliated, chastened and wiser golfer. This process was repeated at Sandwich next door. A better and more experi-

On the King's Course at Gleneagles. The green of the 285-yard 14th hole; with a favourable wind it is in reach of one shot (*G. B. Alden by permission of Scottish Field*)

ABOVE Going down Gullane Hill to the fairway and bunkers guarding the 17th green (*H. W. Neale*)

BELOW Historic turf. The author on the 16th green of the North Inch Course at Perth alongside the River Tay (*George Malcolm*)

OPPOSITE ABOVE Royal Dornoch from the air. The 16th hole is on the extreme left of the picture, the 17th runs back towards the bottom right-hand corner, and the long 18th goes away again towards the town. To the right of the 18th fairway is the first hole, followed by the short second (*Planair by permission of Mearns Publications*)

BELOW The 350-yard 13th hole at North Berwick 'the Pit'. The pitch shot has to negotiate a stone wall close up against the green, a very tricky shot (*Peter Allen*)

ABOVE Links-land on the Channel coast. The 163-yard 7th hole at Rye, a beautiful natural plateau beset with bunkers; the 6th green is just beyond the tee (*H. W. Neale*)

BELOW The view from the top of 'the Maiden' at Sandwich of the 6th green at Royal St George's Golf Club. The bunkers to be carried from the tee shot on the 7th lie just beyond the farther spectators (*The Central Press Photos Ltd*) enced golfer might have realised that these famous links take some getting used to, that Bobby Jones had torn up his card in the 1921 Open at St Andrews in the third round after playing ten holes in 52 strokes and failing to reach the eleventh green at all or that in the Championship at Deal just a year or so before Hagen had taken 48 for the last nine holes, while only two years before our descent on Deal, Sarazen had failed to qualify for the British Open at Troon. Then at the end of this first visit came one shaft of sunlight through the racing cloud-wrack; playing the rather short course at St Augustine's just north of Sandwich, as a reviver, I had a 76, my first round under 80 and so resolved to go on with the game. To round off these personalia I might add that forty years later, on a sentimental journey, I had my first round under 70 with a 69 at St Augustine's and these were the only two rounds I have ever played there.

So for Deal I have an abiding affection, one which could be uncritical if necessary but luckily it need not be for this is one of the *great* golf links, great and difficult. Bernard Darwin says this:

'Deal is a truly great course. I incline myself to think the most testing and severe of all the Championship Courses . . . yet it is not in these stern and almost sombre conditions that I best like to think of Deal or Sandwich. My day-dreams are rather of them on a day of sunshine and light breeze—it is perhaps because it chances that here are the first really great courses that I ever saw, that this smiling corner of the earth's surface has for me something that no other spot, not even perhaps St Andrews, can quite equal. The larks seem to me to sing a little louder and more cheerfully there and the grass to have a more poignantly delicious taste of garlic. I am sure no other cliffs are so shining white as those beyond Pegwell Bay or that there is no view of shipping like that through the big plate-glass windows at Deal. Long may these things remain unchanged for future golfing generations to enjoy.'

And may I say hear hear to that.

In spite of what Bernardo says, I must say I find the view from the club-house windows at Deal a little prosaic. To the right a new crop of council houses blocks out the hitherto uninterrupted view of the gasworks. To the left are the rolling sandhills of the links from which the players emerge after driving from the eighteenth tee whose green on its shallow plateau is straight in front of you. Beyond lie the second fairway and the rampart of shingle protecting the links—all too feebly sometimes—from the pounding of the sea. In the foreground the first fairway, lush and flat and green, runs past the club-house, picked out by a few clumps of rushes.

The course runs north and south at both start and finish, with four holes at the far end near the Sandwich links running at right angles to the general line of play. The prevailing wind, south-west, is off the land and has the maddening property of not helping you going out, for it comes over your left shoulder, and being a harsh enemy coming home. In high summer, with a gentle north-east breeze off the sea, the links plays easiest; then the terrible long beat home is a joy and not a supreme effort.

Now let's go round Deal from the red tee boxes, which take 275 yards off the championship length for which I am truly grateful. The first hole of 328 yards, towards the town, past the club-house windows, should be no hardship; it is flat, verdant and unbunkered, the green is generous in size and a little ridge at the back protects you from going too far. There is just one snag: there is a ditch right across the fairway in front of the green. You have no business going into it, yet like the Swilcan Burn at the first hole at St Andrews many good men have done so, usually when the hole is played as a nineteenth.

At the second hole you turn north and at once you are in the real links-land with plenty of undulations on the fairway and the green half hidden by a low protecting ridge unless you can hug the right-hand edge of the fairway, a very attractive hole. Then to number three, a very great favourite of mine. Off the tee you can see some very broken country in the distance along the fairway and only the top of the pin. Two big bunkers in a ridge across the fairway about 300 yards out are conspicuous, though you ought not to get in them. Beyond them the fairway is almost excessively broken and folded and culminates in a deep punchbowl green, on two levels with a steep step, beyond the last of these folds. At 449 yards even with some help from the wind it takes two fine hits to get there and some luck from the run of the ball too.

The fourth is a fine new short hole, replacing the old blind hole across 'Sandy Parlour'; you play from a tee high in the backbone ridge of dunes which bisects the course here, to a plateau green with severe falls on either hand; you need a good poke with a six- or seven- or sometimes a five-iron.

Five is a long hole, but not excessive for a par five, then comes the unorthodox and attractive number six, which has its plateau green right up against the shingle of the beach. It is only 293 yards long from our tee, but the ground on the way is very bumpy and in front of the green is a really deep hollow out of which you usually have to pitch up sharply without lifting your head. There is a big protective sandhill to the right. In dry weather with a fair breeze astern you can get home with a good shot and what fun that is.

The seventh continues the run to the north with a drive-and-medium-iron hole, at which the green rather helps to gather the ball. The eighth is a heavily bunkered but not too difficult short hole towards the sea. Then come three holes of a duller and more prosaic texture, though the tenth is often selected for high, indeed I think extravagant, praise. All three have a dog-leg element—the tenth very much so—with trouble at the joint, as it were, but the ninth and eleventh, both running inland, are too much alike and while not easy leave no memories and no scars.

At this stage I hope you have got a good score on your card, fours perhaps or better, for if there is any west or south in the wind you are going to need it, for you are in for a straight beat in for the last six holes. There are times when, as Frank Pennink says, you would settle for five fives and a four, but it is really more fun to play them, at any rate for the first time or two, in milder conditions.

The twelfth at 426 yards is par four, though Bogey gets given a five here. The preliminaries are rather flat and dull, but the green, long and narrow, between two little ridges, is quite exceptionally attractive. The thirteenth, a dog-leg of 412 yards, gives you a chance of an iron shot to the green perhaps, but the green beyond the row of bunkers across the fairway is always a little farther off on its up-slope than it seems. Next comes a long tough par three hole, 199 yards, with a hollow on the left of the green and two deep bunkers on the right of it which catch a shot with any fade on it. A fair shot with a two-iron boring into the wind to fall lifeless on the green is a pretty sight here. It was here that that great Irish golfer Lionel Munn, who was walking round, was asked to demonstrate the hole, so he borrowed a club and ball and holed in one stroke while the feat was recorded in a bystander's camera. The picture hangs in the club-house.

The fifteenth at 414 yards is a splendid hole, where your second shot may be anything from a five-iron to a brassie, depending on the wind. There is a slight dog-leg here, with bunkers at the angle, about 180 yards from the tee. The hole is then dominated by a mild sandy hill beyond which lies the green; you can easily run too far if you pitch too far on to the down-slope of this hill.

The sixteenth is to me the greatest hole on this great links—456 yards from my tee and 474 from the yellow tee-box. The green is lodged on a wonderfully-moulded high plateau, rising, as Bernard Darwin says, sheer out of a lush green 'valley of inglorious security' with a protective knob and bunker on its right extremity. You drive past some fortifications of the last war over some bunkers on the fairway, then if you can't get up in two you make for the safe green vale rather left of the line; if you overdo this you are trapped deeply on the left, if not you still have a good stiff pitch to play to this incomparable plateau. But if you can get up in two, as to my surprise I did not so long ago, to the angry resentment of two innocent women putting out, what a superlative joy it is to see the ball racing into the sunset to climb the ridge and give you a putt for an eagle. A hole in a million.

Channel Coast

The seventeenth is shorter, at 364 yards, but the fairway is very bumpy and there is a deep cross-bunker about eighty yards short of the green; the green is a tiny saucer set among bumps and slopes. Finally to eighteen, where you drive out of the sandhills on to the flat ground in front of the club-house, cross a ditch and then fly up on to a shallow plateau. At 396 yards it takes two good shots to get home and if your second is less than fine the ball dies on the up-slopes of the plateau and you take five.

Great events have occurred at Deal. The record stands to Michael Bonallack, who did a splendid 65 in the Brabazon Trophy in 1964, which he won, going out—with the help of two twos—in the astounding score of 31, though his other three rounds didn't destroy the course.

In the Open of 1920 George Duncan, whose first two rounds of 80 would not have survived the 'Cut' in these days, came roaring in with 71 and 72 to snatch the prize from the unhappy Abe Mitchell. Abe, who led after two rounds with the aid of a one at the eighth hole, was a beautiful shot-maker, but could never quite do it in the pinch; he was unlucky enough to be waiting on the first tee to begin his third round rather late in the morning and had to endure seeing the mercurial George with an enthusiastic crowd finishing at the eighteenth; then, his nerve gone, Mitchell started 5.5.6.4.8 and finished in 84, his whole lead of thirteen shots over Duncan gone with the wind. In that same championship Walter Hagen, later four times the winner, made his first appearance in the British Open and finished fifty-third out of fifty-four.

Many great things have happened, too, in the Halford Hewitt Cup games which are played by the Public Schools Golfing Societies each April, and are now so popular that some games even have to be played at Sandwich to relieve the pressure, while others start so early that, to quote Henry Longhurst, 'The lightship moored on the Goodwins was still flashing as we played the second hole'. Incidentally, the Royal Cinque Ports Club has a very generous scheme of membership for all members of Public School Golfing Societies.

Some early opinions of Deal are reported in the Royal Cinque Ports club-house, of which these are some examples:

'I am proud to have won the first Open ever played on Deal links. It is most worthy of such an event being held upon it.' *J. H. Taylor, June 1909.*

'I have had the pleasure of several rounds of golf over the Deal course and think it is without any doubt one of the very finest courses I ever played.' *Francis Ouimet, May 1914.*

'I have just played on all the principal golf courses in the United Kingdom and I just love Deal.' *Ted Ray, 27th November 1913.*

'Je certifie avoir joué à Deal Golf Corse [*sic*]; à mon opinion c'est le plus beau golfe que jamais je n'ai vue en Angleterre ou en Ecosse.' *Arnaud Massy, 19th December 1907* (the first of a long line of foreign winners of the British Open).

And finally, with some mock modesty I fear, this:

'I think Deal a very fine course but much too difficult for me.' *Cyril Tolley, 1st July 1920.*

Littlestone

Littlestone is a most pleasant and enjoyable links, with some considerable but not too emphatic sandhills. The lies on the fairway are less humpy than on the links farther north at Deal and Sandwich or farther south at Rye. Nevertheless, you have to hit your shots well to score properly. My favourite holes in the first nine are the second, where you have to beat your second shot over a hill, a blind stroke but fun, the third, where the green is on a saddle in the same range of hills, and the 'drive and iron' eighth out by the coast road. In the second half you come and go across the course until confronted with a splendid hilly sixteenth towards the water tower, where you can hope for a four but settle for a five. Originally I think this hole had two vast bunkers to be carried from the tee in the face of a rise. The seventeenth is a splendid par three, a good hard iron or even a spoon or four-wood to a green on a ridge above the final plain of the last hole on which we have rather a dull eighteenth.

Littlestone is, I think, a rather underrated course and in my view, as the *Guide Michelin* puts it, 'worth a detour'. Try it some time.

Rye

Rye is a place for tradition. It is conservative, possibly even a little old-fashioned—and none the worse for that. Foursomes are played as a regular thing and it must be just about the only club in the world which puts up a notice saying: 'Three and four-ball matches are allowed, but they have no standing.' Tweedy plus-fours—knickers to Americans—are worn and small flat caps. There are no 'Winter Rules' or improving your lie. The club-house is up to date, though for years a corrugated-iron pavilion was sufficient until the Germans destroyed it, and thank heaven the traditional scrambled eggs are still served at lunch.

The links is first-class, a little short for the big hitters but quite long enough for you and me. There is a main ridge of sandhills running the whole length of the course which comes markedly into play and another subsidiary ridge parallel to it nearer the sea. There have been many alterations to the course since 1894, most of them made necessary by the increasing traffic along the road which runs all along the northern boundary. However, the new holes which were built after World War II, virtually the whole of the first half indeed except for the present fourth and fifth, to replace those closer to the road and beyond the coastguard cottages, which now form the boundary at the end of the course, include some of the best of the whole eighteen.

The three opening holes on the flat to the north of the main ridge are difficult enough, if not spectacular, the short second being far from easy. Then comes the fourth, 430 yards long and surely one of the great holes in golf, with a painfully narrow hog's back to find and hold with your drive and trouble all the way to the green after the drive, sandy hills on the left and a plunge down to the plain on the right. Stay on the ridge and you're all right, but how difficult in a wind—and wind is something you have to expect at Rye.

The short fifth, once the eighth, is a magnificent short hole of 175 yards across a wide gully to a shallow saucer of a green perched up high in the sandhills. The short seventh too, a new hole, is a splendid shot and so too is the short fourteenth.

The second half is less changed since the war than the first nine, though the tenth and eighteenth holes have been remodelled; no longer at the last hole do you drive from below over a vast bunker fortified all the way round by a stockade of black sleepers, a hideous and horrifying hazard; instead you have a hard hole back along the ridge. Sleepers in the bunkers, which were once a feature of Rye, have now disappeared, though the tops of some of them are still just visible, e.g. in front of the seventh and to the right of the fourteenth greens, where bunkers have been filled in or re-shaped.

The second half has some grand holes; at the thirteenth, the 'Sea Hole. of 435 yards, you still have to carry a great rampart of sandhills with your second, if you've hit a good drive or your third if you have not, to a hidden green over the ridge.

The sixteenth is a grand hole with the ridge to be carried from the tee running across your line diagonally; and after you're over that a good stiff iron shot to get home or even a blow with 'The Old Man's Friend', a five-wood.

The course, then, is tough but perfectly fair, the fairways are of the old seaside quality, rather thin grass with plenty of run and dry at all seasons. The greens are also far from lush and indeed can seem terrifyingly thin, even bare, in dry weather and some of the downhill putts can be alarming: but they are true and reward a properly struck ball. And always there is the breeze, which never seems to help you but always to hinder, for the prevailing wind blows across the line of nearly all the holes.

Hayling Island

The course on Hayling Island is a true links and a fine one. On a small island between Langstone and Chichester harbours, close to Portsmouth, it lies on land once beneath the sea and today on the lightest of sandy soils. Even the rough, though it contains heather in places, is sparse, except where the gorse bushes and tree-lupins flourish. The latter, tough as they are, form such an engaging bush with their scented flowers, though they make formidable rough out at the far end of the course where the sandhills are. The English Ladies' Championship has been played here several times but not the British Amateur, though I am sure the links is good enough.

In spite of the very dry soil and spare turf there are some hazards where water can play a conspicuous part, notably the carry from the tee at the 405 yard fourth and the 430 yard fifteenth holes and dominating the splendid second shot to the 428-yard sixth. Nevertheless, in spite of this, the course in all weathers gives an impression of crisp dryness rare in these days. In total the links measures 6,510 yards, quite enough for a middling player like myself. It can, of course, blow like the devil here and then it would be long indeed.

All this area was in the forefront of the battle in World War II and to this day, by a local rule, a ball may be lifted and dropped without penalty from a bomb crater.

I made my first acquaintance with Hayling Island very late in life but was so pleased with this delightful links that although it was raining all the way round there was no thought of quitting. Yet in spite of this, and of heavy rain in the weeks before, the course played with a very reasonable amount of run and the seaside greens were quite fast enough.

The course is fairly evenly divided between the ten flatter holes at the beginning of the first half and the end of the second, and the eight holes starting with the par-five seventh which are among the sandhills and in the very best style of traditional seaside golf. This is not to say that the flatter holes at the beginning and end are not excellent tests of golf, they are, with sometimes small and narrow greens with plenty of subtle slopes and borrows which require excellent shot-making. None the less, the holes out at the far end amongst the hills have the finest flavour. Starting with the seventh, although a par five of no great length (478 yards), there is a small green well cocked up, with slopes carrying the ball away on either hand so that your third shot, even if a short one, has to be very straight.

If you are long enough to get home in two, which I am not, well, good luck to you.

The eighth is that difficult thing, which is I fear disappearing fast from golf, a good short par four—only 345 yards. A line of sandhills across the fairway, though they make the pitch blind or half-blind, nevertheless prevent the big hitters from destroying the hole by their length, which indeed they will need in good measure at the next hole, which is a long par four and alas now barely within my reach: the drive over the sandhills at the ninth is attractive and reminded me of Sandwich.

The tenth is another short par four, indeed a very short par four (272 yards), though for some reason, probably the narrowness of its long green, it looks very much longer than it is. It is reported that the players in one four-ball once holed it in one, two, three and four strokes.

We then have an excellent short hole of 152 yards with a beautiful plateau green and attractive moulding of the protecting bunkers, a really lovely hole. Following this comes a great two-shotter running parallel with Langstone harbour, where, for my capabilities, two exceptional shots have to be hit to get home to the green, which is up a slope, 'defying you to reach it', as Bernard Darwin used to write, with a fall to destruction on the left. The drive is over wild rough, mostly tree-lupins; a four here, even with a rather scrambly little run-up, was a real pleasure.

The next hole, the thirteenth, is famous and justly so. You have to drive uphill over a long carry, possibly not as long as it looks but containing a monstrous bunker known as the 'Widow'. If you clear that with a good shot you then have a not-too-difficult pitch downhill to a green well below you; a less-than-good drive gives you a blind or half-blind second. Having managed to achieve a good drive here, the hole in retrospect looks absolutely splendid, though I suppose one of those drives when, as the American pros say on TV, 'I come off it real baaad', and so cutting the ball into some horrible sandy waste would leave you with a rather different first impression.

The thirteenth green brings you to a unique feature at Hayling Island, and one I am not aware of anywhere else—namely, the secondary club-house. As the club-house proper is a long way round by road from Portsmouth and its neighbouring towns, which are the principal source of membership, and as there is a passenger ferry across to the island close to the thirteenth green, the club has built a small secondary club-house for those that come this way and wish to start their round at the fourteenth hole.[1] This hole, by the way, is a fine par five of 530 yards, with marshy ground on the left which can be water in bad weather to catch a pulled

---

[1] The course on Wimbledon Common has two club-houses, one at each end, but there are two clubs using the course.

second shot, and a finely moulded green just behind a protective ridge rather in the St Andrews style.

Three of the four short holes at Hayling are in the flatter territory, one of them, indeed, the first hole of the course. This hole looks a very dull number from the tee, but the nearer you get to it, the better it is, because you see more and more what an excellently shaped green it has. The fifth hole has its green on a very narrow plateau, which certainly doesn't invite the shot or gather the ball, while the sixteenth is also on a slight plateau where a shot off line will confront you with a most difficult pitch, one of which, to my intense pleasure, I managed to bring off more by luck than judgement.

So much for what was for me an intensely enjoyable round, rain or no rain. An added pleasure was my old caddie, who had been on and around the course for fifty-two years and was known by everybody as 'Sailor'. He was a caddie in the old tradition, who took an interest in the game, 'our' game, needless to say, and was an excellent judge of the shot and his partner's capabilities. He was also reputed never to lose a ball and with the amount of bush around at some places this must have taken a lot of doing. During the war his sloop was sunk off the Nab Tower, within sight of the links, by a bomb that went down the funnel and wounded him in the back. At the end of the game I gave him enough to have a good drink, for he was as wet as I, saying: 'I hope you can get it without much difficulty', to which he replied: 'I always believe in having some in the house, sir.'

One final feature of Hayling is the names which the holes carry: I am not usually much enamoured of named holes, especially if these have been all too artfully contrived, like those revolting Scotticisms at Gleneagles. But here, if some of the names are sadly uninspired like 'Plain' or 'Narrows' or 'Sea', others clearly commemorate some person or event which the little booklet issued by the course entirely ignores. Who, for example, was the 'Widow', for whom the thirteenth is named, and who was the 'Sailor', whose Grave is at the seventeenth? Furthermore, why is the tenth called 'Pan-Ko-Chai'; who are the 'Woolseners', commemorated at the eleventh; what is 'Wharram', named at the sixteenth, and why is the last hole called 'Sinah', or is it just a misprint on the card for 'Sinai'? Though I must say, having contrived to hit two good shots right home at the last hole, I was too pleased to care too much about this one.

Channel Islands

The Channel Islands are part of the BritishI sles, though not part of the United Kingdom, their relationship to the Crown being derived from having formed part of the Dukedom of Normandy in 1066. Be that as it

Channel Coast

may, they are pleasantly different from England and blessed by a rather better climate. Golf is well suited here and Jersey can be regarded as historic turf indeed.

Harry Vardon, Britain's greatest golfer, six times Open Champion and once U.S. Champion, and his brother Tom, who was also a fine player, were born on the edge of the links near Gorey on the eastern shore of the island. Ted Ray, who won the British and U.S. Open Championships, was a Jerseyman, so were the Boomers, Aubrey, a Ryder Cup player for Britain, and Percy, author of a book of instruction which was a classic; add to these numerous Gaudins, Renoufs and Le Chevaliers and the output of this small island, only some ten miles by five, appears prodigious.

There are two attractive courses in Jersey, both of the links type and a third shorter course. The La Moye course, at the western end of the island near the famous lighthouse of Corbière, is on top of the cliffs overlooking the sea. The Royal Jersey course, at the opposite end of the island, is mostly on sandy low-lying links turf on Grouville Bay, though one or two holes in the inward half with protecting gorse are perhaps halfway between true links and downland turf.

La Moye

The La Moye course could be described as a delightful and not-too-long holiday course, with only one disagreeable feature, which I believe is due to be eliminated—a really fierce walk up to the green of the short fourth hole after an uphill tee shot and then nearly as fierce a walk uphill after re-crossing the same gully with the drive at the fifth. Apart from this there is a lot of pleasant—and it is fair to say not too difficult—golf to play in a natural setting with some blind shots, greens in hollows or on plateaux, with some fine views along the coast. The pros play here in a tournament each year and some low scores are turned in.

Gorey

The Gorey links of the Royal Jersey Club is rather different in character, flatter, rather less exposed and tightly compressed into a small area so that there is some interlacing of holes. Again it is a natural setting, with the greens where you find them. The first nine starts out right along the shore and the inward nine is more inland with rather more bush in the rough to contend with. A hole that stands out in my memory—I suppose because I hit a fine shot at it—is the 392-yard thirteenth, where a good spoon or four-wood may be needed to get your second right home over the bumps and guardian bunkers in front of the green. This spot is historic turf indeed, for in this corner stood the cottage where Vardon was born, though it is there no longer. Other fine holes are the two-shot seventh and eighth, the long par-three seventeenth and the eighteenth up on its plateau green hard by Fort Henry.

Guernsey

There is one course in Guernsey, the links of the Royal Guernsey Golf Club on L'Ancresse Bay in the extreme north of the island, which, while not quite so kempt as those on Jersey, is a testing course of 6,200 yards with five short holes. Standing out in memory are the short tightly bunkered second hole and the long two-shot third of 444 yards. The eighteenth, too, is a tester, a 175-yard belt home over a humpy entrance. A fine family of golfers, the Jollys, came from Guernsey.

There are innumerable stories about Harry Vardon and the prodigies of golf that he performed in his prime—that he was never off the fairway in two years or that in an afternoon round he drove frequently into the divot marks he had made in the morning. Suffice it to say he had the unparalleled record of winning our Open Championship six times, interspersed with two attacks of tuberculosis, the U.S. Open once, tying for the U.S. once in 1913 to lose on the play-off and finishing second in it in 1920 at the age of fifty. He played in the first international golf match between the professionals of Britain and the United States at Gleneagles at the age of fifty-one and won both his matches.

Two stories of Vardon and Bobby Jones are favourites of mine. The first occurred at Inverness, Ohio, at the time of the U.S. Open Championship of 1920. Young Jones, then eighteen years old, was impulsive and inclined to be talkative while playing; Vardon was quite the opposite. After a bad pitch shot which scuttled along the ground and over the green Bob turned to Vardon and said, 'Did you ever see a worse shot than that, Harry?' 'No,' said Vardon and finished the round in silence. The other let Bob tell in his own words:

'Looking back on the Grand Slam year, I find that there is one little episode that was of absolutely no importance, yet it is one that I still have a great deal of pleasure in remembering.

'During the Open Championship at Hoylake, Ted Ray, who won our Open in 1920, asked me if I would be willing to play a charity match at his golf club, Oxhey, sometime between the conclusion of the championship and my departure for home. There was something in Ted's manner of extending the invitation which led me to believe that he had not intended that he himself should take part in the match. To me, however, the proposition immediately suggested the possibility of having a most enjoyable game. So I said, "Sure, Ted, I'll be delighted to play, provided you'll play and that you'll get any two of Vardon, Braid, or Taylor to complete the match." These three, of course, comprised the Immortal Triumvirate for which I had long had so much admiration and respect. Ray himself, with his boisterous good humour and slashing play, could not fail to make an attractive addition to any exhibition.

'For my part the occasion could not have had a happier result. Ted got Vardon and Braid to join us. I played one of those easy rounds which are possible only when every sort of thing is working smoothly and right. My score for the round, with a bogey five at the last hole, was sixty-eight, which I understood at the time was the lowest eighteen-hole total ever returned for the golf course. It was not a record, though, because the British quite properly only recognise as records scores made in formal stroke-play competition.

'Above all else, I like to recall an incident on the seventeenth tee. With my newly-acquired skill with the mashie-niblick, I had played a tee shot to within a yard of the hole. As Vardon stepped forward to play, I heard him say in his very quiet, soft voice, "Ah, Master Bobby's 'ot today". Since we had first played together in 1920, he had always addressed me as "Master Bobby". I liked it very much, and I liked also the combination of American slang and Channel Island accent. Old Harry was a very great player and fine gentleman. Every round I played with him was an event in my life.'

I would also like to record Walter Hagen's first impressions of Vardon when he went to play in his first championship at the Country Club at Brookline, Massachusetts, in 1913, that famous championship which Francis Ouimet, who died only the day before I wrote this, won against all the odds.

'In the locker-room a small fellow was pulling on a bright sweater. I recognised him immediately, for he was the defending champion and I'd read plenty about him.

' "You're Johnny McDermott, aren't you?" I asked. "Well, I'm glad to know you. I'm W. C. Hagen from Rochester and I've come over to help you boys take care of Vardon and Ray."

'That brought some laughter, of course, and a lot of kidding from the pros who were listening, but I didn't mind. I was meeting and seeing the greats of the game. I met Vardon and Ray, who'd both won the British Open Championship and Vardon was touted as the best player in the world. As I expected to become the best I decided to keep my eye on him. In fact, I stood around and gawked at him like any other greenhorn from the pastures.

'Harry Vardon was a tall man with huge hands. My own was practically lost in his handshake. He was reserved, quiet, with almost nothing to say. But I learned plenty from watching him swing a golf-club. He had a much more compact and precise swing than I'd ever seen. He had it in a groove and I tried it out in practice and it worked for me too. I did not dare shift into the Vardon swing right then, but I did use it late in the tournament, when I had gone four over par for the first three holes in the final round.'

My greatest regret in golf, I think, is that I never saw Vardon play; when at last in 1936 I woke up and tried to arrange a game with him it was too late and shortly afterwards he died, and, in the plain words of the *Golfers' Handbook*, 'He was buried in Totteridge Parish Churchyard in the presence of an assembly of his fellow golfers'.

Bembridge

It would have been a pleasure to include the little nine-hole links of the Royal Isle of Wight Golf Club at Bembridge in this book, but alas it has been abandoned in spite of a venerable history. The course occupied a very small area near the village of St Helens, protected from the sea by a seawall called the Duver, on which now repose some of the old coaches of the Isle of Wight Railway. The nine holes wove in and out amongst themselves and gave you some fine shots along the dune wall on the seaward side. On the beach here Mr Horace Hutchinson many years ago reported finding his ball lying upon 'a dead and derelict dog'. I only include Bembridge here because a recent visit suggested the possibility that the links might be resuscitated without undue difficulty. I wish it could be.

5 The West and Wales

The north coast of Cornwall, Devon and Somerset on the Bristol Channel has some fine links to offer, whereas the southern coasts have none; links, mind, not golf *courses*.

Lelant

Starting at the far west of Cornwall, near St Ives and Penzance, there is an excellent links at Lelant, near Hayle: this is the birthplace of Jim Barnes, who won both the British and American Open Championships in his day. It is a good spot for a holiday, as you can stay at St Ives, a charming little town, where one of the hotels has an amusing little par-three course in the park.

Lelant has real seaside turf and greens and many attractive and entertaining shots, even if there is not too much wooden-club play through the green. It is indeed rather short, being under 6,000 yards, but there are four bogey threes and two more which par puts in that category, though the Colonel allows four.

You have one of these at the 238-yard first hole, where a four early in the day is likelier than not, and, as Frank Pennink says, 'hinting that the score of 70 net is a far from simple achievement'. You then voyage towards the flanking dunes of the Hayle estuary, up and then down, and then progress past the churchyard to investigate the bottom of the course—'down in the reeds by the river'—well, not that quite, but a lower level where there are two par threes and two short tricky par fours; 'Calamity Corner' is good fun.

Returning to the upper level, we are in for much longer golf and the second nine has two par fives of the fullest potency, and though you have a long downhill stretch in the twelfth, the fourteenth is all uphill to the top of the links, on the landward side.

St Enodoc

Next stop is St Enodoc, near the village of Rock in north Cornwall, over the River Camel by ferry from Padstow, though you can go round by road. In getting here we have to pass Newquay, but I don't know it, so we have to leave it unrecorded.

St Enodoc is pure links-land, with some very considerable sandhills, and has all the irregularities of fairway and stance you can use. It is not long, just over 6,000 yards, but as at Lelant, don't imagine that you are going to make hay here; there are five par threes and plenty of stout two-shotters in the 400-plus category. You open with three pretty stiff tests, the first a par five without sand-trap, but there are awkward hollows confronting the drive and in front of the green and the fairway narrows at mid-point by the encroaching of the sandhills; at the second you have a stiff second shot to a plateau green bearing right and the third hole though running downhill, and at 405 yards the shortest of the three, has a lowering hillside all down your left flank and an awkward angle of shot into the green.

At the fourth, 274 yards uphill, you can, I suppose, allow yourself four shots, and well you may, for if you want to avoid a horrible little pitch you must hold your ball well up to the right and go over the angle of an out-of-bounds fence and the green is up against this fence too. After a short hole we get the 374-yard 'Himalayas', a real old-fashioned links-land hole with a mountainous hill and bunker as a compulsory carry on the second shot; as Frank Pennink says, the 'Himalayas' dwarf the 'Alps' at Prestwick or the 'Maiden' hill at Royal St George's. It's no use trying to sneak by round the left flank, as there are pot-bunkers and rough to defeat that very object. So over we go, or hang our heads in shame and get out our sand irons. I'm glad to say I 'made it', but taking no chances I laid on a four-wood.

This same hill and vast tract of sand confront you on the seventh tee as well, but after that shot you get out into flatter and more open territory, though not necessarily easier golf. The half closes with a short hole entirely beset by bunkers and a mild and rather innocuous par-four ninth.

At the tenth we appear to turn inland under the flank of Brea Hill and the green is close to a brook which has been nagging at us all along the left of the fairway. We then play three rather more prosaic holes, a short one and two par fours round the little old ruined church of St Enodoc, which was at one time swallowed by sand blown in from the beach nearby.

The West and Wales

Continuing home with the fourteenth, the fairway sloping hard from the hills on the left and the green in a hollow we are ready for the run-in. First a mid-iron shot across a valley with ditch, fence and road in it, to a green on a bank beyond; then a good par five, the fairway cut across at about 300 yards by a belt of rough. Seventeen is another par three, a long one, across a vale of tears to a plateau green set among the sandhills and the last a stiff two-shot—or to me two and a bit—to another plateau under the windows of the new club-house.

Westward Ho!

Moving now into Devonshire but still on the north shore, we come to historic turf indeed, the first English golf links and the first outside Scotland at Westward Ho!, named after Charles Kingsley's novel, which was written here. Golf started here in a primitive way in 1863 and the club started in 1864. It lies on some low land called the Burrows, under the wing of the great Pebble Ridge, which protects it from the sea, and Barnstaple Bay. Sandhills march with the Pebble Ridge and come into play in the first half.

The links remains the supreme example of natural seaside golf and it hasn't altered for decades since Herbert Fowler's reconstruction; in spite of that, its difficulties are almost as much with us as in the days of Captain Molesworth, 'Old Mole', and his three sons. The links is still on common land and the commoners can and do graze horses, sheep and cattle on the Burrows and every green is surrounded by a wire fence to preserve it. The unique characteristic of Westward Ho! is the rushes which form the rough at many of the inland holes; up to six feet in height and 'as thick as a hedge', they end in iron-tipped spikes which can impale you with ridiculous ease or spear a ball from cover to cover. You have to play over them or play along them and you pray that you won't get in them. There is no out-of-bounds to this day.

The Amateur Championship has been here three times, first in 1912, when John Ball won for the eighth and last time, at the thirty-eighth hole; then again in 1925, when Robert Harris won, and for the last time in 1931 when a surprise winner—and none more surprised than he—was Eric Martin Smith, just down from Cambridge. But for its remoteness, there is no doubt that more use would have been made of this great course.

Two very great golfers were nurtured on this links: Horace Hutchinson, the graceful and gifted amateur, who twice won the Amateur Championship, and John Henry Taylor, five times Open Champion, who died quite recently in his ninety-third year. And what a splendid character he was, forthright, vehement and brave. I saw something of him in the late 'twenties,

ABOVE Putting on the 3rd green at Deal in its natural hollow; the green of the short 4th hole, 'Sandy Parlour', is in the background (*Sport & General Press Agency Ltd*)
BELOW Peter Alliss driving from the 9th tee on the La Moye links in Jersey (*H. W. Neale*)

ABOVE The 3rd hole at Burnham and Berrow with the green beautifully moulded in a shallow cup among the sandhills (*Frank Gardner*)
OPPOSITE ABOVE The famous Himalayas bunker at the 6th hole at St Enodoc in Cornwall. This is a compulsory carry for the second shot at a hole of about 400 yards, unless the drive is extremely accurately placed on the extreme left of the fairway (*St Enodoc G.C.*)
CENTRE The Harlech links has a most spectacular setting beneath the walls of the castle with the mountains of Snowdonia as a backdrop. The picture here shows the 16th hole (*H. W. Neale*)
BELOW True links-land. The third hole at Aberdovey, 'Cader', a short hole requiring a blind tee shot over a huge sandhill (*P. K. Standring*)

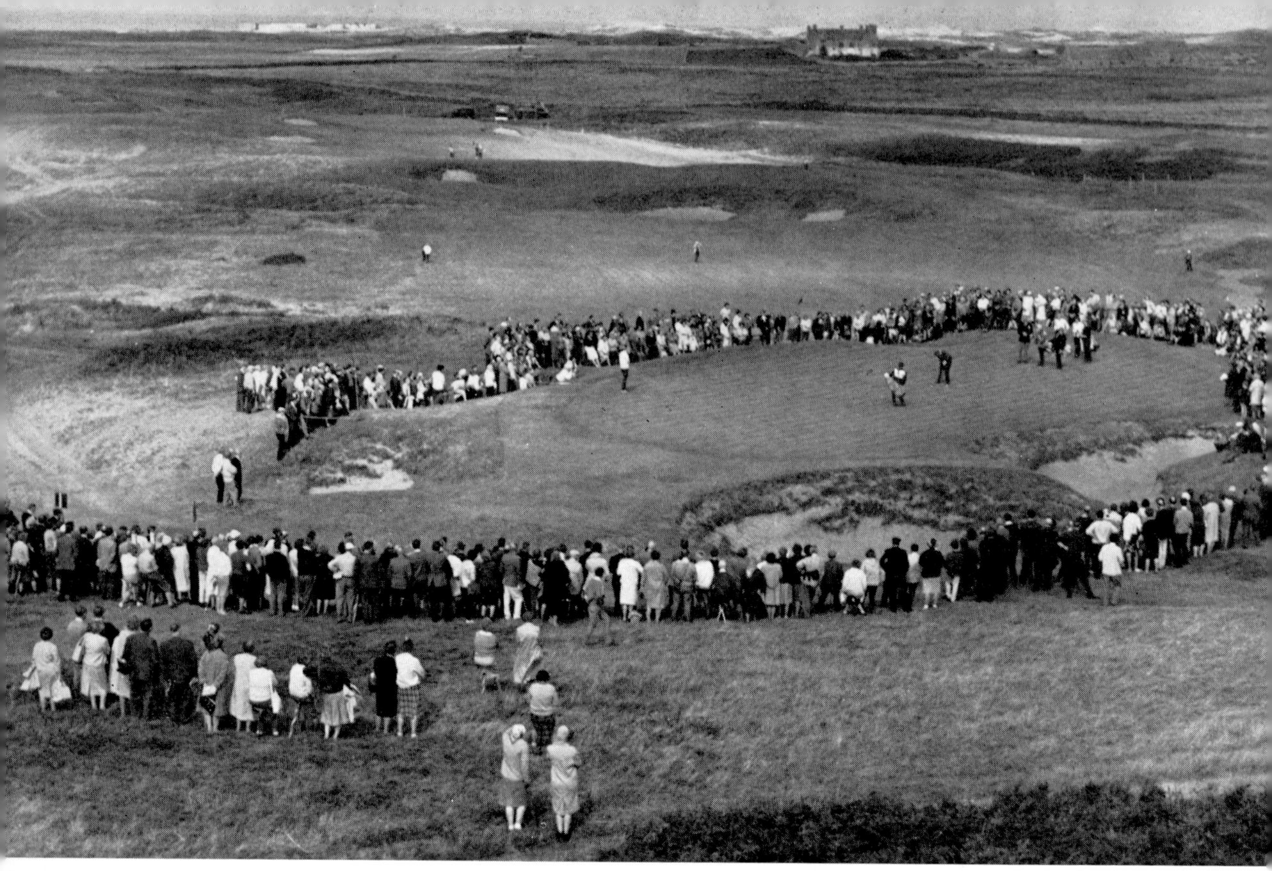

ABOVE The 14th green on the Royal Porthcawl links, a one-shot hole, photographed during the Ladies' Curtis Cup Match (*H. W. Neale*)
BELOW The great Cape bunker at Westward Ho! with a view of some of the famous rushes in the foreground. The bunker requires a carry of something like 170 yards from the tee (*R. L. Knight by permission of Messrs Martini & Rossi Ltd*)

for I used to play golf with his son at Oxford. J.H. was fond of the Johnsonian 'sir' and used to say things thrice for emphasis. In his shop at mid-Surrey was a picture of W. G. Grace, for once not attired for cricket; so I asked J.H. what sort of a game the Doctor played and he said: 'Like a boy, sir; like a boy, sir; like a boy.' Just after he had captained the winning British Ryder Cup side at Southport and Ainsdale in 1933 I was in J.H.'s shop. He said, 'I had a terrible lot of trouble with that fellow Abraham Mitchell, Abraham Mitchell, Abe Mitchell they call him. He came to me on the night after the foursomes and said, "It's no good, John, I can't play tomorrow; it's my back." So I said, "You'll play tomorrow, Abraham, back or no back; you can have Hagen or you can have Sarazen or you can have Dutra, but you'll play"; so he said, "All right, John, I guess I'll take the big bugger", and he murdered him, sir; he murdered him, sir; he murdered him.'

Apart from his distinction as a great golfer in the immortal Triumvirate, he did much to raise the status of the professional, which in his early days was little above that of caddie and often miserably paid. When he retired the profession was on the threshold of the million-dollar business it has now become. He could also be a speaker of rare charm and I will always remember his speech after the University Match dinner at Sandwich in 1928 when he thanked all present with a sincerity and emotion, which none could doubt, for being kind to his son, but in a way which showed that he had learned 'to distinguish between sentiment and sentimentality', so that no one was embarrassed, neither his son nor his son's friends. He always said that his son's election to the presidency of the junior common room at his college pleased him more than any championship he ever won.

Westward Ho! as a golf course has one misfortune: the club-house is on a mild slope above the links near the village of Northam, so that one has to open and finish the round with two holes across the flattest and dullest part of the Burrows. However, they must be played and they are long and, if dreary, hard enough, so if we start 5.4 and end 5.4 we have done well.

Once at the third tee we turn right and the real golf starts. Again the hole is over 400 yards, with a hollow in mid-fairway and a well-bunkered green. Then at the fourth we are right in it; it is like going out of harbour in a ship when she puts her nose down into the first big wave and you hear somebody say, 'Now she's feeling it'. Across the horizon, stretching unbroken it seems as far as the eye can see, is the huge 'Cape' bunker, looking a mile off; in fact it is about 170 yards from the tee and fully 100 yards wide, but it shuts off the view and there is nothing but sandy waste and grassland between you and it and its face is boarded with tough planks with little scaling ladders at intervals to help you out. Once over, the hole is not too tough, the green in a small saucer and not very far off. Four or eight is often the alternative here.

Next a short hole, only 139 yards long and often into a hard wind off the sea, so you may on occasion want a much stiffer shot than you'd imagine; it is a pretty hole with a raised green.

Next come two excellent holes, the first down from a high tee from which you can see the sea for almost the only time; they are both two-shot par fours, running over broken seaside ground and take you nearly out to the estuary of the River Torridge.

Then you have another par three, the 199-yard eighth, the green slightly below you and plenty of trouble in front. You are now at the far end of the links and you start to beat in, against the wind probably, and here on the flatter ground the rushes start to intimidate you. The ninth with its green on a small natural plateau is not too hard, for it is only 471 yards and you are allowed five, but the tenth is another cup of tea. The hole is a sharp dog-leg to the left of 361 yards and your drive is over a sea of rushes on your left where you bite off as much as you can, for it helps tremendously your shot into the small green; this may easily be another eight or four hole. More rushes too at the 372-yard eleventh, to the left and again in front of the tee, and rough to the right, so, to use J. H. Taylor's immortal phrase, 'What's the matter with the middle of the course?'

We emerge, hopefully unpunctured, at the twelfth for a longer par four with a green on top of a slope and well bunkered. Then the thirteenth we can try for another four, for it is 440 yards long, with the green on a small plateau, but it runs against the prevailing wind. An unmemorable short hole with some rushes follows, still heading out to sea, and then turning finally for home the attractive dog-legged fifteenth in reach of two shots. Sixteen is another short hole, only 145 yards, with bunkers left and right and the shot must be most accurate. As Patric Dickinson says, 'Deceptively easy and with a duck's back of a green off which your ball rolls like a waterbead'.

All that is left now is the distressing beat in along the immensely long flat seventeenth, with the third shot having to cross a track and a ditch. Then up to the fence in front of the club runs the tough flat 416-yard eighteenth, which presents you with a muddy ditch to cross quite close up to the green itself. So ends the round and, as Frank Pennink writes: 'Westward Ho! is a historic club in historic surroundings; it is worth every trouble, or any length of journey, to play golf there.'

Continuing up Channel, we must unfortunately pass by Saunton, a most excellent links, by all accounts, which lies on the north shore of the River Torridge estuary opposite Westward Ho! I have not played it and I regard

Burnham and Berrow

So, then, into Somerset to draw up at Burnham and Berrow, near Bridgwater, where one of the most prodigious wastes of sandhills of all is to be found. In this, an excellent golf course has been laid out for which I have a great regard, for I played one or two good rounds there not so long ago.

We start with a couple of two-shot holes up characteristic valleys between the lowering dunes, the second with a plateau green. Then turning left we play a most attractive 378-yard par four, hitting home over knolls and a bunker to a green in a natural saucer. After a modest par five near the shore we have an excellent short hole of 156 yards very deeply bunkered in front. Next a long par four among the hills with a sandy path to cross near the green still near the coast; then two holes in succession at which we are allowed five, rather flatter and duller than what we have had so far. I remember hitting a spoon-shot at the eighth which ran accurately under a Land Rover of the greenkeeping staff by the green without a touch and lay close enough to give an eagle putt. The half ends with a tremendously bunkered short hole, with a plateau green in a setting of high sandhills.

These we have to cross at the tenth and then turn half right to hit a five-iron or so up to the green. After a short par five at twelve along the churchyard wall and across a road, which has to be shortened on Sundays, you get another stiff two-shot up a valley and follow in with a short hole to a high plateau green after crossing a valley. The fifteenth, another valley hole with a narrow green in a dell, is longer than it looks and plays all of 432 yards. Sixteen is a drive and pitch with little room on the green and then comes a full-blooded wood-shot uphill to the seventeenth green high among the neighbouring sand-dunes and fully bunkered in front. I remember needing a driver here against a fair breeze and had the great joy of 'making it', so that I had a putt for a two—which failed—just when I was protecting a good score. The sort of shot of which the pros say 'Get after *that* one'. The eighteenth is a comparatively mild hole if we are content with a five, but it crosses some excessively broken ground and you can hit trouble.

The English Native Championship has been held here, and also the Amateur Stroke Play Championship for the Brabazon Trophy.

Porthcawl

I didn't get to Royal Porthcawl in South Wales until late in 1966 and more's the pity, for it is a mighty fine seaside golf course. However, I *did* get there

The West and Wales

in the end and so completed my tally of all the championship courses of the British Isles, a pursuit which had begun at Deal forty-one years before. True, Porthcawl joined the select band late in the day in 1951 and so became the last but for Ganton to be used for one or other of the major events, but it had its reputation made long before then.

I have called it a seaside course advisedly, for it is indeed by the sea and the club's boast that you can see the sea from some part of every hole is true, but it is not all links-land by any means; the lower holes along the shore and on shore level are links golf, right enough, but there is a distinct hill which you climb at the fifth and on the upper levels from the fifth green to the ninth tee and then again at the twelfth and seventeenth you are on something more like moorland turf with bracken and heather and thick gorse in the rough.

The course is not by any means abominably long, 6,700 yards off the championship tees and 6,400 off the regular tees, so that several of the par fours are under 400 yards, that is until you get stuck into the second half, when the par fours lengthen out and indeed become bogey fives. Don't be deluded, however. The course is not easy, for on the whole the greens are small and the course is richly bunkered; the greens, moreover, have some heavy curvatures, steps and slopes, so that when the game needs to be tightened up some pretty difficult pin positions can be selected.

The location of the course is excellent, with a fine view over the Bristol Channel towards Minehead and Exmoor twenty miles or so away, and on down the coast to Ilfracombe. Inland are some attractive hills and across the bay the Gower Peninsula, with Swansea on its flank. Industry does not too much intrude, save for the emission at intervals of some pink smoke from below the sheltering hill to the west, which betrays the presence of the Steel Company of Wales's Port Talbot plant.

The Porthcawl Club started its golf on a different site on a piece of common land to the east, but for nearly seventy years it has been where it now is, occupying a rough triangle of land, as good a shape as any for a golf course, and especially if, as here, there is liable to be plenty of wind. Then the straight-out-and-home course is at its worst and a layout on a triangle far better. The first three holes run out to the west along the shore, the third, indeed, so close that you can drive on to the shingle without any trouble at all. Then you turn back and play inland to a short hole, well bunkered, with its green sitting up for you, none the less, then at number five with its long uphill pull to the green you are on the plateau. Here, as I have said, you are off the links-land, and indeed this part of the course reminded me a great deal of Ganton, but, after all, isn't Ganton a links inland or something very like it? Up here there is a very short hole, only 125 yards, but it is not easy, for it is heavily bunkered, the green is long

Above The plateau green of the 16th hole at Deal, one of the finest holes in golf. In favourable conditions it is possible to get up in two shots, but against the prevailing wind a pitch to the plateau for the third shot is needed.
Photo: Peter Allen

Below The shot to the beautiful curving 385-yard 14th hole at Portmarnock. The second shot with a medium iron has to cross the ridge with the protecting bunkers, and stay on the plateau green. *Photo: Peter Allen*

and narrow and has some big slopes and borrows. The ninth, with a drive across a big dip, is a splendid hole, with a small much beset green and with some good slopes on it, an excellent medium-length par four. My Welsh caddie, whose vast ginger moustache and whiskers, extending from ear to ear, reminded me of Sir Gerald Nabarro, declared that it was the finest hole on the course and I'm not disposed to disagree.

The par fours in the second half really stretch you, holes like the thirteenth, fifteenth and sixteenth, which I couldn't reach on a soft November day, and there are two fine short holes in this half, the eleventh, which is longer than it looks—where I bolted a putt for a two—and the fourteenth, which is shorter, where I missed a much easier putt. Only the two long holes in the back nine seemed to me to be rather below standard, but the eighteenth is a beautiful finishing hole, with a downhill drive off the plateau straight towards the sea; there is a scrubby hollow across the fairway about 270 yards from the regular tee which no doubt bothers some, but keeping short of that was no trouble to me. The green is long and narrow and literally runs on to the shore, so a shot hit 'thin' can well end up on the shingle.

The greens throughout the whole layout are excellent.

Aberdovey

As Patric Dickinson writes: 'If one dares to write about Aberdovey at all one must begin by letting Bernard Darwin through on the way to the first tee. For this links is his. . . .' It is indeed; for the first holes, with their flower-pots cut into the greens, were laid out in the early 'eighties by his uncle and he played on it in boyhood and loved it with a passionate regard. He also won the first medal competition in 1893 with a score of 100. Let us quote from his famous *Golf Courses of Great Britain*:

'It is the course that my soul loves best of all the courses in the world. Every golfer has a course for which he feels some such blind and unreasoning affection. When he is going to his golfing home he packs up his clubs with a peculiar delight and care; he anxiously counts the diminishing number of stations that divide him from it, and finally steps out on the platform, as excited as a schoolboy home for the holidays, to be claimed by his own familiar caddie. A golfer can only have one course towards which he feels quite in this way, and my one is ABERDOVEY.'

As on so many famous links, the land here is bounded by an estuary, that of the Dovey, and the sea, Cardigan Bay, and as usual there are sand-hills and broken ground along the shore and flatter land on the inland side. The turf is crisp and the greens small.

The West and Wales

After a fairly prosaic start, heading north-west along the duneward side of the links, with a short five and a stiff four we reach the famous short third, 'Cader'. This is a completely blind shot of 165 yards over a huge sandhill; you can look at the match in front through a periscope and they will also announce their departure by ringing a bell. Then grasping your four-iron or five-wood you bend to it and hope to see the ball soaring over the mountain to the green. But if you are short or catch the top you can be in a very tough gravelly bunker with a sleepered face. The green is small, but gently gathers the ball. Next you have a cheerful drive down out of the hills to the plain and a punch home with an iron. After the short fifth come three rather flat holes along the curve of the railway to the far end of the course, where wild iris appear in the rough, a rare attraction on any golf course. You play a short hole across and then come home on the sandhills side of the links. Coming in, I remember especially the odd length sixteenth, 274 yards, but fiendishly difficult driving, with the railway on your left hand, a curving fairway with trouble on the right, and an evil pitch to a small humpy shelf of green with the hills near 'Cader' protecting the right, and a sharp fall off to the left; somehow the ball ran for me here, for I had a fluky three in an undistinguished round. Two rather mild holes bring you in.

Harlech

To end, we should call in at the Royal St David's Club at Harlech, if only for its superb views of Snowdonia and the castle, though I take leave not to care overmuch for the golf. This is doubtless my fault and I certainly played vilely there, which always tends to make you dislike a course.

Considering the territory, I found the course surprisingly flat and difficult—with much less use of the big sandhills than I expected; they really only come into play at the last five holes and then the course becomes splendid, a notable great thump all carry over the vast 'Castle' bunker to get to the 217-yard fourteenth, three stiff two-shotters and another but flatter three.

6 Golf in Ireland

Ireland is refreshingly different from the rest of the British Isles and a visit there makes a wonderful change. The tempo of life, and thank God for it, takes you back forty years, so that even motoring can become a pleasure again. We had an example of this as recently as July 1967, driving from Dublin to Belfast on a fine warm Sunday morning. Whereas in Britain you would have been in a perpetual traffic jam of thousands of cars an hour and the vile hoggish driving that this brings with it, we swished along the narrow adequate roads between the principal cities of Ireland without seeing a hundred cars in all, once outside the capital cities' limits.

That the Sabbath is made for man and not man for the Sabbath is devoutly believed in Ireland, so, provided that you are not pressed for time or trying to cram two days' work into one or something idiotic like that, you can relax and enjoy yourself. The towns are different and not always better than in Great Britain, though Dublin is a city of immense charm; the hotels in Ireland are not worse than here and sometimes very good; the food varies from superb to bloody awful; the scenery is lovely and if it doesn't rain gives as fair a prospect as the heart can desire in blue, green and brown.

The golf is excellent. The Irish love all sports and have produced some splendid golfers—Joe Carr, Lionel Munn, Cecil Ewing, James Bruen, Harry Bradshaw, Christy O'Connor, Fred Daly, Max McCready and the whole Hezlet family.

Good golfers don't come without good golf courses and these Ireland has in plenty. Henry Longhurst puts it this way: 'Some of the Irish links, I was about to write, stand comparison with the greatest courses in the world. They don't. They *are* the greatest courses in the world, not only in layout but in scenery and "atmosphere" and that indefinable something which makes you relive again and again the day you played there.'

Golf in Ireland

The great courses are Portrush, Newcastle and Portmarnock, which stand comparison with any on earth and indeed as a trio are entirely unbeatable; then Dollymount comes close to these. But there are many more excellent and less-known links—Ballybunion in the far west, which I don't know, alas, and Lahinch in County Clare, of which no less an architect than Dr Alister Mackenzie wrote: 'Lahinch will make the finest and most popular links that I or, I believe, anyone else ever constructed'—thus the architect of Augusta National. Rosses Point, near Sligo, a links well exposed to Atlantic winds, I have played with great pleasure and also that most enjoyable holiday links at Castlerock, near Portrush, with its splendid coastal view up to the great Donegal headland of Inishowen. When we were in Dublin recently we heard tell of a splendid and unfrequented links at Baltray, about halfway between Dublin and Belfast, and unfortunately hadn't time to visit it, but it's in the book for next time. Frank Pennink, in his admirable *Golfers' Companion*, gives it high praise.

Killarney

Killarney is as lovely as you can imagine—outside the rather scruffy little town—and it has a famous golf course alongside the Lower Lake laid out by Sir Guy Campbell just before Hitler's War. I've only played it when it was sodden with rain, and while acknowledging the supreme beauty of the mountains and lake, take leave to disagree with almost everybody else about the merits of the course; I found it dull slogging. The eighteenth, a curving water-set par three, is, however, a terrifier. Pat Ward-Thomas can perhaps be allowed the last word here. He says:

'The pursuit of golf has taken one to many of the loveliest corners of these islands, but the beauty of the setting has few peers. All golfers should make a pilgrimage to this enchanting place and know too the charm of a splendid course which can be exacting for the great but never unfair to the weak.'

The Sunday I played it we had the misfortune to get behind four American priests in plain clothes, visored caps and all, who no doubt had fulfilled all their duties earlier, but they made the round a penance for the rest of us with their slow play.

Portrush

Portrush is in the extreme north of Ireland, with a superb view over the Atlantic across the Skerries to the Isles of Western Scotland and the Paps of Jura. Be assured that it can blow violently here. I first played here on the old course with my friend Charles Mitchell in 1927; we drove up from

'Where the Mountains of Mourne sweep down to the sea.' Two views on the links of the Royal County Down Golf Club of Newcastle. The upper picture shows a player making the second shot to the stiff par four 9th (*Bobby Hopkins*). The lower picture shows the green of the par four 13th (*Northern Ireland Tourist Board*)

ABOVE The 4th green at Portrush close to the beach and white cliffs of Antrim. The coarse seaside grass in the rough is typical of links-land (*Northern Ireland Tourist Board*)

RIGHT On the links of the Royal Dublin Golf Club at Dollymount near the entrance to Dublin harbour. The Wicklow hills are in the distance. The players in the foreground are on the 3rd fairway and the 2nd green is

Killarney in the shadow of MacGillicuddy's Reeks is one of the most beautiful places to play golf in the world. The players are on the 3rd green (*Irish Tourist Board*)

ABOVE The last green at Royal Lytham and St Annes with Bob Charles, the first left-hander to win the Open Championship, playing his approach putt in 1963, the year he won (*Blackpool Gazette & Herald Ltd*)

BELOW The short 9th at Royal Lytham and St Annes, 164 yards, with Peter Thomson in play (*Blackpool Gazette & Herald Ltd*)

ABOVE The short 7th hole at the Royal Birkdale Golf Club in Lancashire which measures 158 yards. Some of the enormous sandhills which are such a feature of Birkdale are seen in this picture (*H. W. Neale*)

BELOW The 9th green at Hoylake in a shallow depression. This is one of the oldest and most difficult championship links in England (*H. W. Neale*)

ABOVE The full rigour of the game! The sleepered face of the bunkers at 'Gumbleys', the 492-yard 15th hole at Southport and Ainsdale (*G. H. Loker*)
BELOW LEFT Another Lancashire links, this time the picture is of Formby where the sea-woods are a prominent feature. The play is on the short 9th (*Frank Gardner*)
BELOW RIGHT The second shot to the 345-yard 10th hole at Liphook, a delightful natural course in Hampshire (*H. W. Neale*)

Ganton is the only inland course on which either of the British Open or Amateur Championships have been played. The Amateur was held here in 1964. The picture shows the famous dog-legged 12th seen from the tee (*H. W. Neale*)

ABOVE The shot to the green at the 16th on the Old Course at Walton Heath is very hard if you have not hit an exceptionally good drive. The bunker on the right of the pin gathers many shots that are less than accurate (*Frank Woods*)

BELOW Felixstowe is one of the oldest courses in England and this picture dates from 1887. At that time there were two fairways to the right of the nearer Martello Tower which have since been carried away by the sea (*Felixstowe Ferry G.C.*)

Belfast on a dark winter's day, lunched well, and then with all the careless rapture of youth and kümmel hit two tremendous shots down the first fairway, followed by two scorching irons to give a putt for a three to each of us, after which, and out of sight of a mildly interested handful of members in the club-house, we disappeared into the sandhills and never hit another shot.

When we came back in 1950 to tempt Charles Hezlet out to play, the course had been wholly rebuilt by H. S. Colt and I don't think any trace of the old links remained, certainly none that I could see. In place of the old historic turf is one of the grandest circuits you can name, laid out in stupendous tumbling dune country. After a quiet start and an attractive par three at the top of the duneland you play a long par four and then at number five comes one of the great spectaculars of golf.

You are on the tee, and there, surely much more than 398 yards away and below you, is the green on the edge of the Atlantic, with nothing but a sea of rolling dunes, rough and sandhills in between. Well, it's not as far as it looks and there is a fairway down there, so if you are not hypnotised by the scenery and don't try to cut off too much you can play it as a dog-leg and a very fair and reasonable hole it becomes.

There are some great holes in the second nine, the uphill drive-and-pitch thirteenth, with its little plateau green, is one, to be followed immediately by the 206-yard 'Calamity' fourteenth, an appallingly narrow shot with utter disaster down a violent slope into a dell on the right and below the green and no help from the bumpy hillocks all along the hole on the left. Just about all that will do here is a perfect shot, straight to the green. Then comes a swooping downhill hole called 'Purgatory', after that you are more or less on the level, passing the club-house to go out to the seventeenth green and then turning back.

The Open was played here in 1951 and this was the last occasion on which a British player won—Max Faulkner getting home with an average of just over 71 per round. The course held the upper hand all the way that year and only two rounds in the whole tournament beat 70. The Amateur was here in 1960 and gave forth an Irish victory, as Joe Carr beat the tar out of Cochran, the American, in the final.

Dollymount

The links of the Royal Dublin Golf Club at Dollymount lies on an island on the northern outskirts of the city connected to the mainland by a bridge. One may ask why the Royal title is still maintained in an independent Republic, but this is Ireland. The links is narrow and incredibly compact; like the Old Course at St Andrews it must occupy one of the smallest acreages of any first-class course. The layout unfortunately is straight out, straight home, or very nearly, so that if the prevailing west wind is blowing you have a very fierce beat home. All the same, the links is of the true metal, the ground, though rather flat and without mountains of sand, is of the proper sandy soil and the grass and the rough are 'up to test'.

I think one has to place Dollymount in a category rather below the Irish Big Three of Newcastle, Portmarnock and Portrush, not quite so tough, not quite so interesting, and not quite so beautiful, though the Hill of Howth is an attractive feature and the Wicklow Hills beyond the city make a good backdrop.

The best holes at Dollymount to my taste are the par-four third and seventh of 386 and 352 yards, the latter with a low plateau green. The 179-yard ninth across the far end of the course is the best of the one-shotters I think, though the 251-yard sixteenth makes for a big hit which may give good satisfaction if the wind is not too much against you. On the inward nine the eleventh and thirteenth at 535 and 479 yards need big hitting into the wind but have attractive greens in natural dells which I like, though not as a steady diet. You end the round with a right-angled dog-leg hole, a short par five, which allows you to take a dangerous short cut across a big out-of-bounds carry right up to the edge of the green, which if you bring it off yields you a birdie or even an eagle to go home with.

Dollymount is a bird sanctuary and 3,000 specimens have been identified there, I was told, but what I liked were the hares. The far end of the links is full of hares, big ones, young ones, little ones, loping about on their long legs or stopping with their big ears cocked to look and listen. They are fairly tame and unafraid, as no guns are allowed on the island. I startled a young one which had been lying in the rough with its ears back; it sprang up from under my feet and ran off and you could see the little nest its body had made in the grass.

The Island

The Island is fascinating primeval golf, golf as it was eighty years ago, rough, unkempt, harsh, brutal and short—mercifully it is short or we would surely be destroyed by it.

The links lies on an island across the harbour at Malahide, twelve miles north of Dublin, and you go out to it in a small rowing boat with an outboard motor, the cost of this being part of your green fee.

Once there you see nothing but a tangled waste of sand-dunes covered by the roughest of rough grass, the club-house being hull-down in the endmost group of them. The links is short, only 5,800 yards, with a par of sixty-eight, but it is short in that there are five par threes and two short par fours, otherwise everything is up to full length and there are two holes, the second and the fifteenth, which are over 500 yards; the inward nine against the prevailing west wind at over 3,000 yards has the need for plenty of stout hitting and nowhere more than at the 233-yard last hole, where a slice or even a fade puts you on the beach—from which my friend Rush put a horribly good shot up by the side of the hole—while the broken ground in front of the green can check a perfectly good straight shot like mine; a very narrow and difficult hole.

The early holes along the harbour marshes lie in some of the lumpiest dune country you can imagine; you can't always see where you are supposed to go and there are a lot of blind shots. I suppose the third hole, the 'Andes', is the most spectacular, for here you propel a three-iron or a five-wood shot over a towering sandhill, absolutely blind, with wind-eroded bunkers on its summit; if you succeed in this your ball lands on a furious down-slope and rushes on to the green in a nice gathering hollow—or over it in dry weather; a splendidly old-fashioned hole. The bumps, humps and hollows round the greens of the short fourth and sixth holes are almost as pronounced.

Frank Pennink, whose book of reference is an absolute necessity for the writing of a book like mine, gives the origin of the name of the 502-yard fifteenth, the 'Cricket Field'. W. G. Grace had brought over a team to play cricket in Ireland and on the Sunday they met the Island at golf and lost every match. At lunch the Doctor said it was a pity his side couldn't play the Island at cricket, whereupon the greenkeeper was sent for and told to roll out a pitch. This done, the players went to cricket and W.G. was bowled first ball by Harry Jackson.

Well, it's wonderful to find an old layout like this preserved intact, for this is what golf was like in the time of W. G. Grace—narrow and not very good fairways, really rough rough, sometimes consisting of those tenacious dwarf wild roses, small greens, unwatered, and sand-dunes of spectacular hugeness. Now and then, too, there is a grand view down the coast to the south to the island of Ireland's Eye and the promontory of Howth.

Portmarnock

Portmarnock is a great course, one of the greatest, and there are some who would say *the* greatest. Moreover, it is big golf, the links all of 7,000 yards from the back tees, and yet off normal tees, and with some summer run on the ball, it is not too harsh, even for the elderly, provided that you don't get a wind. The greens are perfect—no other word is adequate—of the finest grass that only prolonged time and the right climate can produce—keen, true and without weed or blemish.

It is an attractive place, too, with water on three sides of it; as you stand in the middle of the course there lies the Hill of Howth to the south; to the east a line of sandhills marks the strand and ocean, and beyond the club-house to the westward you see the sheltered waters of an arm of the sea. Up in the sandhills by the shore you can get a splendid view on a fine day, the islands of Lambay and Ireland's Eye in front of you, Howth to the right, and far up the coast the Mountains of Mourne, sweeping indeed down to the sea. I remember just such a day here on my twenty-third birthday, alas all but forty years ago.

One of the most attractive things about Portmarnock is that there are never more than two consecutive holes in the same direction, so that you tack about all over the ground, constantly changing direction, and when there is a wind of any size—and of course it can blow like the devil here—you don't get battered to death for nine holes on end or blown forward all the way in or out like a leaf on the gale.

The links starts with three par-four holes of moderate length, just to get you going, as it were, but none of them is easy, as they have some nagging bunkers, so that it is all too simple to miss these fours which you are going to need so much later on when the going gets tougher. Four and five are par fours of the full rigorous length, the fourth, at 460 yards, too long for me. Then at six comes the first of the three huge par-five holes, this one 586 yards long. In spite of the third shot being upwards to a hill-top green, this hole, with a following wind, which is not unusual, is manageable, but with a heavy wind across the line from due west it can be a brute, while an east wind makes it inordinately long. A short hole follows of no conspicuous merit, after which you turn for home with a shortish par-four dog-leg eighth with a little narrow plateau green, all too easy to miss, and then a longer par-four ninth by the club-house with another plateau green.

Indeed, plateau greens are a feature at Portmarnock, for the tenth has one—and it can look painfully small—and so has the short twelfth. The twelfth is a standing refutation of the now fashionable belief that all par threes must be 190 yards or more. This one measures only 136 yards, with a small green cocked up in the sandhills by the shore protected by a violent up-slope in front and a big hump on the right; there are also traps about. It is painfully easy not to get on the green from the tee and painfully difficult to chip near the hole from off the green.

The thirteenth is another big par five, 565 yards this time, and this can very easily be dead into the wind as it runs north-west. The same goes for the 525-yard sixteenth. They can make a very tough pair of holes indeed, but in between comes the splendid 385-yard fourteenth hole, back towards the sea with a leftward curving fairway and a plateau green protected by two bunkers in the face of the rise and folds and slopes round the green itself to take off a misplaced shot—a really superb hole and to my mind the best on the course. Henry Cotton, I believe, rates this as the best hole in all golf and I would not disagree. Fifteen is a short hole along the edge of the strand where the green notably fails to gather the ball for you. Arnold Palmer is reported as calling it the best short hole in the world, though I would not go that far.

Seventeen is a long and slightly dull par four, probably because at 466 yards I can't get up in two, but it is made up for by a superb finishing hole, the 398-yard eighteenth, where you have to beat home to a plateau green, the flag at the top of a slope defying you to reach it, as Bernard Darwin used to say. With bunkers on either side of the rise to the green, and the prevailing wind against you, or at least not helping you, you have to hit a fine shot to get home, and then what pleasure you get.

The general appearance of Portmarnock on a fine day in summer I have mentioned, but it is such an attractive spot that I willingly do it again, white water to the west, blue sea and sky, the rough a pale khaki colour, the fairways the light green of an olive, the watered greens the colour of emeralds picked out by black and white posts topped by scarlet flags. What a wonderful place to play the best of games.

But don't forget the autumn gales and the soaking rain from the west, like that famous day in 1927 in the long-abandoned Irish Open Championship, when all the tents were blown out to sea. On the morning of that day only one player beat 80 and that was Jack Smith, who thereby led the field by eight strokes after three rounds. In the afternoon Jack Smith took 91, but George Duncan, well protected from the weather inside and out, had a marvellous round of 74, the only round under 80, and won by one shot from Henry Cotton, who had had 86 and 81 for the day.

There was a similar gale at the Dunlop Masters' in 1965 when the whole day's play was washed out like the tented field, destroyed by the gale, when later Bernard Hunt came from away back in the ruck with a tremendous 66 in the last round to beat out the leader, Peter Thomson, and win the competition.

Let us recall, too, 1949, the only time the British Amateur was held in Eire, when Max McCready won for Ireland, albeit the North of Ireland, and recorded a fine win in the final over an American, one of the great Turnesa family.

Newcastle

The golf links of the Royal County Down Golf Club at Newcastle, under the shadow of the Mountains of Mourne, is to my mind the toughest in the United Kingdom and second only to Pine Valley as the severest golf course in the world. What is more, it is a superbly beautiful place in which to play golf. Behind, to the south-west, as a superlative backdrop, are the Mountains of Mourne, topped by the 2,800-foot peak of Slieve Donard; out to sea to the east and south-east lies Dundrum Bay, with a great arc of strand, across which on a clear day you can see the mountains of the Isle of Man, forty miles away. On the opposite hand is a row of hills by Ballynahinch, while to the north-east along the shore is a tangled wilderness of huge wild sandhills in which the links lies.

I have a great sentimental attachment to Newcastle, for I played there much in my youth with a family of Irish friends, the Mitchells. It is also the scene of my first and almost my last championship in 1927. In those days if you had a handicap of four (worth about six today, I suppose) you were eligible for the Irish Open Amateur Championship and this gave an impecunious undergraduate the chance of ten days' first-class golf—for neighbouring courses gave you the courtesy of the green—for four guineas. A party of us from Oxford used to take advantage of this and even if we failed to survive the first round we had a splendid golf holiday for very little.

Newcastle has two great virtues, first that it is laid out in two separate circuits of nine holes, very different from each other in character, and, secondly, that each hole is separate and private to itself, in its own valley. You can only see the hole you are playing—and not always all of that—so that the sense of solitude and quiet enjoyment is never destroyed, even when the course is busy. In this it is like two other great favourites of mine—Sandwich and Pine Valley.

The claim for Newcastle's difficulty I would make on the grounds that the rough is really rough—seaside grass, heather and gorse on the landward nine and wild roses, sandhills and dunes of uncompromising severity on the sea nine, coupled with heavy bunkering. On top of this there is a carry off most of the tees—not one to terrify the experts, perhaps—but quite enough to give cause for care and thought to the moderately skilled if there is any wind, and there usually is, and sometimes enough to devastate the novice. The bunkering, allied to the fierce rough, is such that rarely does an indifferent shot escape severe trouble. Moreover, the placing of the drive makes a big difference. In consequence, I would rate Newcastle, off equivalent tees, to be two shots a round harder than Portmarnock or Portrush.

Many of the greens are small and, how shall I put it, unwelcoming, like the tiny second green with two dominating pot-bunkers to the left and a fall off the green to the right. I know that this is a short par four and should require a good tight shot, so all right and it damned well has to have it. The greens at the seventh, eighth and fifteenth, to pick three, all seem to be on a little summit with a fall-off in front, on either side and sometimes behind.

You start out along the coast with a friendly fairway and a comparatively easy par-five hole, yet many who have sought a birdie here have retired discomfited with a dull six, for the green is long and narrow and somehow fails to gather the ball as you hoped it would. Number two is the fine 370-yard par four, with a drive which has to carry over a range of sandhills and a pitch over another ridge to a minute green, easy to miss. The third was once a five and is now one of those par fours which only seem endurable downwind. Behind the green is a vast mountain range of sandhills, perhaps the biggest in captivity. On the next tee you can astonish the first-time visitor by suggesting that he tee up to carry this monstrous range and having had your laugh you turn him round to play a comparatively mild par three back towards the club-house and Slieve Donard.

The fifth is a fine right-bending dog-leg with a carry over a ridge of rough illuminated by a characteristic Irish white stone as a marker, a fine two-shot hole with a big hit needed to get home against the wind. The sixth, after a tough carrying drive, is a milder par four altogether. Then comes a minute par three with a greedy bunker just in front of the green, so that any shot which towers into the prevailing wind falls slap into it and any left-tending shot into the wind charges off downhill to two horrible bunkers on the left; behind the green the ground falls away too; it is like playing on to a very small dome.

Eight is a fine two-shot hole of 427 yards, with a small green falling off both left and right, just beyond the throat of a pass, as it were. Then comes the ninth, one of the most spectacular holes in all golf. You drive uphill at a post on the summit of the fairway. If, as you should, you clear all this, you find a superb prospect below you: the hill over which you have driven falls in a precipice to the green fairway far below. From the flat ground below the hill you have to belt your ball hard into the eye of the wind, over two protecting bunkers on an up-slope to the plateau of the green beyond. Behind all this lie the demesne and Gothic brickwork of the hotel, with its dark fir woods, and behind again the whole mountain mass of the Slieve Donard.

Slieve Donard, of course, is the masterpiece of all Newcastle's scenery; now purple in the autumn light, now indigo, now dark bottle green, now half hidden in mist and rainstorm, now glittering with rocks wet after rain has gone by; it is a perpetual gazingstock.

So to the landward nine, quite different from the seaside half. Less spectacular, far fewer huge sand castles and monster dunes, flatter lies, less awful bent grass but more heather and gorse in the rough; but alike in maintaining solitude and privacy with each hole on its own.

Golf in Ireland

After a short overbunkered tenth hole you have a fearsome carry over a vast sandhill at the eleventh, after which the second to the flattish green is not too exacting. Similarly the twelfth, a short par five, which could perhaps be called the only easy hole on the course, is very much on the same lines, though here your drive by contrast has to carry a pit. The thirteenth, however, is a beauty, with a curling fairway, not really a dog-leg but more truly a banana hole, up a valley with hills of heather on either hand, going always to the right so that if you don't hit a good drive you have to bite off a deal of trash in the rough to your right to get home.

A short hole comes next of fair merit but not one to be remembered on one's deathbed, save by my friend Wallace Collie, who did it in one, followed by a splendid tough two-shotter uphill and back towards home with a small green which does nothing to gather your ball. This is almost as hard a four as the thirteenth at Pine Valley and I can't speak higher than that. After that you coast in with a short par four of 267 yards on a plateau which I wish I was still young enough to reach with one great blow from the hill-top tee, a modest seventeenth and a long tough par-five eighteenth into the wind again to get home.

Of course, as at all famous golf courses, great deeds have been done at Newcastle, notably, perhaps, Eric Fiddian's two 'aces' in the thirty-sixth-hole final of the Irish Open Amateur Championship in 1933, in spite of which he had to give way to the late Jack Maclean, who so nearly won the U.S. Amateur Championship in 1936.

The remoteness of Newcastle and the absence of facilities for players and spectators on a massive scale has so far kept from it the British Open and Amateur Championships, and more's the pity, but now the Amateur Championship is coming here in 1970. Newcastle has been a great place for women's championship golf, however, and a course which for some reasons has been particularly rewarding to French girls, three of whom have won the British Ladies' Championship here.

7 North by West

Hoylake

I suppose there is no famous links which offers less encouragement to the first glance of the visitor than Hoylake, except perhaps St Andrews, where the view from the club-house is seemingly the ultimate manifestation of non-golf.

The view from the smoking room at the Royal Liverpool Golf Club on the first floor of that supremely plain Victorian club-house in red Ruabon brick shows a vast flat space, apparently without character or guile, bounded by some singularly uninspired examples of later Victorian and Edwardian domestic architecture to the west—and unrelieved even by that foursquare Victorian barracks, the Royal Hotel, now that it has been destroyed—while only far away on the horizon to the south and south-west is a distant range of sandhills to remind you that this is a links, after all.

Don't be put off: the reality is greatly different. First of all this is a long, tough, supremely competent golf course, one of the toughest and most searching of the great links. You don't get away with anything and, what's more, the great long pros don't make a fool of it either. The 1967 Open was played here under almost unbelievably easy conditions. The ground was hard and the ball ran; then just as this looked like making it all ridiculously short there was a storm in the night and two inches of rain, so that a decent respect for length was reimposed while the greens lost any risk of becoming too fast; there was never any wind and yet—and yet—the course passed the test; it emerged in charge of affairs. Only twelve players averaged less than par for the four rounds and there were only nineteen rounds under seventy out of 370 played. The great Nicklaus, who had slaughtered the vastly long Baltusrol a few weeks before, did not slaughter Hoylake.

Well, what does this rather dreary field, with incongruous knee-high banks of turf called Cops, really do to you? First of all these knee-high banks define out-of-bounds and already the unseemly clamour against this dire ruling is gaining ground. The hideously severe out-of-bounds between the first fairway, almost a right-angle dog-leg, and the practice ground is under fire from the Levellers who have succeeded in abolishing another severe out-of-bounds over the cop to the left of the third and totally destroying for the duration of the Open Championship the terrifying nature of the short seventh where the out-of-bounds cop is the boundary of the left-hand edge of the green. It seems possible that the artificial difficulties made by out-of-bounds at Hoylake will go and be replaced by sheer length, as in America—what a pity.

But there's length at Hoylake and plenty of it, a full 7,000 yards for the Open, plenty of bunkers too, though fewer than there were thirty-five years ago. The greens are beautiful and the fairways less uneven than on most links; the rough on the other hand, with dwarf rose and low-growing blackberry in places, is formidable. The fairways are often narrow and require the drive to be exactly placed or else the hole remains inexorably difficult. For example, if you drive down the left side of the second fairway the hole is not too tough, but drive down the right side and you never seem to get on terms. At Hoylake if you put your drive in the right place, the green, while not quite welcoming the second shot, does not seem unbearably hostile as it does to a misplaced drive. The greens are often tucked away at an angle, as at the twelfth and seventeenth, to make entry difficult. The genius of Hoylake is not one of these things separately but just the stringing together of hazards and penalties with good tees and lovely greens, the rewards for excellence and the penalties for incompetence which make this such a great and such a just links, the Final Honour School, together with Muirfield perhaps, of British golf, where luck enters into it to the minimum and justice is not only done but manifestly seen to be done.

The Royal Liverpool Club has not been afraid of change and alterations have been made several times at Hoylake since golf started there in 1869. After World War I H. S. Colt was brought in to make momentous changes, a new green at the eighth and entirely new holes at the eleventh, twelfth and thirteenth, and playing there today it's a wonder that these excellent holes were ever criticised and disliked.

After World War II a lot of bunkers were got rid of, such as those across the fairway at the eighth and the little pots to the right of the seventh green, no doubt to reduce maintenance, for assuredly these changes didn't make the golf any easier. Some 'modernisation' took place too, with the cross-bunkers at the sixth and eighteenth done away with. This I rather deplore, for a good cross-bunker here and there makes an essential uncompromising demand on the player which you can't easily argue is bad for him. The cross-bunker on front of the eighteenth on the Old Course at Walton Heath is just such a one, and so was the bunker at the last at Hoylake.

In time for the championship of 1967 the third hole was completely altered from a straight par five right into the eye of the wind to a slightly longer dog-leg hole to the old fourth green, better and prettier. Then the new short fourth up into the flanking sandhills to a plateau green is a great improvement on its dull predecessor.

So now let's set out on our game. The first hole can be a horror, for you can go out-of-bounds from the tee and even after a good drive at any point between your lie and the green. As a first hole it's a beast and as a nineteenth or thirty-seventh terrifying; the sharpness of the angle of the dog-leg is most unusual and the closeness of the out-of-bounds cop and its sandy ditch to the entire fairway and green severe in the extreme. Robert Hunter, the American who wrote *The Links* forty years ago, says:

'At the very first hole one is taught not to treat Hoylake with contempt. It is without doubt the most uninviting first hole on any first-rate course in Europe, but one has only to play that hole once to approach it ever afterward with profound respect. The sailing appears smooth enough but something always seems to be a bit wrong and after one has holed out one suspects there has been treachery somewhere—no obvious treachery but some subtle influence that makes what seems quite easy a very difficult performance.'

Dire disasters have happened here, one of the classics being Bernard Darwin's loss of his match in the Amateur Championship of 1910 by running out of ammunition. On a minor scale a friend of mine reported only last summer that he had started out in a stroke competition with a fourteen and that on top of returning from holiday the night before to find his house had been burgled.

The second requires an accurate drive or you're in trouble all the way, as the green is infested with bunkers. The new third is a long slog into the wind, as long at least as the old third, at which I once remember, in the days when I could hit the ball, playing the hole into the gale with a drive and four cleek shots—and who has a cleek today—the last of which pitched on the green and was blown back off it. But Hoylake wind is a subject in itself, suffice it to say that after that game we calculated the par for the day in the bar and it came to 86.

Next is the new short fourth, a better-looking and more exacting hole than the old 'Cop'. Five is a straight-forward and fairly undemanding par four, needing no superhuman placing or length and usually down wind.

The sixth, the 'Briars', with the drive over a corner of the playing fields of the Leas School, is a fine and famous hole guarded in the old days by a cross-bunker and now by two close-lying pot-bunkers. The hole was halved in nine during the final of the Amateur Championship of 1906. Bernard Darwin's description of J. H. Taylor slashing his second shot up to the hole side here with a cleek into the teeth of the gale and rain which ravaged the last day of the 1913 Championship is famous.

Then comes the short seventh, the 'Dowie', to my mind one of the great holes of golf, one which absolutely fits that test of a great hole, that you begin to worry about it before you get to it. The shot is a level one and about 190 yards; it is rare for the wind to be against you—or with you—though it is often totally unhelpful. The green is pear-shaped, the bulbous end the nearer—perhaps triangular is a better description, with an out-of-bounds cop all along the hypotenuse—the chances of being blown or racing over which are painfully easy. In front of the green are a few wild patches of rushes. The other edges of the green all run down into a narrow shallow valley outside of which is semi-rough. To pitch on and stay on requires a shot of supreme merit, while to kick in from the safe region to the right needs a degree of luck allied with skill which is often absent, so you are left with a putt out of the little shallow valley or an approach across it out of the semi-rough.

The eighth takes you out to the far end of the links with a good hummocky par five without a single bunker except for a small pot under the right-hand side of the green. Here at this most straightforward hole Bobby Jones's pursuit of the Grand Slam in 1930 almost came to grief. After nearly reaching the green in two fine shots he contrived with all the ineptitude of you and me to take a calamitous seven, fluffing two chips and taking three putts—and then had to wait a full ten minutes on the ninth tee while the rampaging mob was brought under control. A friend of mine, Tom Dobell, was watching through glasses and says that it was one of the most painful things he had ever witnessed on a golf course. Bob pacing up and down the tee, lifting and replacing his cap, lighting a cigarette and throwing it down and fighting the appalling possibilities of the situation. Then he was off, technique and courage in command, with a smacking drive down the humpy fairway of the ninth towards the green in its dell, a par scored and then home in triumph with hardly an error in the back nine.

So here we are on the tenth, a splendid two-shot hole, bearing left all the while, with a plateau green up in the sandhills. It was at this point in the championship of 1924 that Hagen, not on the green in two nor dead in three, learned that he had to come home in 36 to win—which he did in spite of having to recover thrice from bunkers.

Eleven is a fine one-shot hole with a pear-shaped green, facing you this time, and twelve, the 'Hilbre', is one of those excellent Hoylake bending two-shotters where the entrance to the green only accommodates a really well-placed drive, this time long and well out to the right. Thirteen is another attractive par-three hole, not very long but heavily trapped and usually played downwind as well as downhill.

Now comes the gruelling finish, the last five holes measuring 515, 459, 529, 418 and 400 yards for the Championship and a bit less for ordinary days, the Field, the Lake, the Dun, the Royal and the Stand. Well, at least they don't all run the same way—fourteen, sixteen and eighteen run east and the other two exactly opposite. Depending on how you view it, this can be the most demanding finish in golf or a dreary weary slog up and down a vast flat field, up and down the old race course in fact. To be fair, I think it's a bit of both. The first two holes of these five I think are really a weariness of the flesh, but the sixteenth, with the out-of-bounds eating into the fairway on the right, just where you don't want it, is a splendid hole—and who will forget who saw it, Roberto de Vicenzo's spanking great spoon shot over the lot and home to the heart of the green to clinch the 1967 Championship, or Jones's first serious shot with a sand wedge from the bunker on the left of the green to get his third close to the hole for a vital four in the last stages in 1930.

The seventeenth, too, is a beauty, with traps to the right just where you need to put your drive, so as best to avoid the traps on the left of the green and the hard high road to the right and beyond it. The last is the mildest of the five and well it might be after the beating the others have given you.

As on all great courses, great things have been done at Hoylake, many of them by John Ball, whose championship experience spanned the period from Willie Park and Bob Ferguson to Bobby Jones and Walter Hagen. Here in 1902 the rubber-cored ball came into its own, both championships being won at Hoylake that year with a Haskell for the first time. Here the first foreign golfer, Arnaud Massy, won in 1907.

Well, that's Hoylake, an examination paper, and A-level at that; not my favourite links, for many others would prevent it as a place to play my last round, *but* if you do manage to play a good game there and score tolerably well you have earned some warm feelings of self-satisfaction.

Formby

Formby, along the Lancashire coast, north of Liverpool, is much less severe than Hoylake, but in the opinion of many a more enjoyable place to play golf at. True, the railway runs all along the eastern edge of the course, but it doesn't really bother you as a hazard once you are past the second green. Apart from that you are in unspoiled links-land, with big sandhills and some fine sea-woods to give you some shelter occasionally.

You start a little dully north along the railway for three holes, playing on that flat sandy soil, which all around here produces that admirable fine green asparagus. Then back for a drive and pitch to a shallow bowl, followed by a formidable par three to a high plateau green. After that it is out into the big hills, with limited flat areas among them on which we play to greens masked or protected by the dunes. Holes eleven thru' fifteen, as the Americans say, are all fine two-shotters, the eleventh, with its plateau green sandwiched between two higher mounds, a great favourite of mine, but all five on broken difficult terrain. Then all at once it's over, sixteen is a short hole of no great difficulty, judging by the number of twos scored there in the Amateur Championship of 1967, and there is a flat, flat finish, a long seventeenth and a well-bunkered 412-yard eighteenth with a big green, where Marty Fleckman of the U.S. Walker Cup team had an outrageous two to take out one of Britain's last hopes who was lying close to the hole.

According to its own handbook, Formby is the club where the original club-house was a small thatched hut and the bar consisted of a loose floorboard concealing a bottle of whisky and a collecting box on which was written: 'A moderate go, 3*d*.'

Wallasey

Wallasey, near the mouth of the Mersey, where the qualifying rounds for the Open at Hoylake have often been played, is another fine links with some huge and splendid sandhills. It has recently been reconstructed and improved; formerly it began and ended nobly in the dunes but had a flat sector in the middle which was not in keeping with the rest. The new layout is a big improvement.

All along the coast north of Liverpool from Crosby to the other side of Southport is a rich belt of links-land with a fine diverse crop of golf courses, West Lancashire at Blundellsands, Formby, Hillside, Southport and Ainsdale, Birkdale and three more on the other side of Southport itself.

Birkdale

Of these Birkdale has the most illustrious place in modern golf, having housed the Open Championship in 1954, 1961 and 1965, the Amateur in 1946, the Walker Cup in 1951 and the Ryder Cup in 1965. It is a great and justly famous links, 6,678 yards off the medal tees and stretchable up to

7,000 for the championships. Moreover, it lies in the heart of a great belt of links-land and towering sandhills are to be seen on every hand. However, in practice the sandhills are much more an ornament than a hazard, for rarely do we play over them, certainly not in the Sandwich sense; much more often we play along valleys with the great dunes flanking us, and valleys being what they are, of course, gather what moisture there is, so that some of them are almost lush in their greenness. These valleys *are* the Birkdale scene, then, and if all the big dunes were miraculously removed the course, apart from exposure to the winds, would be affected not at all. The lies here are much flatter than is usual on links-land, so bunkering and sheer length have to play a greater part, these and tougher than usual rough, creeping blackberry—whose fruit carry a matt blue bloom like an American blueberry—and utterly tenacious willow scrub amid the seaside grasses illumined in the season by yellow Evening Primroses. From this gluelike rough Arnold Palmer played an almost miraculous six-iron shot to the present sixteenth green (then the fifteenth) in the 1961 Open after an errant drive and saved at least a shot at a critical moment. This notable stroke is today commemorated by a marker planted on the spot.

The first hole of 450 yards is mildly double-dog-legged, a sort of shallow 'S' in shape, as a sandy ridge comes in from the left to influence your drive away from the ideal position and another comes in from the right to protect the front of the green.

The second hole, a good stiff par four, is away out towards the sea and into the prevailing wind; there are plenty of bunkers round the green and a little sea-wood behind it, a very pretty hole. On the third you reverse direction and fire down a valley between the highest sandhills on the course and play to a green in a shallow depression. Number four is the first short hole, not one I admire much, a good thump down from a tee up in the hills to a flat green with wing bunkers, tight enough in all conscience for a hole of 212 yards.

Next we have a drive and pitch of 320 yards parallel to numbers two and three out towards the sea; the green, as you would expect, at this length is very heavily bunkered. I remember seeing Stranahan in his Walker Cup foursome in 1951—when he and Bill Campbell were playing Ronnie White and Joe Carr in the top match—hit his pitch off the socket, almost at right angles into a bunker. I'm glad to report that Stranahan, who was inclined to take things rather grimly, threw his head back and roared with laughter; so did the other three—and the gallery.

The sixth is a really big two-shotter of 456 yards, with a ridge of low sandhills across the fairway for once, and five is good enough for you and me. Then comes the second short hole, again down from the tee to a very well-bunkered green.

Eight and nine at 413 and 410 yards are two dog-leg holes, the first swinging to the left up a valley in the sandhills and the second to the right. The ninth in fact is a very attractive hole, a good drive over a stiff carry putting you on a plateau overlooking a big hollow in the fairway across which you belt your second shot to a markedly steep plateau green.

The tenth is a sharp dog-leg to the left, the green being tucked away in a corner almost, amid surrounding hills; unless you hit a good drive out to the right you have a hellishly difficult second.

Eleven is a most attractive hole, for you can see it all from the tee and you have the pleasure of hitting down from a rise. The green is small and set across the line, which is fair enough for a 368-yarder; there are cross-bunkers too on your way to the green.

The twelfth is a new one-shotter of 180 yards from a tee in the hills across a shallow valley to a green up in the next range; the green is narrow and looks very small, especially as it is beset with four deep and hungry bunkers and flanked by sandhills. It reminded me of one of my American books on golf architecture which has a photograph of the tenth at Pine Valley with the caption, 'There is no welcome here'; well, there's no welcome here either.

Thirteen at 437 yards I think rather dull, a flat hole with a flat fairway, though the surroundings are agreeable they don't affect the hole; it's not easy, of course.

The short fourteenth is rather longer and rather easier than the twelfth, which it somewhat resembles. The shot is more downhill and the green is larger. I found it a good hole for my five-wood from a forward tee. Now you have to gird yourself for a big finish, the last four holes measuring 530, 343, 507 and 473 yards. The fifteenth is on flat ground again, but three little traps *en echelon* threaten your drive on the left and it is heavily bunkered across the course where your second and mine want to go as well as at the green itself, a pretty tough par five, this one, but I would have liked a few more undulations in the fairway. At sixteen you have a blind tee shot over a sea of rough and little humps to a flat green fairway; then you have a really tight shot on to a high plateau green with half a dozen guardian bunkers; the green is not large and does nothing to gather the ball; how Arnold Palmer made it out of thick willow scrub defeats me.

For ordinary players the tee shot at the seventeenth is dominated by two big sandhills between which you drive; they give you a very narrow gap of less than thirty yards, at 230 yards from the medal tee. The rest of the hole I found too flat to be inspiring—flat and difficult. If you can get up in two shots, which I can't, it's a different matter.

The same arguments apply to the 473-yard eighteenth. I can't get it in two and so have a not very tough pitch to the small green, but if you can get up in two then what a splendid hole it becomes; bunkers to skirt from the tee, others, and two small ridges on either side of the fairway on the way along and then three small traps, two on the left and one on the right on the very edge of the green itself. What a hole to have to be sure of getting a four at to win the championship! Well, it doesn't seem to bother Peter Thomson.

So ends a big golf course, but to me my last visit left a tinge of disappointment; the valley fairways are just a little too green and grassy and too flat for this old Tory.

Southport and Ainsdale

Southport and Ainsdale lies one side of the electic railway and the fine Hillside links, which I don't know, on the other. S. & A., as it is always called, has twice been host to the Ryder Cup match in 1933 and 1937 and is a full-length circuit in authentic links-land. It has its quota of big sandhills and these come into play quite a lot, notably at the third tee where you drive from a great height and at the 492-yard sixteenth, called 'Gumbleys', where you have to hit a second shot with wood over a vast hill fortified with a wall of black sleepers with two bunkers below into which you bounce if you hit your second too low. As at Birkdale, the fairways here are rather too flat for my taste and the seventeenth hole is flat indeed. However, the narrow humpy eighteenth fairway makes up for it with an attractive shot to a plateau green where Easterbrook in 1937 holed the last putt of the game, on which the entire Ryder Cup match depended. An attractive links, this, and as much as anything I like the unorthodox opening of a 200-yard shot to a very narrow-looking heavily bunkered green.

Blundellsands

Like others on this coast, the West Lancashire, this course at Blundellsands has recently been remodelled and brought entirely to the links side of the railway and a startling new club-house of ultra-modern style built. The links is in flatter land than its neighbours to the north, but is of the real stuff and hard by the shore at that, with the shipping channel out of Liverpool close in at this point.

Lytham and St Annes

The most northerly of this great chain of championship golf links along the coast of the Irish Sea is at Lytham and St Annes, near Blackpool, on whose links golf has been played now for some seventy years. In this period the area has suffered major changes and what was once a piece of natural agricultural and links-land, bounded by the railway and blown over by wild breezes and flying sand from the dunes along the shore, is now an oasis in a wilderness of modern housing, of rather unprepossessing style in the great and growing conurbation of Blackpool and St Annes.

Inevitably the character of the course has changed in this process, as have so many of the great seaside links, and it has become more 'inland', softer, fatter and lusher. With a desire for better lies and softer greens, water and fertiliser have been applied and much of the bone-hardness so characteristic of St Andrews, Hoylake and here have gone for ever. With all this, Royal Lytham and St Annes remains a great course and it is now firmly established in the championship rota, with the Open here in 1926, 1952, 1958 and 1963, and due again in 1969, the Amateur in 1935 and 1955 and the Ryder Cup in 1961.

Here in the mists of the past the first Ladies' Championship was played; here Bobby Jones won his first British Open in a dramatic finish after a daylong struggle with Al Watrous and here the first left-hander to win a major championship, Bob Charles of New Zealand, triumphed in 1963 after a tie.

The links is approximately out-and-home in that the first nine run south-east with one diversion and the inward nine work back with rather more holes across the general line of play. The result of this is that the outgoing half, if the prevailing wind is blowing, is where you must build your score and the inward half, which is also longer, where you must strive desperately to defend it.

The course is rather flat, especially at the club-house end, and many of the 'seaside' hillocks and dunes are in fact the work of man not nature, fashioned by countless spades and cartloads long before the days of the bulldozer but done with a skill which matches the folds and humps and hollows of the natural links-land across the railway nearer the shore. The far end of the course out by Ansdell railway station is in natural links-land with some notable sandhills and plateaux.

The round opens with a par three, which is a start disliked by many on principle, but it has its advantages and often makes for a freer start than, say, a 450-yard par four, where every novice waits swinging an inadequate brassie for the unreachable green to be cleared. The first at St Annes is tough enough at 208 yards to be respected.

Two and three run out along the railway and at 426 and 456 yards are a formidable pair; you can slice on to the line or if you pull away you can be bunkered or get yourself a harder second shot. At the fourth you reverse direction with a carry over shallow hills and a shot to a tightly bunkered green. Then the fifth is another par three, difficult enough in all conscience at 188 yards off the medal tee and off the far back championship tee whence

I would need a driver just horribly long. Two par fives in succession put you back along the railway again and then you play the splendid eighth hole from right up by the boundary fence to a high high-plateau green with a big swale in front which is not visible as you line up your second shot; you've got to hit right up to this perched up green and risk going over the back or you will inevitably run off to the bunkers guarding the front of the green; at 394 yards a grand hole.

So too is number nine, a short hole of 164 yards, tightly and grievously bunkered so that only a full carry to the green will do any good. A grand hole this, but alas spoiled by its ugly urban surroundings.

The tenth, now 376 yards, is being lengthened by sixty yards to teach the professors a lesson and in consequence a gap has had to be cut in the range of sandhills which you previously had to carry off the tee. I don't think this spoils the hole and it does give the ordinary members a fair chance with the greater length; the green is an attractive cocked-up plateau, with deep guardian bunkers especially on the right.

The eleventh is also being stretched for the next Open from 483 yards to over 550 and this into the prevailing wind.

From twelve thru' seventeen, as the Americans say, the course beats to and fro with a par three at twelve and two huge par fours at fourteen and fifteen, too long for my taste. The sixteenth at 356 yards, with a bunkered hill to carry off the tee, is more merciful. So we come to the famous and historic seventeenth, where in 1926 Bobby Jones played the famous shot out of a rough sandy scrape—not, I think, a formal bunker, as there is there now. Looking today from where this shot was played it seems a fantastically difficult stroke, even from a good lie. The hole is a flat strong dog-leg to the left with a flat green and on the corner where the drama was enacted was a wilderness of rough, sandy spots, and today bunkers, while the line to the flag is guarded by a trap in front of the pin. Al Watrous, who was destroyed by Jones's shot, taking three putts from the front of the not very big green, had driven right up the centre of the fairway and played a seemingly safe suitable shot in; Jones in trouble took out his 'Old Equaliser', a mashie-iron, about the loft of a number four today, hit the perfect shot out of a good lie in the scrubby scrape, drawing the ball in from the right to lie plumb in the middle of the green, and the Championship was his; as Watrous said, seeing the shot, 'There goes a hundred thousand dollars.' A plaque in the bunker of today marks the spot from which he played. The club with which the deed was done is in the big upstairs lounge which has such a fine view over the links; it is by no means the clumsy iron monster which is often implied. The thick hickory shaft looks coarse to our eyes today, but the head is in my view a beautifully shaped deep-faced iron characteristic of the 'Pipe' brand clubs of Stewart of St Andrews.

North by West

So, like Jones, we are 'only' left with the eighteenth hole of a modest 389 yards to do in four—but what with bunkers to carry and others threatening the tee shot to the left, a spinney to the right and greedy bunkers guarding the pear-shaped green—three each side—and a narrow entrance to it, a four is all too often missed; ask Eric Brown, O'Connor and Ruiz, each of whom had to do it in four to win or tie the 1958 Open and failed, leaving a tie to Peter Thomson and Dave Thomas.

So possibly a little chastened in spirit let us repair to the big hospitable club-house for some of those delicious local shrimps for our lunch.

The Amateur Championship has been twice at Lytham and St Annes, the first time in 1935, when Lawson Little beat Dr William Tweddell in the final after a brave fight which went to the last green, for the Doctor at one early stage had been five down. Of Tweddell when he won the Amateur at Hoylake in 1927 this immortal verse was created:

> 'At Worplesdon and Leatherhead
> they speak of Jones and Wethered
> but Stourbridge, happy Stourbridge
> are going to strike a medal
> to celebrate the victory of
> Dr William Tweddell.'

The Amateur of 1955 also went to America when J. W. Conrad won.

Ganton

This northern tour ends at Ganton, five miles inland from Scarborough, where the Amateur Championship was played in 1964, the first time it had been held away from the seaside. The Ryder Cup match was played here in 1949.

It is on the lightest of sandy soil and resembles a seaside links as much as any inland course can; only the trees, which are sparse, and the surroundings reveal the truth.

You start out with a couple of par fours of no great length, though you can, of course, bunker yourself if you wish. The third was reachable with a big hit from the tee, but a new back tee for the Ryder Cup has put the championship length up to 335 yards.

The fourth is a beautiful two-shot hole across a gully and a sharp rise to a plateau green. Then comes a short hole with water hazards, which somehow seems to exact a four much more often than it should. There follow three big holes over 400 yards, of which the sixth is really outside my reach, while the seventh, with its curvature and bunkering and the green on the crest of a rise, is just at the limit of my strength.

The half closes with the long ninth, 510 yards, parallel with the main road. This is followed by an excellent short hole, just rather further than it looks and well bunkered. Then the eleventh with some deep bunkers and a keen green and after that a decidedly 'inland' dog-leg hole round the end of a row of trees.

The par-five thirteenth shouldn't bother you unless you top your drive into a sea of gorse. Then comes the second of three big one-thump holes—if you include the third—a 270-yard beat downwind to a small green infested with bunkers with a choice of a drive and pitch to the right. Two excellent holes around 458 yards follow, reachable in two in the right conditions, the sixteenth with a big cross bunker to carry from the tee and a line of pines on the right, a particularly pretty hole.

The seventeenth is a 250-yard shot across a road to a cocked-up green with all too many bunkers to evade which yields more fours and fives than threes. Finally you have a splendid testing last hole with a big diagonal carry off the tee over a huge sand-dune—for no other word describes it—and the need to get well across to the right before you can get a clear shot home through the aforesaid line of pine trees to the long, deep-trapped eighteenth green.

Ganton has had its long line of famous players, notably Harry Vardon, who was pro here in its early days, and that great pipe-smoker and champion of Britain—and the U.S.A.—Ted Ray. Ray, a genial giant, was once pestered by an importunate member to impart the secret of his great length from the tee; removing his pipe for a moment Ray replied, 'Hit it a bloody sight harder, mate.' And while we are on quotations, here is one from Harry Vardon himself, who, when approached by a 'temperance' worker, replied, 'Moderation is essential in all things, madam, but never in my whole life have I been beaten by a teetotaller.'

8 Others in England

The problem of this chapter is severe, for it is the decision of what to leave out, rather than what to put in, so in the end it will have to be a personal choice again, but there are many, many fine and enjoyable, if not historic, courses and links that should go in and most of them I have played.

For instance, I would like to have included a most attractive group of heather courses near Bournemouth—Parkstone, Ferndown and Broadstone —but they have all had to be omitted. Frilford Heath, where we used to go on Sundays from Oxford, is out alas, and so is Huntercombe. There is no room for the links at Seaton Carew or for my old course at Sandiway in Cheshire, of Alwoodley and Moortown at Leeds, even though I saw Britain beat U.S.A. in the Ryder Cup there in 1929. I would dearly have loved to include that relatively humble circuit West Byfleet in Surrey, for there I began forty-five years ago to learn the game from that fine teacher Fred Hedges, who tried and occasionally succeeded in making me hit my iron shots like he did, with a click like 'the shutting of a knife'. Happy days under Fred Taylor's eye at Southfield at Oxford should be in too, but are not.

When we come to the London courses the dilemma is worse than ever. Why on earth are Woking, where I was once a member, and Wentworth and West Hill and Worplesdon and the two fine courses at the Berkshire, which have always been good to me in competitions, and Addington and, almost the best of the lot, Colt's classic at St George's Hill, all left out? I can only say in a small quiet voice that I'm very sorry, there wasn't room for everyone and I've had to show a preference for seaside links and be just plumb arbitrary. I would just make one more apology and that is at having to leave out Swinley Forest near Ascot, for although it is not a demanding course it is charming and lots of fun to play, with some splendid holes, and very beautiful as well, especially when the rhododendrons are out at the back of the twelfth green in June or when the heather is blazing in September. The plain well-cooked English food is so good too.

So we have got to get down to the hard decision of what goes in and I am going to make perhaps a surprising start in giving pride of place to East Anglia, which has some excellent and historic courses in its compass. Even then we will be leaving out Woodbridge, an excellent heath course and one of special joy to me, for I once holed it in 72, and also Aldeburgh, with its gorse, and Thorpeness, fine courses both. There is no place for Cromer, on the cliffs, although the first international match in golf was played there, between the ladies of Great Britain and the United States in 1905, which our girls won handsomely. And, incidentally, the two Curtis sisters, both later to be U.S. Ladies' Champion, who later gave the Curtis Cup for the international contest, played in the Cromer match. Sheringham is out too, I'm afraid, but the final distillation has left us with four courses of rare interest and distinction.

Felixstowe

The first of these is Felixstowe on the Suffolk coast, one of the oldest clubs outside Scotland, which was formed in 1880. While on this subject Robert Browning, in his excellent *History of Golf*, while acknowledging that there can be and is much argument about such dates, puts the oldest clubs outside Scotland in this order:

Blackheath	1766
Old Manchester—Kersal Moor	1818
Calcutta—the first outside the U.K.	1829
Bombay	1842
Pau—the first on the Continent	1856
The Curragh—the first in Ireland	1856
Westward Ho!	1864
London Scottish—Wimbledon	1865
Hoylake	1869
Alnmouth	1869
Adelaide—the first in Australia	1870
Montreal—the first in Canada	1873
Clapham Common—no longer in existence	1873
Quebec	1874
Royal Jersey[1]	1878
Felixstowe	1880

[1] Added by the author.

Others in England

There seems to be some doubt about the validity of claiming Manchester, for there was a big hiatus in its life, while claims for two defunct clubs in the southern states of the U.S.A. and the one on Clapham Common would seem to me invalid; if Manchester is excluded on that score, then Felixstowe would appear to rank sixth in the order of date of surviving English clubs, otherwise seventh.

The course has been altered several times, for when the club has not been taken over because of war with the Germans—for this has always been a potential invasion beach—it has been continuously at war with the German Ocean. A perpetual erosion of the coast has been going on for years and whole fairways have disappeared since the first layout. Two Martello towers grace the links, the nearer one is now on the edge of the sea having originally had two fairways to the eastward of it and the battle is being continued today with expensive works under construction.

The first layout was a nine-hole links on sandy soil running both sides of the first Martello tower which once served as the club-house. The course was later extended to eighteen holes. Then after the military and marine damage of World War I had been made good an entirely new layout was devised by Dr Alister Mackenzie, embracing some flat estuarine land on the far side of the road to Felixstowe Ferry and some cliff-top land behind the club-house. World War II saw a complete shutdown and occupation by the soldiery, after which, again confined by the inroads of the sea, the present entirely new layout was made by Henry Cotton, abandoning the cliff-top holes, which had gone anyway, making the most of the sandy soil near the shore and extending the number of holes in the riverine plain. It could be said, therefore, that the first nine holes today are links-land, with thin turf, keen greens and some ' 'umps and 'ollows', while the inward nine is flat and inclined to be much softer. The first six holes make a loop and come home to the club-house, then the course runs right out to the second Martello tower, then across the road and then in again, but it is all so compact that agreeable variations can be played to give you almost any number of holes you like to play.

My knowledge of Felixstowe is confined to a bitter cold winter's day when I was afflicted by a weight-reducing regimen I was undergoing which left me ill-equipped to beat off the shrill wind or hit the ball at all well, but I enjoyed the few holes I played, notably the first, with its true seaside fairway and lightning green up by the Martello tower, the short par-four second on its plateau and the short eighteenth, well guarded; most of the brookside holes are for another and warmer day, but it is a good and enjoyable-looking course and I want to go back.

The north of Norfolk is a strange and remote place, and, except in a short holiday season, sparsely inhabited. It is flat and open and you get the

ABOVE The famous view on the Old Course at Sunningdale, looking across the green of the short 4th to the two-shot 5th and 6th holes beyond (*H. W. Neale*)
BELOW LEFT A fine natural hole on the links at Hunstanton with a plateau green amongst the sandhills. The hole is the short 7th (*H. W. Neale*)
BELOW RIGHT A delicate approach to the 8th green at the Royal Worlington and Newmarket Club. The tricky short 5th green is just behind the line of pine trees (*Royal Worlington and Newmarket G.C.*)

The green of the short 127-yard 15th hole at Spyglass Hill, a big new course laid out on the Monterey Peninsula of California. This hole has one of the many water hazards which Robert Trent Jones has introduced into this spectacular course (*Julian P. Graham Studio*)

ABOVE One of the most photographed holes in the world is the short 16th at Cypress Point which can measure as much as 230 yards off the back tee. The route of inglorious safety is towards the weather-beaten cypress tree on the left (*Julian P. Graham Studio*)

RIGHT A much photographed hole at the Mid Ocean Club in Bermuda. The players on the 5th tee have the opportunity to bite off as much or as little as they care to. The hole is a two-shotter of 415/433 yards (*Bermuda News Bureau*)

ABOVE The 7th green at Pebble Beach, a short hole of about 110 yards with the green close to the shore of Carmel Bay (*Julian P. Graham Studio*)
BELOW The green at the 13th hole at Augusta National with the azaleas in bloom. This hole, though rated at par five, can be reached in two shots, but Rae's Creek in front of the green is a most disturbing hazard (*United States Golf Association*)

impression of immense horizons and huge skies. Off the coast the sea is shallow and great sandy beaches stretch for miles; it is bracing, and, truth to tell, rather cold. The hinterland is often protected by marshes and saltings and there are many wild birds. You might be in Denmark, and that goes even for a lot of the domestic—but not ecclesiastical—architecture. You either take to these wide open spaces or you don't. I happen to like them and not least because two very fine classical golf links lie on this coast.

Hunstanton, a little resort town, lies on the Wash and on a clear day you can look across to Lincolnshire. Last time I was there, checking my facts, was in January 1968 when a brisk north wind was blowing straight off the Pole with alternating sunshine and snow showers. I remember few colder days on any golf course, but I remember, too, warm holiday golf there in July when the weather was perfect and one day when the temperature reached 90°F.

Hunstanton

Since its start in 1891 Hunstanton has had many alterations, the first from its original nine-hole layout. After extension to eighteen holes James Braid had a hand in tightening things up and in 1925 James Sherlock made several improvements. More recently the seventeenth and eighteenth on the low land on the inland side have been replaced by two new holes among the bumps on the seaward side. It is now a fine full-length links of 6,723 yards off the back tees and its own brochure claims it as being 'said to be the finest test of golf between the Humber and the Thames'. I think they are too modest; I think you could say 'between the Tweed and the Thames'.

The links lies between the shore, with its huge beach, and the little River Hun and a straight irregular range of shaggy sandhills divides it into two parts, the flatter low-lying holes on the inland side and the exceedingly humpy holes on the seaward side. The ridge itself is used extensively for siting greens or afflicting tee shots.

Many tournaments of importance have been held here except for the two major championships, and the ladies have often used it for the English and the British titles, the English Amateur has been here thrice and the Amateur Stroke Play Championship has been held here once. Oxford has met Cambridge here on several occasions.

My only regret at the recent alterations has been that the old first tee is now occupied by the new eighteenth green with the first tee pushed over to the right. As a result, the great intimidating bunker which has demoralised so many over the years is now only a menace if you hit a pretty quick hook. The rest of the hole on the flat inland side is not exciting; nor is the long

Others in England

second in the same area. The third, a long par four, is much of the same, though you can cut your second into the Hun without much difficulty.

We then play a short fourth towards the sandy ridge and the sea, well beset by bunkers, fifteen I think. Then back with a two-shotter on to the plain again. Well, so far, not much, and you would be pardoned for thinking that there was nothing special to crow about. However, from now on things are on the up and up and the remaining thirteen holes are first-class. The change starts with six, a drive and pitch hole towards the ridge, of 336 yards. The green is set on a high plateau guarded by bunkers on either hand in front and a deep pit of short rough to the right of the green which runs precipitously into it; it was once the old green but doesn't look like it today. The green is none too big and is well sloped; putting can be a problem. To my taste a lovely hole.

The next is even better, a gem of a hole, 164 yards from plateau to plateau with a long deep trough of rough in between and a bunker in front of the green. To the left are the sandhills of the main ridge and very broken bumpy seaside ground and a similar but lower ridge on the right; these combine to give the perfect setting of what a true links-land hole should be.

You now have to prepare yourself for some pretty resolute hitting if you want to score, for No. 8 is 493 yards long out to the end of the links, then the ninth is 515 yards back to a green under the seventh tee. Two tough uncompromising holes, these, and you can't have the wind helping you at both; indeed, with a norther blowing it won't help you at either. Ten is out towards the sea, and the eleventh runs back again along the shore; these are among the newer holes at Hunstanton. At the twelfth we are attacking the ridge again, this time from the sea, and cross it with a 359 yard par four. Then we immediately recross it with the unorthodox thirteenth, 390 yards long. You drive over the ridge and then run out of fairway, for the green is an island and the second shot in has to clear a belt of rough and some sandy hillocks round the green. Patric Dickinson regards it as 'one of the greatest two-shot holes in golf'. At fourteen it's the ridge again, this time a blind one-shot hole, once so fashionable, now so rare. I hope they don't change it. There are bunkers in the ridge face and round the green so at 225 yards that's quite tough enough. Then comes a short par five and then another short hole down from the ridge on the seaward side; a pretty good stiff iron shot is needed here. We finish with two new holes among the sandhills which were opened in 1951, the seventeenth a fierce two-shotter of 448 yards to a shelf green with a hillside to the left and a drop to the right. The last hole is shorter, 397 yards, but again the green is a plateau and a small one at that, protected in front about fifty yards short by a sandy road where you can get a distressing lie—but then you have no business to be there.

Perhaps Hunstanton's most famous character was the professional James Sherlock, who died in his ninety-second year, who served the club for many years. He was near the top in professional golf and beat Vardon in the final of the *News of the World* Match Play Championship in 1910. More remarkable, perhaps, he won the over-seventies' Seniors' Cup in his eighty-second and eighty-third years. When a mere lad of sixty-one he did two holes in one in one round. He also played in the first match against the American professionals at Gleneagles in 1921 and won both his matches. One of his greatest sorrows was the death of John Lyon, one of the promising young men of English golf, who used to play at Hunstanton; he was killed in the war.

Brancaster

Moving east along the coast road a few miles to a still more remote spot we come to the links of the Royal West Norfolk Golf Club at Brancaster.

Whereas Hunstanton has undergone many changes in seventy-five years or so, Brancaster has had few, except where the sea stole two holes of the links in 1939 and 1940. As my friend Laddie Lucas wrote to the Yates family in Atlanta, Georgia, 'the links was laid out in 1891 and has been unchanged ever since'. So here you may see a museum-piece in a sense and yet find a most enjoyable and testing links to play. I love it. A lot of it does look very old-fashioned, sure it does, especially those huge wooden sleepers lining the faces of the bunkers. But they put the wind up you, none the less; they are alarming to play over and terrifying to play out of and even after thirty-three years I can remember starting out 4.10.4 on my first round here.

Brancaster has much in common with Hunstanton, ten miles away, many similarities and many differences; the links lies between ridge and marsh but the ridge this time is right along the edge of the shore and the marsh is wetter, indeed it may be flooded at very high tide, like the road leading to the club-house! The grass is uncompromisingly seaside, spare on the fairways and painfully thick in the rough; the greens are of a seaside keenness but true to the properly struck putt. Wild sea-lavender and sea-holly grow in the marsh.

We start out prosaically enough with a drive over a chasm which was once a huge sand bunker and then turn half left to hit up into the hills, but it is 400 yards, so we'd better hit a good drive. Two is not too tough, either, in spite of Allen's ten, though we meet the sleepers here for the first time with a big boarded bunker to catch a pulled drive. At the third we really have a facer, a 401-yard hole with the green on a narrow plateau guarded about forty to fifty yards in front by a huge boarded cross-bunker.

Others in England

If you don't hit a good drive you've got to go for it with wood—and there's no way round. Even if you get over, the green is not welcoming and may shrug you off into a bunker under the escarpment.

The fourth is a little terror; a pitch from a high tee over a vale to a very high plateau green, guarded in the face by three deep bunkers, revetted with sleepers; with a strong north wind you might even have to take wood here! Normally it is about a number seven, but there's no temptation to be short.

Keeping near the marsh, we play the next three in 4.3.5, we hope, but you can get into the saltings if you hook at the short sixth or slice at the long seventh.

At the eighth we have a celebrated hole, with two arms of the marsh to carry—it is not out-of-bounds—or two arms of the sea, as I have once seen it. The first carry is from the tee and diagonal, so the more you can bite off, the better. If you've hit a good one you can bear down on the green with your second over the second inlet. However, par allows five here, so you can adjust your efforts to your drive and if need be poke one along the arm of fairway and then pitch up to the plateau green.

You drive over the marsh again at the 462-yard ninth and then have to hit a firm second over a huge sleepered bunker to the new green, slightly to the right of the old one devoured by the sea.

You now turn for home on the seaward side of the links with a 150-yard short hole on a plateau green. There follow two more holes among the dunes, the 480-yard eleventh and the 375-yard twelfth, with their greens in natural dells, then a new post-flood short thirteenth from plateau to plateau again, the green up in the sandhills. Then comes a famous old hole along the bumps and hollows of the links land close to the shore; it is 430 yards long and that would be all right if there were not a big swale full of short rough about fifty yards short of the green; so your second shot is all carry and that to a pretty small target area. The green here is cheek by jowl with that of the short fourth, and mishit shots at either can finish up on the other.

We then face another desperate shot at the fifteenth, or so it seems. The hole is 190 yards long and it looks—only looks, it is true—as if the green were immediately beyond a huge enormous pit of a bunker, deep, dark and cavernous with a boarded face. Reality is rather kinder, for the green is about fifty yards past the trap, so your carry is only about 140 yards instead of what you first guess; even so it is not easy, for the green, on the inevitable plateau, is small and easily casts your ball aside.

The sixteenth is a nice short par four of 335 yards slightly dog-leg up into the hills; the guardians here are only small pot-bunkers! At seventeen you cross the play to the second and you may drive into the bunker, sleepered of course, which catches drives off that tee, but otherwise at 375 yards the seventeenth is not too tough. At the last, 380 yards, we do need a good drive, as we have to carry a boarded bunker which forms the front edge of the green and yet stop on a keen surface, remembering there is another sleepered bunker at the back. So ends Brancaster and if you think the inward nine at 2,879 yards is going to be short, try it against a westerly wind.

Have I given an impression that Brancaster is impossibly severe, too harsh in its punishments and too brutal with its cross-bunkering and ancient style? I hope not, for in fine weather it can be amazingly beautiful, the sea birds wheeling and crying overhead, the marsh with its own flowers and, perhaps, after a blow, the sea making a continuous roar on the sands out of sight beyond the rampart of dunes. Remote, serene and unspoilt, may it long continue. As Tom Scott, the editor of *Golf Illustrated*, says:

'It has a quiet and restful beauty and when you leave the club-house and drive across the marsh to the main road in the dusk of a summer evening, look back for a minute and perhaps you will be rewarded, as I have frequently been, with a view of the red sun setting over the sea with a golden glow. You will see too, the long shadows cast by the great sandhills, and you will hear the call of the many birds across the marshes a sound to my mind typical of Norfolk.'

Well said, and even on a bitter January day, with snow flurries, a walk out to the fourteenth green and back with a game leg was a rewarding experience.

Worlington and Newmarket

Royal Worlington and Newmarket in West Suffolk is the home course of Cambridge University and a fine place for young men to learn to build up a strong game. It lies about seven miles north of Newmarket in a surprising belt of sand, when all around the land is East Anglian clay or chalk hills, and in consequence the course is always dry and is a splendid place for winter golf. The greens are keen and fast, too, at all seasons.

Royal Worlington is a nine-hole course and astonishingly compact at that. It has often been described as the best nine-hole course in Britain and occasionally as being the best nine holes; by that I judge the claimant to mean that they constitute the best consecutive nine-hole stretch anywhere in Britain.

Well, is it and are they? In my view the answer to the first is yes, though if an old favourite of mine, the little nine-hole links at Bembridge, the Royal Isle of Wight, had survived I could have disputed the matter. As for

Others in England

the wider claim, fine course though it is, the Royal Worlington and Newmarket certainly isn't the best nine-hole stretch in the country—among courses of the same type I would put in claims for Liphook, Ganton, St George's Hill or Sunningdale—and most certainly its holes are not the nine finest individual holes in Britain.

Having said that, let no one deny that this is a splendid golf course. You open with a 484-yard par-five steering up a fairly wide fairway sign-posted with traps on either flank. The shot to the green is deceptive, as there is a hollow of dead ground in front of it. So there is at the second, which has an 'inverted saucer' green which pushes aside or over the back any shot that is not really well hit; a most difficult long one-shotter to find from the tee or to chip back to from the sides.

Driving back across the second green and over a big cross-bunker you have a very narrow tee shot, the hogs-back fairway constricting just where you wish it wouldn't. The shot to the green which lies beyond a marshy valley is a light iron but quite tight owing to the traps on the left; a very attractive hole this.

Number four into the west wind is a 480-yarder, a short par five for the hitters, but the green is protected by a bank just in front of it, which makes it uncommonly hard to get a shot of any length close to the hole; moreover, the green is hard up to the boundary fence.

The fifth is a famous hole and so it should be. It is 170 yards long and it is without a single bunker or obstacle between tee and green; it is slightly uphill, with a pleasant line of pine trees behind the green, but the green is fiendishly narrow and contoured to take your ball off to the stream or rough on the right or to a large deep hollow, which my caddie assured me was called 'Mugs' Cottage', on the left; from either of these positions it is abominably difficult to get the ball to stay on the narrow green let alone near the hole. On medal day I think most of us would settle for a four and walk to the sixth tee.

The sixth hole is a long two-shotter of 455 yards with the same row of pines which frame the fifth green along the entire right-hand side of the fairway; the left side is trapped extensively, but that is the side to be on unless you can fade a long shot into the green past the last pine of the row. This is a really splendid hole for someone who can hit the ball just a bit farther than I can.

Next comes the unmemorable short seventh of no great difficulty or merit, though for some reason one often underhits and gets stuck on the rise in front of the green.

The eighth runs back along the pine trees parallel to the sixth and is a tough 465-yard hole, too long for me to regard as a par four. There is a cross-bunker about 120 yards short of the green, but this is only a bother if you've been in trouble already, and a big bunker eating into the left side of the green. You end the round with a drive and pitch hole, the drive across the stream—and you can easily slice into it—and a pitch across the road with a tough deep bunker at the back of the green for the shot hit 'thin'. The green here is fiercely contoured, so that this 300-yarder is no pushover as a finishing hole.

So supposing you have holed in 37 or 38 strokes, which is not beyond the powers of many of us, you have to do it all over again, and that's not as easy as you might think, perhaps you make a new set of errors or even do the same ones once again.

Walton Heath

It is now time to move to the London area and first I think we should try to tackle Walton Heath, if only because it was my home club for ten years. It lies twenty miles due south of London and is 650 feet up on the North Downs, so every breeze that blows is available. It is open heathland golf in the widest sense, even more now than a few years ago, as a lot of intrusive thorn trees and bush have recently been cut down to restore its former bareness.

There are two very fine courses here and, as happens so often, the New Course, good as it would be anywhere else on its own, is just slightly inferior by comparison with the Old—and about three shots easier—that it gets scant praise and less than it deserves. So it is to the Old that we must direct our interest, but don't forget the New and if you can play thirty-six holes in a day, which alas I can't, try both.

The Old Course at Walton Heath, like the New, was laid out by Herbert Fowler, the first in 1904; it was altered somewhat after World War I and some further changes have just been made. It sets out to be, and is, totally uncompromising: the fairways are narrow when they should be narrow and the rough is *rough*. Walton Heath's heather has been notoriously tough for years and now encroaching bracken is providing an even worse rough and killing the heather as well; it would be a good idea to get rid of it. Cross-bunkers are plentiful and those that don't compel a carry are deep and steep faced. The greens are often just cultivated and mown terminations to the fairway, full of subtle slopes and borrows, difficult to judge an approach to, fast and hard to read. Luckily they are as true as velvet. Altogether Walton Heath sets as strict an examination in golf as any in the United Kingdom and is certainly the hardest inland course in the country.

It is also very good for your golf; you don't have to fear it, just respect it. If you can drive straight you won't do too badly; you just have to learn to drive straight, and Harry Busson, an excellent teacher, is there to help you. One thing is certain: if you play regularly at Walton Heath any other course you go to will seem easy. In the evening of my golfing life, when I was in my fifties, it had a most invigorating effect on my poor game, so that for about five years I was playing as well as I ever had in my life, which I attribute entirely to this course and some tough games there.

The name of James Braid, five times Open Champion, is indissolubly linked with Walton Heath, for he was the professional there for forty-five years until he died in 1950 aged eighty. He used to hole the course regularly and ritualistically in his age or less on his birthday and his vigorous austerity was a good match for that of the course. Patric Dickinson puts this well: 'Perhaps it is fanciful but Walton Heath itself seems to be very like James Braid, for it is strong and modest, positive and forthright, yet never ostentatious. Walton Heath, by saying nothing, will give an opinion of your golf. If you *ask* for an opinion you will get one and there will be no mincing matters.'

Many tournaments have been played here, the English Close Championship twice, and the *News of the World* Match Play Championship many times; indeed it has come to rest here.

Well then, praying for a good day of driving straight, let us go out to sit the examination. The first hole is no guide, for it is a very short par four of 300 yards in a little annex to the heath; there is a pond in front of the tee but most people don't know it's there. However, unless you hit your drive to a precise spot you have a tricky pitch to a green that runs away from you, over the protecting bunkers. It is a less innocent hole than you'd expect and makes a good nineteenth in a match, as I well remember one evening in the Heathens' Foursomes competition. Our opponents on leaving the fifteenth green had unwisely said, 'That makes us dormy three, I think', to which my friend and partner, Maurice Allom, replied, 'Oh no; it makes you three up and three to play', and he then proceeded to hole four putts of highly doubtful length, one a long one, to win the match for us at the nineteenth.

The second was a most difficult hole, a par four of 445 yards or more off the *News of the World* tee, for it had a great gully of humps and heather right across the fairway about 250 yards from the tee; you played short, of course, and then usually had a full wood shot off a hanging lie to get you anywhere near the green. Now two-thirds of the gully has been smoothed out and in my opinion the hole is not as challenging for the ordinary player as it was.

The third can be driven, but usually isn't unless the tee is forward; it is flat with the green merging into the fairway. Flat, too, is the fourth and it can be reached in two, but very often is not.

The splendid 18th hole at Pebble Beach in California. This great hole of 530 yards hugs the shore of Carmel Bay in a majestic curve. This is surely one of the great finishing holes in golf.

Walton Heath

The golf now begins with full rigour. The fifth is a lovely two-shotter, driving downhill to play up to a bunkered green on a slight plateau, a very pretty hole. The sixth isn't pretty, it's just long and straight, with a bunker to catch a slightly pulled drive just where you don't want it. You can always feel delighted if you do this and the fifth in four.

The seventh is one of the hardest short holes I know, especially with the greater length of the new tees; for me it is a five-wood played to fly high and pitch right on, for if you pitch in front to the right you're in one trap or another, while the other half of the entrance and the rim of the green kicks your ball down into a little valley running round the green or even into the rough.

Up the eighth we go, 'hard pounding, gentlemen', 470 yards to the top of the course and now about 800 feet up we can pause for breath. The ninth has a cross-bunker in front of the tee and another on the right entrance to the green; at 420 yards you want a stiff shot to get home to the low plateau and the putting is tricky.

The tenth is a pretty two-shot hole curving up to the right to a green on an up-slope. Then another short hole the 175-yard eleventh, which is much more from the back tee. The hole is guarded on the left by a big bunker and the shot across a vale of heather is all carry. A few years ago I had the supreme pleasure of hitting a number four iron shot into the hole from the tee which put my score of 'aces' just one ahead of Harry Vardon's. Later in the club-house Harry Muirfield Braid, the great man's son, and a very distinguished amateur golfer, said a kind word of congratulation, so I asked how many he had done and he replied, 'None', which only goes to show that holes in one don't go by merit.

The twelfth, a drive and a pitch, is a real round-the-corner-to-the-right hole, though Henry Cotton in a big challenge match once drove right across the chord to the green. However, you and I drive downhill to the fairway like good boys and then come up with a seven-iron. The thirteenth, a long curving par five, and the fourteenth, another par five downhill, take over 1,000 yards and we should be content with ten for the pair.

Fifteen is a tough par four into the prevailing wind with the second over a cross-bunker; the green is particularly unmoulded and slopes evilly.

So to the 478-yard sixteenth, which is a great hole whether we can or cannot get up in two shots; the fairway runs down right to left and cross-bunkers menace the way; the cream of it, though, is the shot to the green, a big bold plateau, or rather shelf, with a bunker under the right of the ascent into which any poorly hit shot inexorably rolls. On a favourable day the smack of a wood shot held up properly to the left, but not too much, which breaks right towards the pin gives a supreme pleasure.

The seventeenth, a shot of 167 yards, has recently been altered by

Others in England

removing the small gap by which you might just run on and having bunkers all the way round the front of the green. Not an improvement I think.

The last hole is a splendid one. You drive over a gully full of rubbish on to a perfectly flat wide fairway; the second shot—the hole is 410 yards—has to cross a full-size deep cross-bunker, so deep that small ladders assist your egress. What's more, the green is apparently hard up to this grave, but it isn't in fact, so the shot always needs one more club than you are prepared to give it. The cross bunker is uncompromising, you've got to go over it sooner or later, there is no way round. What the pros make of it from the new back tee when the hole becomes 490 yards I can't guess, but anyway they never make a fool of Walton Heath.

Sunningdale

Sunningdale somehow seems to have become the leader and the best known of all the London clubs; others might not agree, but at least all will accept that it offers you a very fine game of golf.

As at Walton Heath there are two full-length sandy heather courses, but the New, which is less highly regarded than the Old, is out on the open heath, while the Old is almost entirely among fir trees. On both there is plenty of good heather in the rough.

Many events of major importance have been played at Sunningdale and it even had a connection with the Open Championship when qualifying rounds were held there in 1926 and Bobby Jones played the perfect round—perfect with one small flaw like an emerald—of 66, 33 out and 33 in, 33 shots and 33 putts, twelve fours and six threes.

No professional at Sunningdale has matched Braid's fame, though Jack White won the Open Championship at Sandwich in 1904 with four rounds each lower than the one before. The fame rests more on the former caddie-master James Sheridan, as salty and forthright a character as ever left Scotland who has just shown that he knows how to write a book.

Although the New, laid out by H. S. Colt and remade after the devastations of World War II, is a very fine course, with many magnificent holes, it is to the Old, laid out by young Willie Park in 1900, that we must go if we've only time for one round.

The 492-yard first hole is undemanding, slightly downhill and no rough or bunkers of great import. The second, with a semi-blind shot to the shelf green—it runs down sharply at the back—is a tougher proposition if you want a four. The third insists that you carry a cross-bunker on the right-hand side of the fairway if you want the easiest pitch into the green, but at 292 yards you should get a four.

The fourth hole, 165 yards rather steeply uphill, doesn't give me any pleasure, but it is followed by three superb par fours, each slightly over 400 yards. At the first two you drive over a thick belt of heather, downhill at the fifth, and at the seventh you have to hit over a high menacing mound right in front of the tee. The second shots are all lovely, the fifth has an absurd little pond on the right which becomes an infuriating great lake when you get in it; at the sixth which is a two-island hole—you have to cross a second heather belt to get to the green—and there is dire trouble to the right. The seventh gives a lovely shot home to a plateau green with a protecting mound on the right flank. Three fours running for these is grand golf.

The eighth is a prosaic short hole, but the ground in front and the green itself slope considerably to the right, more than you think, and the bunker there works overtime.

You can drive the green very nearly at the ninth and it is not a hole of great character or joy. The tenth, however, is a charmer, with a great belt needed off a high tee right down and down to a wide fairway below; it is 470 yards on the card, but you can get home or near if you keep out of Braid's bunker on the left, from which he once hit a prodigious iron or cleek shot to the green and holed for a three to wipe the smile off Ted Ray's face.

The eleventh is only 321 yards, but the fairway is narrow and the little plateau green small and hard to stop on. The drive is across a cross-bunker and a hook into the heather or a fade into the trees makes a four very difficult.

Next comes a very fine two-shot hole with the second shot uphill to a plateau green, a handsome hole too. The thirteenth is a rather indifferent par three, a downhill shot. The distinction it has is that Jones's only flaw was here as he got into a bunker; but he chipped out and holed the putt.

We are now faced with a very fair, just and stiff finish starting with the 506-yard fourteenth; I like this hole because, off a more lenient tee I scored my last eagle here, probably the last I'll ever do, which is a sad thought.

Fifteen is a very tough par three, 229 yards out of the trees to the edge of the heath. It is also the best of the par threes by far, I think. At Sunningdale they are the weakness and the two-shotters the strength.

Three of these carry you to the finish and difficult they all are. The sixteenth is a hole where you can never seem to drive far enough, for your second shot is uphill, with cross-bunkers to carry, some way short; I have to use wood now and the hole stretches me exceedingly.

At seventeen you drive downhill and length is not a problem, but for some absurd reason you tend to fade the drive, to keep it out of some trees at the bottom I suspect, and then you're trapped and bang goes your four. The green is closely bunkered at this hole.

Others in England

Finally at the eighteenth you have an uphill drive and woe betide you if it is all cut, for then you're in dire rough while a pull bunkers you. Then home over the cross-bunkers, aiming at the great oak tree by the green for a tough finishing hole. A splendid course and one where you hardly see another game except at that long vista from the fifth tee over to the sixth green or from the hill-top at the tenth tee.

After lunch don't fail to go across the road and play a round at the Sunningdale Ladies' Club, a separate club, by the way, and requiring another green fee. This is a most amusing little heather course of 4,000 yards and a par of 61. The shots are not long, the longest hole is 321 yards, but the greens are small and you don't race away with such a low score as you imagine; one enjoyable exercise for me is to try to play twenty-seven holes in under 100 strokes. There are plenty of narrow shots, an occasional out of bounds and carries of heather off the tee. I've played dozens of rounds here and thoroughly enjoyed it. There is one story of an irascible and unpopular member of Sunningdale who did the first seventeen holes of the course in three apiece, a really great performance, and then hit a prodigious drive and reached the eighteenth green—where he took three putts.

Liphook

The course I'm going to end this chapter with is another sand-heather-and-pines course a little farther out at Liphook. This, apart from its painful name, is one of the most charming courses that I know, very natural and unforced with small difficult greens, and some beautiful short holes. It was laid out at a minimum of cost and so makes the greatest possible use of natural locations and the best lie of the land with few bunkers. About forty miles south of London it is a good place for a day out. Frank Pennink calls it 'an outstanding course' and I go along with Frank.

The course requires accurate placing of the shots and the architects Croome and Tom Simpson set out to make the tigers scratch their heads. Since the war the course has been changed around and you no longer play off from a pub on the Portsmouth road; as a result, the first half roughly is the old second half and vice versa.

For my money the most enjoyable holes are the short third, 'Milland', the short seventh to a very folded green, 'The Bowl', and even more the highly picturesque and photogenic eleventh, a short hole of 165 yards, with a low plateau of green and a clump of straight pines behind it on a knoll.

There are some very shrewd dog-legs among the shorter par fours, notably at 'Hollycombe' and the 'Quarry', which run parallel as numbers fifteen and sixteen and at the 330-yard 'Pulpit' hole, number fourteen. The long par fours are long enough for any man and if the total yardage is rather short because of five par threes don't think you will burn it up; I rather think not, for as Henry Longhurst says, 70 has only once been beaten here in competition, in spite of its relative shortness. Quoting Frank Pennink again: 'Liphook is one of the two courses in the south of England of which Bobby Locke thinks most highly, and on which he plays regularly when in this country (the other is Hankley Common). Anyone who can play to his handicap at Liphook is doing well.'

I shall always remember my first visit to Liphook, forty years ago, for a dramatic moment. We had played all day under grey lowering skies, with a high wind. As we drove back to London over the high ground of Hindhead it was close to sunset and at that moment the grey cloud-wrack lifted and the whole sky became a swiftly moving mass of small scarlet clouds racing past us borne on the wings of the gale.

9 Golf in America – South and West

Golf in America has many notable differences from golf in the U.K., historic, climatic and temperamental. The differences often seem very great, though I suggest that all things considered it is perhaps remarkable—and a tribute to the good sense of the governing bodies of both nations—that the games are as similar as they are. You have only to look at football in the two countries to see what differences could have developed.

True, we play with a different-sized ball, but it would not ruin our game here to play with the U.S. ball and might even improve it. The Americans like to keep score—and they keep it correctly too—and they like to play complicated and elaborate matches with several other sets of players simultaneously, all of which takes time compared with our more casual match play, sometimes as much as five hours for eighteen holes. But often they play in hot humid weather, which makes a leisurely eighteen holes per day enough compared with a bracing thirty-six holes here. The game in America, too, is often conducted in a more luxurious manner than with us, with locker-room attendants, bathrooms, barmen, restaurant staff and club managers, though rarely a secretary in the British sense, added to electric carts—a godsend for arthritics—and a pro shop selling all manner of clothing and equipment. This tends to make the game a good deal more expensive than here and while we tend to reduce amenities to the bare minimum, and sometimes below that, in order that the local schoolmaster can afford to play, the Americans, with a higher standard of living than ours, expect in the natural way of things to be able to afford their dearer game in due course.

When we get out on to the course American golf and ours differ rather less than they do in the club-house. The climate in which golf is played is usually distinctly warmer than it is here and good fine grass is very hard to grow, but since World War II the Americans have made some remarkable strides in grass cultivation, even if it sometimes means sowing a summer grass to come up when the winter grass dies down. The game usually is played with less wind than we get, though Pebble Beach in March can blow you down. All greens are watered, but so are ours now, and most fairways too, so that you are playing nearly always with comparatively little run on the ball and the greens are soft and stop an iron shot abruptly; the fairways are often very 'fat' with coarser grass than ours, so that a bigger ball is a necessity. The greens, with some notable exceptions, are not of quite the fine texture of our best though true and fair. On the whole I think one is playing among trees a good deal more there than here and their rough is much less severe; there is nothing like the heather of Walton Heath to contend with.

The courses themselves haven't the same variety as ours. Most of them are in what we would call parkland; very few stretches of links-land exist, and the heath courses, like ours in Surrey, are rare. But there *is* variety and more than you might be led to believe; after all, Pine Valley and Augusta National, both great courses, are totally unlike in both idea and layout. Baltusrol is quite unlike Pinehurst or one of the desert courses of the far south-west.

In their playing quality and interest the great American courses are second to none and compete on equal terms with our great ones, different as they often are. Oakland Hills is a far cry from old Prestwick, a totally different type of golf course, but in this excellent game of ours both can be splendid golf and testing and enjoyable in equal measure. Golf, after all, is the only game into which the ground enters to any notable extent—one billiard table should be exactly like the next and one football pitch like another.

Championship golf in America follows a rather different pattern from in Britain; more courses are used in order to hold the meetings in all parts of the country, though some of the more famous ones, such as Pine Valley and the National Golf Links of America, are not on the rota at all. Augusta National, too, which stages its own champions' meeting each year, the Masters' Tournament, has never housed the Amateur or the Open Championships because it is not open for play in the summer. None the less, the American championship courses are an impressive list and several of the most famous ones have been used several times. Nearly all of them are inland park or grassland courses, long, well-protected by rough and toughly bunkered; for the U.S. Open the rough is quite different from what you find ordinarily; it is cut to a predetermined height and made to grow out into the fairways at appropriate points and around the sides and backs of the greens. Tees are put back to a total length of over 7,000 yards and so you are in for an ordeal unless you are both long and straight. There is no likelihood of an aggregation of scores in the sixties in the U.S. Open such as the promoters of the Piddle Creek Open so enjoy; the United States Golfing Association sees to that.

Mid Ocean

Golf as a mirror to life has its full quota of disappointments and one of these in my golfing journeys I'm sorry to say was Mid Ocean in Bermuda. It was one of those unfortunate situations in which I had heard both too much and too little about the course and seen only the seaside photographs. In fact the course, apart from some fine cliff-top holes along the coast at the start of the round, is predominantly an inland layout and this was too much of a reversal of expectation to make appreciation of it at all easy. Let it be said straight away that the setting of the club and the views along the cliffs for the first three or four holes and at the eighteenth are splendid, a sparkling sea of all shades of blue and turquoise near the shore, bluff rocky cliffs and beaches of pure white or pink sand. Somehow the golf ought to mix in with this much more instead of staying aloof on the high hilly ground inland which fails to create for us the illusion of a links or even of a seaside course.

This doesn't mean that the holes are short or easy or any sort of a happy-go-lucky holiday layout; it is a stiff test of golf and a good test of your legs as well. The first, a tough two-shotter with the drive across bunkers, is a fine hole, so is the long second, with its play downhill and then up. The third is a difficult short hole near the edge of the cliff and four runs uphill inland with the second shot over guarding bunkers, farther than it looks. The best known and most spectacular hole is the fifth, with a drive over and along the edge of a big lagoon which gives you an option which may land you in disaster, and then you play a long shot to a huge folded green, one of Trent Jones's monsters, on which I had the satisfaction of holing one of the longest putts of my life, 123 feet over hill and dale, borrowing about ten feet on the right from the extreme front of the green right into the hole. After this interest rather wanes, though some fine and exacting shots remain—the short seventh over water, a tight second shot to the eighth and another such at the tenth. So it goes over slopes and rolling ground until at the seventeenth, a long one-shot hole, we are close to the ocean again and finally play the two-shot eighteenth along its edge from a tee, perched on the very edge of the cliff overlooking the blue water.

Coming now to the mainland of the United States this chapter and the next, while describing famous and historic courses, those, that is, within

ABOVE The view from the picture-window of the men's locker room at Capilano, North Vancouver, in British Columbia, showing the 16th green in the left foreground, the 17th green in the centre background, and the 18th fairway on the far right (*Commercial Illustrators Ltd*)
BELOW Another beautiful Canadian mountain course, this one at Jasper Park, Alberta (*Canadian National Railways*)

One of the most beautiful and spectacular golf courses in the world is at Banff Springs high up in the Canadian Rockies. The short 8th hole is perhaps not quite so formidable as it looks (*Canadian Pacific*)

ABOVE Links-land in America. The green of the short 3rd hole on the new Spyglass Hill Golf Course on the Monterey Peninsula in California. In the distance is part of the Cypress Point course (*Julian P. Graham Studio*)
BELOW Another links hole in America. The green on the short 15th at Cypress Point, California (*Julian P. Graham Studio*)

ABOVE Sam Snead playing to the 8th hole, 346/374 yards, at the Peach Tree Club, Atlanta, Georgia (*Shell's Wonderful World of Golf*)
BELOW The short 17th hole on the famous No. 2 Course at Pinehurst, North Carolina. This is one of many holes in America based on the 'Redan' at North Berwick (*United States Golf Association*)

my personal knowledge, are not confined to the same extent as the British chapters, to championship circuits, for many famous and splendid courses have never been host to a championship and don't intend to be. We start in the south, for although the evidence is scanty, it seems incontrovertible that organised golf, of some sort, somewhere, was played in Charleston, South Carolina, and Savannah, Georgia, a hundred years before the gentlemen of Yonkers, N.Y., began their operations in the cow pasture in 1888, or even the unsung pioneers of Oakhurst in West Virginia in 1884 and revolutionised American life and leisure.

Augusta National

So where better to start than at Augusta National, one of the newest as well as one of the most celebrated courses in the United States? The idea of a first-class championship course here came from Clifford Roberts, the New York banker, who had wintered in the genial climate of Augusta, Georgia, and when he confided his idea to the most famous of Georgian golfers, Bobby Jones, who had just completed the Grand Slam, the idea got enthusiastic support.

Although the great Depression was in full force, the idea caught on and enough backers were found to give the idea a fair wind so that the famous architect Dr Alister Mackenzie could be retained to lay out the course on an ideal piece of land, an old nursery garden full of flowering trees and shrubs, with an attractive old manor house to serve as a club-house.

In Jones's words the idea was to form a club with only a small group of local members and then 'to develop a golf course and retreat of such nature, and of such excellence that men of some means and devoted to the game of golf might find the club worth while as an extra luxury where they might visit and play with other kindred spirits from other parts of the nation. This policy has never been changed, and I am happy to be able to say that the club apparently has adequately fulfilled this mission.' And speaking as the only non-American member at the time of writing I would say that this aim had been admirably successful.

The first thing, of course, was to get the golf right, and here Jones and Mackenzie worked splendidly together. It was their first essential that the ordinary man should be able to get round without hardship yet with a layout which could be stretched and twisted to give the professionals a thorough run for their money. In the latter category are the four par-five holes which are designed to give the great players a chance to get up in two and collect a birdie, which they often do, while not destroying the club members by sheer brute force.

The result has been a unique layout, unique in that there are only forty-four bunkers on the entire course, unique in that while you and I can bumble round in say, 84, because there are no savage carries or penal hazards, to get round in 72 even off the forward tees is a notable achievement. After all, there is no rough to speak of, very few bunkers, as I have said, trees, yes, but the scrub underneath them is cleared out to enable you to play out; but the folds and slopes of the fairways and greens are subtle and exacting and with the pin positions of the last day of the Masters' Tournament and the back tees you have as gruelling and difficult a course as I know. In other words, this is the strategic course *par excellence*, relying on accurate placing of the shot compared with the penal type of course, with its condign punishment.

You start with a mild enough hole, driving over a ravine but if you don't quite hit your drive you're in trouble for your four. The second should get you a five for it's downhill, but the green doesn't exactly gather the ball and you can have a hideous long putt from the top of the green. the shorter par-four third doesn't gather you either, for the small green on its plateau runs away from you.

The fourth is a big one-shot hole into the prevailing wind to a wide green so that three putts and a four on these slopes is not unusual. The fifth is a long par four to a plateau green, out of my reach now, though I was once over it in two shots. Six is a short hole steeply downhill to a very folded green; some very difficult pin positions can be picked here.

The seventh, a drive and pitch, is the shortest par four and also the most bunkered, and it is always one club longer on the second shot than it looks. Eight is an uphill par five which the pros can reach in two—though, alas, I can't—and the ninth back to the club-house is a difficult par four in spite of a drive downhill; the second shot for you and me is often off a hanging lie to a very sloping green.

After refreshment at the tenth tee—Bourbon and milk is very good on a cool day—the next hole is a beauty, down down down from the tee between trees but needing a placement to the left to get positioned for a shot over the big 'picture bunker' to the plateau green framed by trees, 460 yards—a tough hole this. The eleventh with a pond eating into the left-hand edge of the green is a terror off the back tee and quite difficult enough off the regular tee as you have to pitch in over a hump which blinds the shot so that you rarely hit your shot far enough.

The twelfth, the famous short hole over Rae's Creek, is a very tight iron shot as you play to the narrow width of the green very close to the water. Thirteen is one of the spectaculars of golf, a curving short par five with the creek running up the left-hand side of the fairway and then across the front of and to the right of the green; behind the green are some traps and a high bank covered with azaleas; many disasters and many eagles have been gathered here; to get home in two is one of the supreme moments in golf as my friend John Kitchin found on his first visit here.

The fourteenth is a contrast, a very folded and difficult par four without a single bunker but with a heavily contoured green and an infinite chance of three putts.

The fifteenth is the last par five, with the green guarded by a pond; it is 520 yards long and often in the Masters is reached in two shots. Jack Nicklaus was over the green with a drive and an eight-iron in 1964 and in 1935 Sarazen holed it in two with a drive and a full spoon shot to gain a tie for first place and win the play-off.

The sixteenth is a short hole over water with a beautifully moulded green; although the green is difficult, it is not usually a killer hole, indeed few at Augusta are. The seventeenth is a long par four for you and me and you have to mind the trees, but for the tournament pros the second is not long though the plateau green is small and usually fast. Eighteen is a tough par four uphill to a sloping green and it has seen its fair share of birdies and distress in the tournament; on the last day with the pin just behind the left-hand guarding bunker, the approach is tough. As Bob Jones writes:

'Overall, Augusta National is not intended to be a punishing golf course. It is, however, a course which under tournament conditions (that is with green surfaces firm and keen) severely tests the player's temperament. The difficult greens demand fierce and unremitting concentration and determination. When the golf course is wet and the wind quiet, it is easy. We always hope it's not that way during the first week of April.'

The Masters' Tournament is something quite simple; it is the greatest golf tournament in the world.

First, it is held in surroundings of great beauty, when the azaleas and dogwoods are in flower, it is above all the tournament that the professionals want to win, quite apart from the fact that the first prize is $20,000. Once the British Open was 'the one to win'; later, as the world centre of golf became the United States, the U.S. Open became the more important. But now the Masters has somehow become the greatest of them all.

This is rather hard to explain, for it depends on that undefinable thing —atmosphere. Somehow at Augusta the sense of a great sporting occasion is generated, hard to describe but impossible to miss, like that of a Lord's Test match or of the Cup Final at Wembley or Epsom on Derby Day. The huge crowds—estimates say 40,000 people are present on the last day— have been milling round the course, and a big friendly vociferous group of them, probably well over 2,000, have sat round the last green the whole day long, generous with their applause and commiseration. Every player gets his round of applause, every good putt gets a hearty handclap and every putt missed a deep heartfelt groan. Then at last the climax is reached as in the last pair the expected winner comes striding up the long hill of the eighteenth greeted by tremendous applause, doffing his cap in acknowledgement and then bending over his last approach putt. And if, as happened in 1964, it was Arnold Palmer, and if, as happened then, he sank it for a birdie 3, then a storm of cheers goes up which could be heard in Atlanta, 160 miles away.

All day this climax has been building up just as the tensions have been rising in the players, but Americans being what they are in the pinch, these tensions on the last day have produced some incredible spectacular finishes without which someone else would have been the winner—things like Art Wall's finish of five birdies in the last six holes to win by one stroke, Doug Ford's holing out from a bunker at the eighteenth green for a winning birdie, and Gene Sarazen's two at the 520-yard fifteenth hole. In this fierce cauldron of competition, it was good to see Britain's Peter Butler and Tony Jacklin holding their own here.

Another reason why the Masters is such a great event is that it is impeccably run. First of all, it is run by the club; they, the members, run it. They run it as an invitation tournament and they invite whom they like and omit anybody who is unacceptable. A pro who refused to meet a very reasonable request not to practise on the course found himself without a partner next day and unable to play. Good amateur players are encouraged, old heroes and past winners are asked back and foreign players are made welcome. Yet the great pros are all there and one of them always wins it. The list of winners sounds like the Hall of Fame of American golf; indeed, only one foreign golfer, Gary Player of South Africa, has ever won it.

The Masters' Tournament has grown from modest beginnings in 1934 into the great event it is today and, as the event has grown, so have the crowds and so have the facilities for them. Unobtrusive mounds have been built at strategic points which don't conflict with the play, but make it easier to see, grandstands of scaffolding are put up and afterwards removed, plumbing has been installed, and hot dogs and beer counters abound. There are huge car parks, as there have to be when 10,000 cars come on the last day. There is a fine shop for golf goods and souvenirs, and the Press are handsomely looked after, with the leading players after each round describing what shots they hit so that the newspapermen can report correctly whether Chichi Rodriguez used a six-iron or a seven at the sixth hole and what Jack Nicklaus thought of his socket at the twelfth—he laughed.

Yet so well are the spectators catered for, that the course never seems unbearably crowded. With a little anticipation, one can see any player play any one stroke; the only thing you can't do is to see every stroke played by any one player. But best of all for the spectators are the scoreboards at strategic points which show the ten leading players' scores relative to par, so that at a glance you can see how each man stands against the others and his score at every hole of the round. Then as the players come up to each green their names are put in a frame and their score relative to par for the whole tournament up to that point.

And so we come to the final moment of the tournament, after the cheques have been handed out in Cliff Roberts's office, when, in the cool of the evening, the members in their green blazers and a small residue of the great crowd are gathered in front of the old stone house which is now the club-house. Then after some simple speeches, last year's winner invests the new winner with the green coat and another Masters' Tournament is at an end.

Peach Tree

Another Bobby Jones memorial is the excellent course to the north of Atlanta, Georgia, at Peach Tree, which I played in the early spring when only the greens were green and the fairways were covered with the buff dead grass of winter which gave a deceptive air of pace to the ground.

Laid out by Robert Trent Jones in consultation with the Master in rolling pine-clad country, it struck me as a beautiful course from start to finish. Many of Trent Jones's principles, with which I don't always agree, are present here, including greens with definite 'pin areas' and very long tees. The first hole with its cluster of bunkers to carry off the tee and then a punch with a mid-iron to a slight plateau is as good a starting hole as you could want and the par-five second is a beauty. After a downhill tee shot you hit your second over a brook on to a peninsula and then pitch over the water again to a small green.

The short holes are good, the fourth a moderate iron shot across a valley, the sixth a big hit across another valley with bunkers close to the green and the fourteenth a four-iron shot with a diagonal water hazard protecting the green. There are some excellent two-shot holes too, notably the uphill eighth of 346 yards, the downhill crafty twelfth of 433 yards with a ditch across the fairway, the long seventh and several others. The 503-yard par-five tenth hole has an exhilarating downhill drive and then a long beat uphill with big menacing bunkers near the green. Altogether a fine and graceful layout, in harmony with its century-old ante-bellum club-house.

Sea Island

Before we leave Georgia we ought to look in at Sea Island, where there are twenty-seven holes of pleasant seaside golf, arranged in three nines all of much the same length with a par of 36 so you can take any pair of them to make a round. In late April when I played there the spring flowers on shrubs and in flower beds, in the rough even, were a joy although we had a fearful thunderstorm, which had followed us from Augusta, and soaked us to the skin. However, it was succeeded next morning by the most intense sunlight that I can remember which gave me a sunburn on my arms which I carry to this day over six years later.

The Plantation Nine is the inmost one and apart from its light sandy soil has no conspicuous seaside characteristics, plenty of trees though, pines and live oaks, hung with grey wispy Spanish moss and a pretty water hole, the fifth.

The midmost nine is called Retreat, nearer the sea but still not quite on the shore; there are plenty of trees on this loop too and a big lake in the centre which affects the play at three holes and a smaller one over which you should go at the short second if you want to get on the green.

Best of all the circuits at Sea Island is the Seaside Nine, which lives up to its name and gives us something approximating to links turf out by the shore, as well as some exacting shots over inlets of the sea, creeks and bayous. One of these provides a lovely diagonal carry off the tee at the fourth, a fine two-shot hole with an army of bunkers marching down the far side of the fairway. The next hole too is a beauty, a short par four of 325 yards with a tight shot to a plateau green guarded by two big shallow bunkers full of dazzling white sand; this hole lives in my memory, I suppose, because I managed to get a birdie to help redeem a poor start. More than just holiday golf, this, but a grand place to have a holiday.

We now move north out of Georgia, with only a backward glimpse at Florida where alas I only know the two pleasant holiday courses at Clearwater.

Pinehurst

So next stop Pinehurst in North Carolina, a golfing phenomenon. While it would not be quite true to say that Pinehurst is wholly devoted to golf, any more than is St Andrews, golf plays a major part in the activities of this little town. After all when this resort was developed other activities were prominent but now golf is the leader. It was about seventy years ago that it was discovered that this sandy pine country where no worthwhile crop could be grown made excellent golfing territory, just like the sandy pine country in Surrey. Indeed the country round Pinehurst is very like Chobham Common and the country round Sunningdale and Swinley Forest except that heather is not native to North Carolina; the pines, though of a different breed, are very similar and a scrubby rough gives many of the troubles we get from heather. I found the atmosphere and the golf at Pinehurst entirely charming and enjoyable and would gladly pay a return trip. The pioneering here was done by that excellent architect Donald Ross from Dornoch who settled in the United States around 1900 and built many famous courses; according to Charles Price, Ross regarded Pinehurst No. 2 as his masterpiece and while I cannot claim to know many others of his design other than Oakland Hills and that much modified, I must agree at once that No. 2 is indeed a masterly and excellent golf course. And it has been so used; the U.S. Amateur has been held here and the Ryder Cup was played on No. 2 Course in 1951, when we received our usual towelling, and such major competitions as the North and South Championship.

The reigning monarch of Pinehurst over the years has been Richard S. Tufts, one of the pillars of the U.S. Golf Association and a great protagonist of the idea of a single set of rules for the whole world of golf, and what a blessing that has been.

It might perhaps be observed that once Pinehurst had shown the way others followed and now there must be something like fifty fine golf courses in this belt of scrubland in central North Carolina with such names as Pine Needles, Whispering Pines, Pine Cones, Pine Trees and I know not what.

There are now five full-length courses at Pinehurst, a modest club-house and some comfortable hotels. I was there 'out of season' in mid-December and was pleasantly surprised at the moderation of the charges. The courses vary in length from the 6,044-yard No. 3 to the 7,051-yard No. 2, the Championship course. In a week-end I managed to play the shortest, No. 3, which is an excellent, enjoyable course for the upper echelons of age, a rain-reduced round on No. 5 which is the second longest at 6,461 yards and another splendid course, a full round on No. 2, three holes on No. 1 including a birdie two on the eighteenth and one shot on No. 4! By all accounts, No. 1 and No. 4 are the least exciting, No. 3 good fun and No. 5 the second greatest, but Pinehurst No. 2 is the big one, the one you must play, though in scenic beauty and ingenuity of layout the others go along with it very well.

You start No. 2 with a big two-shot hole of 414 yards, then a bigger par four of 454 yards with a plateau green—a great Ross feature, no doubt in recollection of Dornoch—followed by another plateau green at the shorter par-four third. Then comes a par five up a long valley and after that the 438-yard fifth a really big par four with cross-bunkers in front of the green. So we come to the first short hole, a good thump with a spoon. The seventh is a par four with a big dog-leg bend to the right over a bunker at the angle. Then after a par five comes the par-three ninth, a beautiful hole of 162 yards on the top of a ridge with bunkers to carry. So it goes with a huge 600-yard tenth and then four hard long tough par fours up and down until there is some relief at the fairly mild though long par-three fifteenth. This is followed by a really beautiful par-five hole of 504 yards with a water hazard, white sandy bunkers, scrubby rough, emerald grass and a generous gathering green. We end with a good punching iron shot to the seventeenth, 187 yards, over an encroaching bunker on the right, a sort of reverse 'Redan'. Then at the last after driving uphill you belt it home to a plateau green for your four. I missed it, but a lucky pitch got me down in one putt for 39 home, which really delighted me. Nothing is more enjoyable than to play a good game on a great course on a beautiful day.

I'm sorry that as we fly west we can't stop and try some of those amazing golf courses of the hot south-west where a little water will make the desert blossom like the rose—and in just a few weeks too—but they are unknown territory to me golfwise in spite of visits to Las Vegas, the Grand Canyon and the spectacular and lesser-known Oak Creek Canyon, with its vermilion rocks, on one notable holiday.

So out to California we must go, and where better to start than the Monterey Peninsula, which thrusts out into the Pacific like a shoulder about 150 miles south of San Francisco. There are few more delightful places in the world—when the fog doesn't roll in off the ocean—with a grand climate, wonderful cliffs, dunes, and coastal scenery and splendid golf; trees abound, notably some exceedingly gnarled and twisted cypresses leaning away from the prevailing west wind, and out to sea seals, sea-otters and sea-lions grunt and cough on the rocks and honk with incredulity at one's bad shots. The sea-otters dive and bring up a clam in one paw and a stone in the other; then they lie on their backs in the water and crack the shell with the stone against their chests and eat the fish. Add the delightful little town of Carmel, with its artists' colony and old Spanish mission church, and you've got a place which it is a joy to visit. The Del Monte Lodge at Pebble Beach is splendidly comfortable with a view over the eighteenth hole to Carmel Bay and the hills beyond a vista of green and blue which is sheer delight.

Pacific Grove

Before we visit the big courses here we'll just look in briefly at Pacific Grove near the town of Monterey itself and its airport—and for this reason: this unpretentious municipal course, with one nine a very mundane affair inland, possesses nine holes of pure links-land, thin hard turf and seaside greens, dunes, sandhills and undulating fairways and appalling rough of ice-plant and tree lupins. This is so rare in the United States that it must not pass without mention. I first noticed this phenomenon as we flew in over the links to the airport and when I mentioned it to several friends nobody had ever heard of it. Just the other day I got together a four to go over and play the seaside nine—the Ocean Course. The holes were not particularly exciting but it was a rare and enjoyable experience.

Pebble Beach

With that tribute paid let us turn to Pebble Beach, a great golf course but in no sense a golf links, save that possible exceptions could be made of the seventh and eighteenth holes. Although several excellent holes lie close to the sea along the cliffs, with a wonderful view of Carmel Bay, the turf, the rough, the greens are not links-land, while many of the more inland holes among the pines and cypresses could be anywhere.

The course was conceived as part of the development of a wild 5,600 acres of scrub and woodlands by the far-sighted head of Del Monte Properties, S. F. Morse, whose later plans included also the splendid courses nearby, Cypress Point and the Monterey Country Club and now the tremendous new course called Spyglass Hill. Monterey, by the way, has two courses, the Shore Course which is near the beach but barely links-land and the Dunes Course which is largely among the trees but with a few true links holes.

Pebble Beach, however, was the first and in its layout it has a connection with Britain for one of its 1915 architects was Douglas Grant, who though a Californian spent much of his time after World War I in England with a house near Sandwich. Grant was a fine golfer, not quite at the absolute top of British amateur golf in the 'twenties but very near it; later he lived in a house near Cypress Point until his tragic death in 1967.

So let's see what Grant and his friend Neville laid out for us. The first two holes are of no special note, the first an undemanding par four with a plateau green and the second a short par five of about 470 yards with a deep gully with sand in it short of the green.

At the third things liven up for your drive is across a wide deep chasm full of rough grass and a bunker; you have a diagonal carry and the more you bite off the easier your pitch to the green.

At the fourth you can slice into the sea but apart from getting your drive over the cross hazard it is not a very exacting hole for its length, 300-odd yards, though the green is surrounded with shallow traps.

Five is an unattractive short hole uphill through a gap in some thick trees but perhaps I just don't play it well. However at number six you get the first of several fine holes; this is a 500-yard par five on two levels. If you hit a good drive slightly left of centre but not too far over to risk the large trap, you have in front of you a big rise on top of which and some way from the crest lies the green; the snag here is an encroaching arm of the sea whose verges are clad in thick atrocious rough so that a sliced second can utterly ruin you.

Next comes a little short hole, a pitch of 110 yards down to a green on the water's edge with bunkers all round and the waves bursting on a group of rocks just off shore—a very attractive and photogenic hole.

Then at number eight you are confronted with the most famous and spectacular hole at Pebble Beach. It is 400–425 yards long and from the tee you don't see much, a rising swell of ground which closes off the view until you march up to the ball. And then what a spectacle greets the eye, a huge deep in-running arm of the sea lies between you and the green, rock bound and furious; it must be 150 yards across at the shortest point and the green below you with five traps hardly welcomes you. Supposing you have hit a smacker off the tee near to the edge of the chasm; you then have to hit a three-iron or more likely for me a wood shot of 180–190 yards to get over. Well I did it once but now I have to trundle round the route of inglorious safety far to the left and play for a five.

The ninth and tenth both run along the top of the cliffs one rather over and the other rather under 400 yards with the green of each very close to the edge, beautiful holes, fine holes—both of them—but too alike to be consecutive.

Well we have just had five excellent holes in a row and now we turn inland and the quality of the golf in my eyes diminishes sadly. The holes continue tough and uncompromising but they lack charm and *memorability*. Even with the aid of the guide book you can't easily unlock from your memory the essential differences between eleven, thirteen and fifteen and only the long bending difficult par-five fourteenth hole stands out of this group of five.

However, we do get a stirring finish. Sixteen is a fine dog-leg with the way to the green barred by the same deep bunkered gully which runs along in front of the third tee and trees on either side of the entrance; the green looks too small for the shot somehow.

Then the seventeenth is a long one-shot hole of about 200 yards straight towards the shore and the eye of the wind; in rough weather it can be out of reach. The difficulty here depends on the placing of the pin relative to the bunkers guarding the left side of the wide shallow dumb-bell-shaped green.

So to the eighteenth one of golf's famous holes, a 530-yard par five hugging the rocks and the shore which run the whole way up the left-hand side. The hole is curved and the chances of getting on to the pebbles and rocks of the beach by a simple pull or by trying to cut off too much are all too great and innumerable disasters have been recorded here. The final shot to the green is none too easy with two bunkers on the right, one partly masking the approach, and another on the left right on the edge of the sea wall. How best to sum up Pebble Beach then? Eight splendid holes would be my verdict and ten of much lesser quality but needing to be treated with great respect—all adding up to a very difficult course but not a really great one. But it must be said that it ranks high in the list of beautiful places at which to play golf.

The U.S. Amateur Championship has been played at Pebble Beach thrice, in 1929 when Harrison Johnston won and Bobby Jones was put out in the first round, in 1947 and in 1961 when Jack Nicklaus won for the second time and our Joe Carr got into the semi-final. Many other tournaments have been played here of which the best known is the Bing Crosby Clambake, a huge pro-amateur affair held in January when some spectacular weather and spectacular golf, birdies, eagles, tens, twelves and fourteens have been recorded.

Cypress Point

Well, if I've damned Pebble Beach a little with faint praise how about Cypress Point? That's another cup of tea, a magnificent course with even a patch of true links-land which might be at Sandwich covering the eighth and ninth, and from the twelfth to the seventeenth holes while the rest are like a sort of seaside Pinehurst with pines, white sand in the bunkers, intense green grass and good but not alarming golf. The club itself is highly select with 100 members who I believe divide up the bill at the end of the year and casual visitors are not admitted to the club-house even with good antecedents; you have to change in a subsidiary locker room of the standard usually reserved in the United States for caddies for which a green fee of twenty dollars is extracted at week-ends and fifteen during the week. Indeed a day's golf here with a cart for my dud leg and caddie and so on costs just about as much as my annual subscription to the R. and A.

For all that it's a lovely place to play golf; there is never a crowd, the course is beautifully kept, the greens are perfect, as good as the best at home, the holes are interesting and sometimes spectacular and there is the intense blue Pacific beating on the rocky shore to be seen from every hole.

You start with a nice downhill drive to a two-shot hole of no alarming properties; somehow it reminds me of the first hole at Portrush. Then you turn inland and play six holes in among the pines and charming they are, the 531 yard par-five second with a drive up over a diagonal carry, the mid-iron shot to the third with its encroaching bunker on the right is delightful as the green has the backdrop of a huge sand-dune, and the fine 371-yard fourth with trees lining the fairway. The fifth is a most attractive short par five, uphill, but with many traps of white sand to mark your way; somehow it is always a little longer than you think.

Six is another longer par five, over 500 yards downhill to the green this time and bunkered to the left. At the short seventh you play from one hill in the sandhills for 160 yards across a valley to a green perched up in the hills on the opposite side. So far everything has been tidy, pleasant and not wildly exciting, but at the 318-yard eighth comes a dramatic change for on the tee you are confronted with a big sandhill which might be at Burnham or Newcastle; you drive across this on to a narrow fairway and must watch that you don't go too far and run off, for you must now turn half right and hit a tight and accurate pitch shot uphill to a small two-level green in the broken links country. At the 291-yard ninth we are still in links-land, very much so, and drive downhill down a narrow fairway with a most exacting pitch to a tiny hard narrow green like the eighth at Pine Valley in the old days, in a wilderness of sand, splendid.

Then comes a par five heading inland again and then a long two-shot hole down towards the shore on 'inland' soil; then at twelve the links holes return with an excellent curving two-shot hole to a plateau green. At thirteen we are in the heart of links-land with a beautiful hole of 339–361 yards with a closely bunkered plateau green of seaside keenness right by the shore and the pounding surf. After that comes an uphill par four, a longer one, with a spinney of battered Monterey cypresses on the right. From there you walk across the road to the tee of the short fifteenth, a grand little hole with the green on the very edge of the sea and an arm of it in front as well; there are lots of bunkers all round but the green is of generous size for a seven or eight-iron shot and you should get a three all right.

Then comes the 'ordeal hole', the 'great photographic spectacular', the 217–233-yard sixteenth, all carry, if you want to go for it. The green is on a small rocky peninsula or appendix connected to the mainland by a very narrow neck thirteen yards wide, between the guarding bunkers. The worst rough in the world, mesembryanthemum is here in places. The green is a fair size and so it should be for most of us are going to need a full belt with a driver. The view from the tee is I suppose one of the most formidable in golf, nothing between you and the green except the shore, rocks and the sea. There is a way round of course, to the left where a prod with a four-iron or a five-wood will put you up on the fairway by the gnarled cypress leaning over at 45 degrees, from which a pitch will get you on; it is only at this point that the extreme narrowness of the neck of land holding the green is apparent. The first time I played here the state of my match required me to play safe and I even got an inglorious three out of it but after hitting my match ball I had a go with my driver. The first shot was cut, splash! The second I thought was a winner but just slightly drawn. I said to the caddie, 'It's just on the left of the green'; he said, 'It's in the ocean'—and it was.

The stories of disaster here are legion, scores in double figures, shots off the beach, cards ruined and the rest. It's nice to know that Bing Crosby has done it in one stroke. For all this I think the hole is a freak and I don't really admire it. I fear it of course.

In contrast the seventeenth from the peninsula of the sixteenth back over the ocean is a grand hole for you have another spectacular tee shot with a diagonal carry over the water and cliffs of the mainland and you can pick your line; the light iron shot up to the green is less exacting unless you cut the shot then another inlet of the sea will grab it.

The last hole is disappointing, downright silly I've heard it called because you have to drive over or through, if you're lucky, a row of cypresses; then you have a long pitch or light iron shot uphill to the club-house side. All in all, though, a wonderful round on a wonderful course but let's hurry back to Del Monte Lodge so that we can have a drink.

Spyglass Hill

The new course laid out by that distinguished American architect Robert Trent Jones at Spyglass Hill is big in every way; 7,000 yards long from the back tees and 6,600 from ours, it swings uphill and down dale between the Pacific shore and its dunes and the wooded summit of the hill dotted with tall thin pines. The area and many of the holes are named after *Treasure Island* characters or places for Robert Louis Stevenson spent some time here. The first five holes are fiercely laid out in pure links-land with acres of sand and formidable carries as tough and penal and severe as they come; the rest of the course in the trees is more subtle with few bunkers but sharp slopes and several water hazards. It was said that Trent Jones had declared that he would make the first five holes to match Pine Valley and the remainder to match Augusta National. If this is true it is quite a fair description of what he has done here for there is a hint of Pine Valley in the links holes and a distinct resemblance to Augusta with the spare use of sand, the bold slopes and the water hazards in the others.

We played Spyglass in half a gale of wind which ultimately freshened to something like a full gale accompanied by driving rain so that we perhaps didn't get full value out of the first visit. Towards the end two trees were blown down within a few hundred yards of us and the woods were crackling and snapping in the gale like a rifle range.

Trent Jones has indulged his taste for unorthodox green shapes and heavy slopes, some of which I thought altogether too extreme. For example, the green at the fourth is sixty-four yards long and only twelve yards wide at the maximum and there are kidney-shaped greens, greens like boomerangs, greens shaped like Africa, wide greens across the line, small greens and large ones, as well as plateaux among the heavy folds and slopes.

You start with 'Treasure Island', a big par five downhill, curving to the left out of the tall pines and confronting you in the end with a small green on a little plateau amid a Sahara of white sand. Again you think of the eighth at Pine Valley in its early days. At 570 yards off our tee it would tax the longest pros to get on and stay on in two; a five here is very good going. At the second of 355 yards you have a fine hole driving over a big carry of white sand and rough while a huge dune covers the left flank. For the second shot, again to a small green, a medium or light iron gets you up across a belt of sand across the fairway.

Number three, the 'Black Spot,' is a pitch shot downhill towards the sea. The green is small and sits among the sandhills and bunkers like a small green oasis in the desert, a very pretty little island hole. The fourth is all right if you clear the carry of rough—tough seaside rough—in front of the tee and keep on the fairway which slopes vigorously downwards and to the left. The green looks tiny among its protecting flanking hummocks, but it is, as I said, sixty-four yards long so you can get quite a putt here. This again is a fine two-shot hole of moderate length.

The fifth, 'Bird Rock', is a beauty, a light iron shot of about 150 yards, all carry, to a plateau green perched up in the sandhills and bunkered tightly in front; this hole might be at Rye and I thought it was most attractive. It is the one on the PanAm calendar for 1968. One leaves these five holes full of admiration—I might almost say limp with admiration—for a splendid and spectacular start. I only wish that the links holes had continued. The holes in the trees don't please me nearly as much, difficult and beautiful as many of them are. I just don't like big curly greens and artificial water hazards—there are five of them—all too artificial to be convincing.

Thus, there is a long pond flanking the approach to the par-five seventh and another in front of the par-five eleventh. The par-five fourteenth, whose plateau green looks from afar like a three-bladed propeller, has its right flank below the green guarded by a pond too. There is water at both the short holes in the back nine. First is the spectacular twelfth across a valley with a narrow green sloping upwards and white bunkers on the hill to the right and water to the left. The other is the short 127-yard fifteenth with a kidney-shaped green and a big pond in front to the right.

The holes I liked best in the second half were the long par-four thirteenth, 'Tom Morgan', at the far end of the course with a plateau green shaped like Africa and the short par-four seventeenth, 'Benn Gunn', with a small green in a minefield of bunkers. So to the last hole, 'Spyglass' itself, a two-shotter with a green at the end of a small rise; two good bangs are needed here.

Well, that's Spyglass—a big course, tough and exacting. If you have a choice I wouldn't recommend trying it in a gale. I only wish the links holes had gone on and on.

Before we head north to Canada let us look in at San Francisco—one of the great cities of the world and one of the most attractive. As Fred Warburg said so wisely 'all Englishmen like Boston and everybody loves San Francisco'. Hills always make a city attractive, even such violently steep ones as there are here, and it has many other claims to fame—its food —the cracked crab is delicious—Chinatown, the harbour and sea, fine bridges, pale unusual colouring of the houses, cable cars, good hotels, spectacular views and some pleasant all-the-year-round golf.

San Francisco Golf Club

The oldest club is the San Francisco Golf Club, laid out by A. W. Tillinghast on rolling country among pine trees at nearly every hole, with a lot of mimosa and some Mediterranean heather bushes in the rough as well. Just by the short seventh green the last duel in America was fought in 1859 between a U.S. Senator and the Chief Justice of the California Supreme Court. The first half of the course is good and long and as we played it after rain we were constantly having to give the ball a lot of stick to get near the par fours in two. The most memorable holes were, I thought, the one-shot seventh down into a narrow valley to a small tightly bunkered green and the shortish par-four eighth up the valley to follow it. The second nine is shorter and therefore a little easier, though the big eighteenth home into the wind was a long haul; the two short holes in this nine I liked and also the dog-leg 325-yard fourteenth very much.

One feature of this hospitable club is the 'gangsome', a game made up of an indeterminate but large number of players; it originated from the friendly idea that no one should be left lonely in the club-house. San Francisco's 'most famous son' has been Harvie Ward, who twice won the U.S. Amateur Championship and ours once.

Golf in America – South and West

Olympic Club

Perhaps the Olympic Club is the most famous in San Francisco as the U.S. Open has been played here twice on the Lake Course and each time has produced the wildest and most improbable drama. In 1955 Ben Hogan, then at the top of his form, seemed to be home and dry with his fifth U.S. Open safely won and I believe that some papers printed the result with him as the winner. Then a totally unknown player, Jack Fleck, came in at the end of the game with a 67 to tie the great man. However, as everyone said, the play-off was a foregone conclusion, but it wasn't as Fleck, now in a hand-to-hand struggle with the greatest player in the land, beat him fairly and squarely by three shots.

Then in 1966 Billy Casper, playing in the last game of the last round with Arnold Palmer, caught up seven shots in the first eight holes of the second half and so forced a tie. In the play-off Palmer led by two shots after the first nine and again Casper rallied and made up six shots on him on the run in to beat him by four strokes; two such calamitous runs of nine holes as Palmer's at Olympic or two better ones than Casper's have rarely been seen in the Championship.

The Lake eighteen make a most formidable golf course, long, tight and hilly. It runs among thick woods of red pine and cypress trees and they lie close in to the fairways at every hole; there are, however, very few bunkers except round the greens, the trees and the rolling hilly terrain exercise the necessary control from the tee. The par fours, eleven of them, make as formidable a battery as I have met anywhere with many uphill shots, like the second and fourth, and many with raised or plateau greens like the fourteenth; add to this the famous short third which rates among the Eighteen Best Golf Holes in America and the other most difficult tightly bunkered short holes and three par fives, one all but 600 yards off the ordinary tee, and you can see that you've got a lot of golf on your hands.

When I played Olympic it was damp and lush and there was no run on the ball and the greens were in a coarse state. I think I played more wooden club shots than in any round of ninety-odd that I can recall and the par fours seemed interminably long. I longed for my mis-spent youth and to get the ball to 'go'.

The famous short third is steeply, almost violently, downhill, but the green looks very small in its nest of bunkers for a 220-yard shot. Almost as famous is the 316-yard eighteenth which, unless you hit your drive hard so that it goes well over the hill and down into the valley bottom, gives you an intensely difficult shot to the bunker-set minute green, a very difficult hole indeed for its length.

The second and fourth are two particularly fine holes both steeply up-

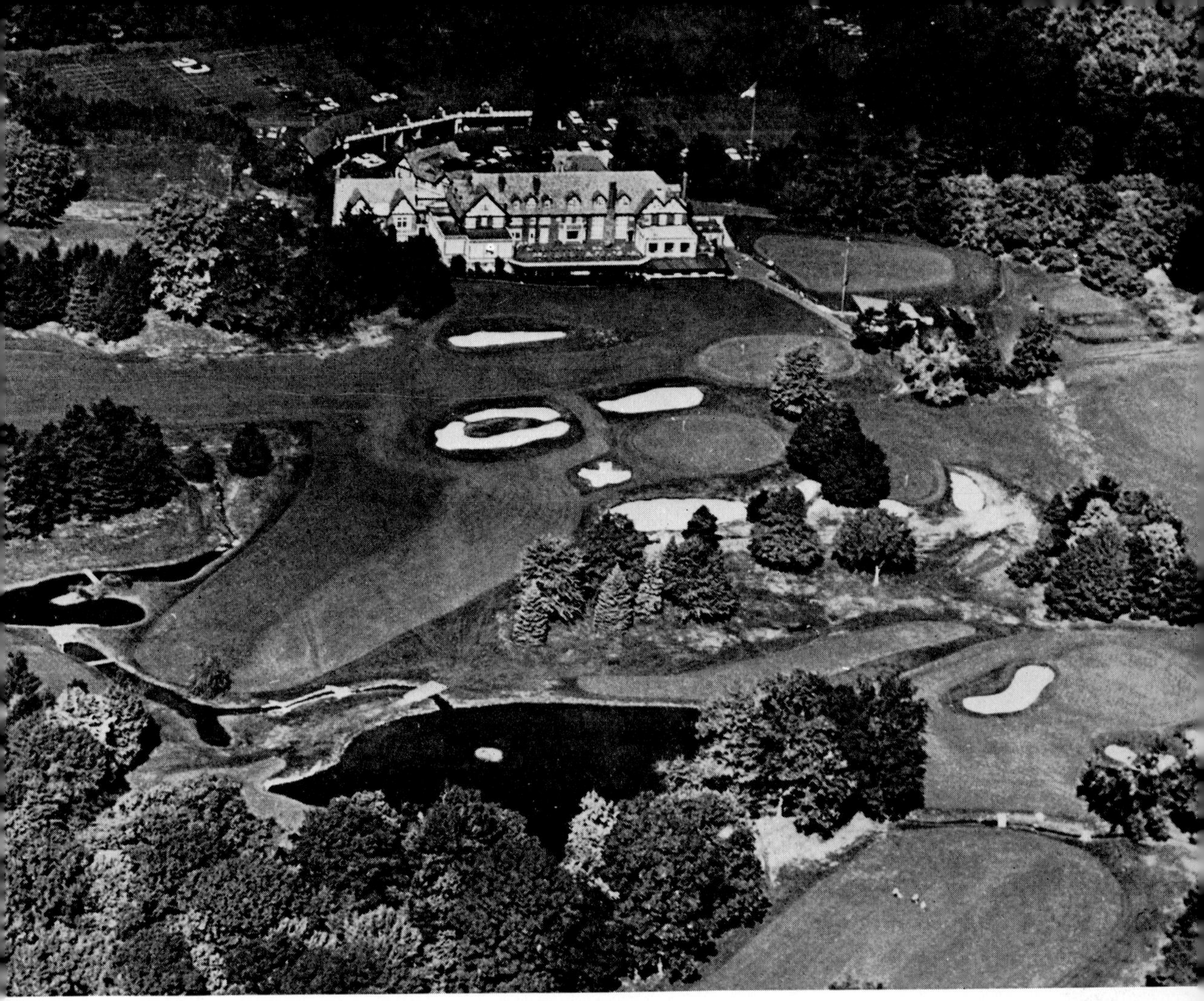

ABOVE Aerial view of the Baltusrol Golf Club in New Jersey, showing the third green on the lower course on the right of the water hazard guarding the 4th hole in the centre foreground. By the club-house are the 18th greens of the two courses (*United States Golf Association*)

BELOW On the National Golf Links of America. The tee shot to the 2nd hole which resembles 'the Sahara' at Sandwich. The picture shows the windmill before it lost its sails in a gale (*United States Golf Association*)

ABOVE The Oaklands Hill Golf Club near Detroit, showing the 15th green in the foreground and the dog-legged 16th with its water hazard guarding the green. A most exacting hole (*United States Golf Association*)

BELOW The 17th hole at the Country Club at Brookline near Boston. The bunker in the foreground is still known as Vardon's bunker where he finally came to grief in his famous battle with Francis Ouimet in 1913 (*Peter Allen*)

ABOVE The second shot, a pitch, to the 8th hole, at Pine Valley as it is today (*Warner Shelly*)
CENTRE The same shot as it was in the early 1920's when the course was new, a much more terrifying prospect than it is now (*Peter Allen collection*)
BELOW The beautifully moulded green of the short 10th hole at Pine Valley, with the 'D.A.H.' conspicuous in the centre of the approach to the green (*Warner Shelly*)

The 10th green on the Red Course of the Jockey Club in Buenos Aires with the 11th green beyond. This course played host to the Canada Cup in 1962

hill at the end and a long, long way to get in two shots. On the whole, I thought the Lake Course commanded immense respect but relatively little affection.

The Ocean Course is shorter and far more open than the Lakeside. It has three charming holes on the top of the cliff overlooking the Pacific coast, not quite links holes but seaside holes indeed. Of these, the fourth is a spectacular and splendid hole, downhill off the tee to a rolling fairway, with endless trouble all the way along the left-hand side as the fairway falls down sharply there on to a rough warren full of mesembryanthemum. This was once another fairway, before the great earthquake of 1906 shook it down on to the shore. The inner holes on the Ocean Course have less charm than the few along the cliff top and there are far fewer trees than on the great championship circuit next door. The spectacular fourteenth, 240 yards down a steep, steep hill to a small green far below, is noteworthy. On the whole, though, I like the Ocean Course rather more than the 'big one'.

It amused me to ride around Olympic in a Harley-Davidson petrol-driven golf cart. I had always associated this name so far with huge police motor-cycles or in older days with big eight-valve racing bikes on the dirt tracks of the 'twenties.

The next two courses I am going to describe, Capilano and Oak Bay, are both in the west of Canada, in British Columbia in fact, where the climate is good for golf and golfing turf and play is possible all the year round.

Both these courses have housed Canadian championships and in 1967, Canada's Centennial Year, Oak Bay was host to the Commonwealth Tournament.

Capilano

Capilano is in North Vancouver, in the hills to the north of the Lion's Gate Bridge which crosses the harbour exit at its narrowest part. North Vancouver and the bridge owe their development to the Guinness family of brewing fame who developed the British Properties north of the harbour long before shorter-sighted citizens could see any sense in it. Now the whole hillside is covered with 'desirable residences' with many homes and gardens of exceptional charm and beauty. The golf course does nothing to spoil the effect, far from it.

It is, I think, one of the delightful places in the world in which to play a game of golf and the view from the huge picture window at the end of the men's locker room over the fifteenth, sixteenth and seventeenth holes to the tree-covered hills and the snow-capped mountains beyond is unsurpassed anywhere in the world that I know. The course presents many other fine vistas through the huge fir trees that line the fairways, towards the harbour and city of Vancouver or the hills round it and at one hole gives a view of the snow-covered 10,000-foot cone of Mount Baker, forty miles away over the U.S. border with as fair a shape as Fuji itself. In places the dogwood trees with their six-petalled white or pink flowers illumine the fairways.

The golf is good without being exceptional. There are plenty of par fours that take all you can give—and more, but some of the par fives, except for the overpowering 575-yard uphill-against-the-prevailing-wind eighteenth, are rather on the short side. There are five par threes, one of them too long to be a good hole—it would be far better as a short difficult par four—with the result that the total par score of 72 off the regular tees is not exacting. Off the back tees and with some tough pin placings it can be a different affair.

Capilano is most ingeniously contrived as you seem to be going downhill far more than you come up. For example, there is an exhilarating first hole down towards the harbour, then after three more or less level holes it is downhill again at the fifth and sixth. Yet you only seem to be coming up at the short ninth and the long eighteenth. This, of course, is not so for the tenth and thirteenth are uphill too but gently and unobtrusively.

True some of the walks from green to tee are uphill but the general effect is still surprising. Another ingenious and perhaps unsought effect is that the fairways are not as narrow as they look; they only seem so on account of the huge fir trees that line the fairways.

With all this there are some excellent golf holes at Capilano, the attractive par-four second with a fold of ground in front of the built-up green, the beautiful short fourth across a water hazard, the big long par-four seventh, again further than it looks with a long narrow green and a fine single tree to give you the correct line for your drive.

The short eleventh is a good hole but too like the shorter downhill fourteenth and as I have said the short sixteenth at 255 yards should be shorter and tougher or longer and tougher. The tenth is a fine sweeping dog-leg uphill to the left, rated at par five but within reach of two big cracks, the twelfth at 368 yards, a fine hole over a water hazard to a plateau green, and the thirteenth hole of 401 yards, just a beauty. If you hit your drive right you don't have too hard a shot but if you cut your drive or drive short the shot to the narrow thin green lying across the line of play at the top of a steep rise out of a gully in front of the green is something 'to remember for years, to remember with tears'. The finish is fierce, the 426-yard curving fifteenth needs two fine shots, the sixteenth as I have said a full belt with a driver (and then some more), the seventeenth, downhill again, with that incomparable view of forest and mountain, is a hard long par four. Finally, as you clamber up that Burma Road of an eighteenth you realise that you have had a round on a course in a thousand. The club-house is delightful and the members friendly and considerate in the fullest measure.

Oak Bay

Oak Bay, on the outskirts of Victoria on Vancouver Island is totally unlike Capilano and only resembles it in being also one of the lovely places in the world to play a game of golf. It has comparatively few trees, though some fine trees and shrubs adorn the nearby gardens, but is well provided with gorse and broom which in May add brilliance to the rough. The course is hemmed in between the sea, roads and the gardens of houses. So the ground doesn't lend itself to any extension of its limited length. Indeed every available inch has been used so that alarming experiences from parallel holes can arise when the course is crowded. Moreover, the lie of the land results in some departures from orthodoxy in the layout, such as three short holes in succession at the end of the first nine and two together in the second half.

But what a staggeringly beautiful place this can be on a fine day—and fine days are frequent here—with the sparkling sea, which so often is a deep dark blue, of the Juan de Fuca Strait and the Haro Strait separating Vancouver Island from the mainland and over the straits and beyond, the glittering snow-capped Olympic Mountains forty miles away at the northern end of the State of Washington. Off the rocky shore is a small island with a lighthouse and every morning in the season close to noon up comes the *Princess Marguerite* of the Canadian Pacific fleet from Seattle with another load of American tourists to buy British woollens and china in Victoria and take tea at the splendidly Edwardian Empress Hotel.

There are some excellent holes on this rather short par 70 course, notably the horribly narrow 410-yard third with an all too easy shot from the tee on to the hard high road which runs along the whole of the left-hand side; the green here is steeply banked with two steps and indeed resembles the green at the shorter par-four fifth. The seventh is a fiercely difficult downhill 205-yard hole with the green literally on the beach, and very hummocky and folded the green is too, while inglorious safety to the right is guarded by two bunkers. Needless to say, the prevailing wind here, and it can prevail in no mean way, tends to sweep your ball on to the shingle on the shore. Here, if you are lucky with the visibility, you can also see the white cone of Mount Baker across the straits.

The tenth is a fine two-shotter uphill and so is the eleventh down towards the sea except that for ordinary mortals it is rated at par five. The finish is good; a very sharp dog-legged 405-yard fifteenth, a drive and pitch sixteenth under the club-house windows, then a shortish par five runs out from the club-house again after which you turn and play a very good par-four last hole to a plateau green which needs a good firm iron to get you home.

Only one thing is lacking for some reason, in spite of the climate, soil and proximity to the sea, Oak Bay is not on links-land but otherwise it is a wonderfully good place to play a game of golf. Again, as in Capilano the club is friendly and the members hospitable.

Banff and Jasper Park

Before we leave the Canadian west there are two courses which we must visit, owned by the rival Canadian Railways at Banff and Jasper Park.

It is not that the golf is exceptional—they are both holiday courses—or that any great tournaments or dramatic golfing events have happened here but they are both in the most superb and spectacular environment in the eastern or Alberta slopes of the Rocky Mountains.

This is largely unspoiled country and for all the wealth and transportability of North Americans these places are still comparatively empty and unvisited. There is therefore a wonderful cleanness and freedom about the whole area which makes it immensely refreshing. Then add the most glorious mountain scenery, peaks, lakes, glaciers and the wild life of a huge National Park, bears, elk, moose, wild goats and sheep, coyotes and a dozen others, this is one of the chosen areas in the world.

The ideal way to see this favoured land is to come from Calgary by the Canadian Pacific Railway and get off about ninety miles on at Banff and put up at their huge baronial hotel; here you are I suppose about 4,000 feet up in the Bow River valley and the first big peaks are now near neighbours. You play some golf, the summer evenings are particularly attractive for this, on a delightful course—but don't top your first drive into that brawling fast-running stream in front of the tee—and you can also do some sightseeing round Lake Louise, Peyto Lake, Moraine Lake and up to the Continental Divide in the Kicking Horse Pass where you can stand with feet astride in a not too exaggerated stance across a small stream which splits in front of your nose, one arm running to the Pacific and one to the Atlantic.

Then hire a car and drive to Jasper, about 160 miles on a splendid brand-new highway. Of all the roads I know in a million miles of travel I think this comes out top, certainly top for mountain scenery. So to Jasper, putting up at the admirable Canadian National Lodge with its cabins around the park.

The golf here is very like that at Banff, holiday play but not short nor easy if you want to score well but with the mountain scenery round you, you hardly care. There are expeditions of all kinds into the mountains too of which I would nominate the boat trip to Maligne Lake as one of the high points of a lifetime.

From Jasper you can take the C.N.R. train back to Edmonton, about 220 miles, and from there you can fly almost anywhere—a nice round trip.

10 Golf in America – the East

While golf in North America seems to have begun in the Southern States of the U.S., only to disappear and re-emerge in the 'eighties further north, a start had been made in Canada before this revival. To quote Robert Browning's *History of Golf* 'Ignoring the claims to pioneer honours of a young Glasgow sailor named William Dibman, who, finding himself in the Port of Quebec in 1854 "carried his clubs to the Heights of Abraham and there entertained himself in solitary contentment", we can say that the history of golf on the American continent began with the founding in November 1873 of the Royal Montreal Golf Club.' The club has been in continuous existence since, though it has changed its fields of play twice, first from Fletcher's Fields on the eastern edge of Mount Royal where Park Avenue now runs, out to Dixie west of the city in 1897 and then out to the Île Bizard to the north of Montreal Island in stages from 1958.

Royal Montreal

Its new premises can hardly qualify Royal Montreal as occupants of historic turf for all that they now have forty-five highly sophisticated holes laid out by Robert Trent Jones. Jones's architecture I feel is like a highly seasoned dish, you either like it very much or not at all. I'm afraid I'm in the second category. I really don't like the immensely long tees, the almost excessive use of water and the huge greens with their exaggerated slopes between the various 'pin positions'. However, others like this style very much.

Of the two main courses I suppose the Blue ranks first and it has some exceedingly difficult and tricky holes in the second nine. Working back from the long tough par-four eighteenth with its plateau green, there is the short difficult pitch to the tiny green at the seventeenth, the double carry over water at the sixteenth, first with the drive and then back over the same pond to the big plateau green, and the tough mid-iron second shot over water guarding the fifteenth green, you have got to play as hard a finish 'as you can shake a stick at'. Not a course to be taken lightly for there are plenty of other tough ones in the rest of the round but for me not much charm.

Just over a year after Royal Montreal started, Royal Quebec was founded and started life on the Heights of Abraham, moving later to Montmorency Falls. However on the course on the Plains of Abraham the first inter-club match in America took place in 1876 when Quebec entertained Montreal and beat them by twelve holes in the aggregate. Alas, Royal Quebec and I are strangers, so no more can be said here.

Kanawaki

My course in Canada was Kanawaki over the St Lawrence from Montreal in the Caughnawaga Indian Reserve, a sept of the Iroquois Tribe. Here the caddies and staff are Indians from the village and excellent they usually are with a proper pride in their rights to have first refusal of the jobs in return for allowing the club to use their land. When the Canadian Amateur Championship was being played here in 1953, the other Montreal clubs suggested sending caddies over to help out; this was indignantly refused as Chief Poking Fire had sent out a message, not by smoke signal, I fear, to Caughnawagas all over Canada who had flown the coop asking them to arrange their holidays and come back to carry in the Championship. And they did.

The Kanawaki course lies close to the St Lawrence Seaway, the building of which considerably altered the natural drainage of the lower parts of the course but it was and is a fine long test with some long tough par fours, notably the fifth, tenth and the eighteenth with its steep rise to the green under the club-house verandah.

The course is on two levels with a sharp escarpment separating them. This steep bank, while giving you an enjoyable drive at numbers one, four and thirteen gives you a very stiff second at two, seven and eighteen and a tricky problem of placing your drive at eight. Then if you like a fun hole now and again—and why not—there is the ninth, a full belt with a driver to a green in a deep crater. Not only is Kanawaki an enjoyable course, but I have an affection for it going as far back as 1933; so I think I got more pleasure out of winning the Senior Club Championship there in 1961 than from any other prize in an undistinguished golfing life. Kanawaki also has some splendid maples on it, of all trees the most spectacular in autumn foliage and the most lovely in sheer shape. When I first knew the club it was very isolated except by rail and to get home after dinner you had to flag a New York Central train with a burning newspaper, a strange wild experience for an unsophisticated young man but now the new bridges have finished all that.

Pine Valley

I suppose that almost everybody who is interested in golf has heard of Pine Valley even if he has heard of no other American course. I have had the good fortune to know and love the course for thirty-five years. Those who had not had the good luck to play there have heard tell of appalling bunkers, terrible carries, water hazards, thick and menacing forests, often wildly exaggerated, all building up a picture of some inhuman monster which devours the innocent handicap player. You tend to start out already beaten as I did in 1933 and so recorded a round of over 100 for the first time in years, a dismaying experience for an aspiring young player.

The truth, however, is different though without a doubt Pine Valley is one of the most conspicuous examples of the penal golf course, just as Augusta National is one of the most conspicuous examples of the strategic course, that you can find anywhere in the world. Pine Valley *is* severe, very severe, but even if it *is* the hardest golf course in the world it is essentially fair and just and not a freak, a monster or an impossible task. So even if it is, as I believe, the most difficult—and also I think the greatest course—as opposed to links—in the world, it is also a delightful and exhilarating place at which to play golf—provided and always provided that you can propel the ball 175 yards off the tee. With this modest performance you can play the course enjoyably, ignoring the par of 70, against a 'personal par' of, say, 75 or 76. If you can hit the ball 225 yards, there is no hole beyond your reach in the correct par figures so that sheer length is not a *necessity* at Pine Valley. Length helps, of course, it always does, provided that you hit straight, but at Pine Valley moderate length and straightness pay better than erratic might.

Why then is Pine Valley different, how is it a unique layout? It lies in this, I think, that, like on some early links layouts in Britain, you are either on the fairway or in a hazard; there is very little rough as such and indeed you are either in the trees, in a bunker or on the fairway or green. Then the bunkers themselves are to say the least of it extensive—one runs up to three-quarters of an acre—and well occupied by bush and scrub as well as footmarks and divot holes in the unraked sand. They are not so much bunkers as surviving areas of the original sandy terrain. The trees too are painfully close at hand at times and water menaces at five holes. But let it

The 3rd hole at Pine Valley, a one-shot hole of 172 yards downhill to a beautifully moulded island green in a Sahara of sand. The green, though large, can give some very difficult long putts. One of the great holes.

Photo: Warner Shelly

also be said that the fairways are very reasonably wide, the shots from the tee present a diagonal carry or a way round or past the hazards and the greens are of a very fair size, indeed some are very large, with one or two notable exceptions.

The general appearance of the course, with serried ranks of pine trees and hardwoods, its flowering shrubs and brilliant fall colours, the numerous and beautifully shaped and moulded bunkers, the carries confronting the teeing grounds, is formidable indeed—totally uncompromising in fact —but let this be said in a very small quiet voice, 'It's not quite so difficult as it looks.'

Pine Valley lies in scrubby sandy pine country near the village of Clementon in New Jersey between Philadelphia and Atlantic City. The club is tucked away up a bumpy side road with a number of comfortable houses among the trees overlooking parts of the course, all rather like the St George's Hill estate at home; indeed of all the English courses St George's Hill is the nearest to Pine Valley in appearance. The club-house is modest and it is purely and simply a golf course; nothing of the country club atmosphere is encouraged here, ladies especially taking a back seat.

Pine Valley was the idea of a Philadelphia business man called George A. Crump who was resolved to make in this excellent countryside the most difficult and exacting golf course in the world. Crump is also famous for originating the term 'birdie.' According to Charles Price in *The World of Golf*, Crump was playing at the Atlantic City Country Club with the brothers Smith back before World War I. He did a hole in one under par after hitting a bird with his drive. His partners said that his shot was 'a bird' and from then on he and his friends always called a hole in one under par a 'birdie hole' and the name caught on.

Crump's idea at Pine Valley is just about what has been achieved, though he died before the full eighteen holes were completed. Work started in 1913, eleven holes were completed in 1914 and the whole course finished at the end of the war. Britain's H. S. Colt was also brought in in consultation and I think his characteristics are to be seen in places on the course; one notable contribution of his was the lengthening of the fifth from a mashie pitch to a full shot. The general layout at Pine Valley whether from the brain of Crump or Colt is a masterpiece, never more than two consecutive holes in the same direction; four totally different short holes, and a superb variety of second shots of different length and type, the finest set on any course in the world.

So after a lunch of a cup of snapper soup, a slice of cold beef and— because we are near to Philadelphia—a little ice-cream,[1] let us sally forth to tackle Pine Valley. Don't be too sure by the way that you will be offered

[1] It is said 'the nearer to Philadelphia the better the ice-cream'.

a host of bets that you won't break 90 or 100, according to your handicap, or that with five strokes a hole you won't succeed in finishing eighteen up on par. In all the thirty-five years that I've known and played Pine Valley, I've never been offered any such bet and only heard of very few being offered to others, though undoubtedly one such was won by Arnold Palmer just after he had won the U.S. Amateur Championship in 1954, for the $800 he won enabled him to buy an engagement ring, elope and live happily ever after. Remember as I said, Pine Valley is not quite so difficult as it looks but also prepare yourself for one major disaster at least during the round. One last word before we start: don't be tempted to play off the back tees until you've had two or three rounds and got the hang of things somewhat. Although the difference in length is only 307 yards, it makes the course a great deal harder.

The first hole at 415 yards off the regular tee is by no means a killer though there is a carry of rough sandy rutty ground in front of the tee; only if you cut your tee shot you may well be in a deep bunker. The hole is a sharp dog-leg to the right with the green large and long and a steep fall on either side and over the back so it's like hitting a shot from midships to the bow of a ship; the shot to the green can vary from a spoon to a seven iron depending on the wind and your drive.

The second hole is a beauty, 348 yards up to a green above the fairway which plays far longer than its length. There is a carry in front of the tee, not too long, and serried ranks of bunkers in the rough along both sides of the fairway and especially on the right-hand side. But suppose we've hit a smacker up the middle, we still have a stiff iron shot, perhaps a five-iron, up over three rows of deep tough bunkers in the face of the hill on top of which is waving the distant inaccessible flag. To hit a good one home here and hole the putt for a three on the big heavily folded green is an ecstatic pleasure.

The third hole, 172 yards, downhill to an island green set in a waste of sand is one of the supreme holes in golf. The green is large but beautifully moulded and sculpted with sweeping curves which give some acutely difficult 'borrowing' putts to judge. The first time I played the hole I had just got to the top of the swing as an Atlantic City express came by and the engineer pulled the whistle-cord for the level crossing; I topped it and took eleven to the hole without hitting another bad shot.

Number four, a long par four back to the club-house is not exceptionally severe other than from its length. Your drive is over a big hill but provided you hit it straight, and avoid the long bunker on the right side of the fairway, you have a fair shot over cross-bunkers down to the green or at least to the apron.

We must mention here the famous game in which Wood Platt started off by holing a putt for a three at the first; at the second he holed an iron shot for an eagle two; at the third he holed his tee shot for a one. Back to the club-house at the fourth, Woodie Platt got another birdie. So at that point, and six under par, Platt and the party retired to the club-house and very properly remained there.

The fifth is another great short hole, 217 yards uphill to a sloping green perched up there with a lake in front of the tee, then rough grass and a road before you get to the bunkers in front of the apron. On the left is a steep hillside pockmarked with bunkers and on the right a drop to perdition in the woods. Gene Littler collected a seven down there in one of the Shell television matches for all to see. The extent to which this hole runs uphill can be seen if you sit at the end table in the dining room, then when you get on to the tee, take your driver, no less.

The sixth tee is a formidable sight with a long diagonal carry as far as the eye can see, over sand and bushes with only a thin strip of fairway visible. This fairway is indeed the highest point on the course. However, you can bite off as much or as little as you like of the big carry and once-over, the shot into the green is not too long or tough unless you pull into the traps to the left or hit a wild slice fifty feet down into my friend Warner Shelly's garden.

The long seventh, 550 yards, is one of the great par fives in golf and so laid out that no man has ever reached it in two shots. This is due of course to the intervention of the great bunker, Hell's Half Acre, across the entire width of the hole, at about 260 yards from the tee. If you hit a good drive and then succeed in carrying the great Sahara, which is about 150 yards wide, with your second shot you still have a further demand on you as the green is an island in a pool of sand and further off than it looks.

The eighth is only 314 yards long and the tee shot lands on a down-slope. The difficulty lies in the tiny size of the plateau green to which you have to hit a pitch often off the aforesaid down-slope. The slopes of the green don't gather the ball—they shrug it off—and needless to say it is beset with bunkers. Once, long ago, this hole destroyed a fine round by Bernard Darwin and he never got over it. Personally I have never found this hole as tough as had been regarded by others; I think the reason is that the growth of trees, grass and bushes round the green area has wetted the ground and made the green softer and more holding and the vast wilderness of sand round the tiny green has to some extent grown over. The hole looks much mellower and cosier now than the oasis in the Sahara looked forty years ago.

The ninth is a grand two-shot hole with two alternative and quite different greens to play to; the grouping of the trees, especially when they are in their fall colours, with the white sand and green grass makes this hole one of classic beauty.

The tenth is another superb short hole—the four par threes at Pine Valley are unmatched anywhere—this one, 130 yards, the shortest on the course. The green is small and full of strong slopes and the bunkers grasping and proximate. A picture of this hole in one of my American books on golf architecture says, 'There is no welcome here'; there certainly isn't. One little pit, with an unprintable name—let us just call it the D.A.H.—is so placed that after pitching on the green you can roll back into it or you can even putt off the green into it and once in it you can only play out backwards.

After the efforts exacted by the tenth, the eleventh and twelfth holes are a slight relief; both are par fours but both under 400 yards, the twelfth with a pitch at an awkward angle for the second shot is quite a bit shorter. However, a new back tee is now available at the twelfth which makes fifty yards longer and harder.

Thirteen is another superb two-shotter, one of the greatest holes in all golf, but at 439 yards with an uphill drive is now too long for me. After hitting a good drive, without pulling it for heaven's sake, you have a full shot to a big green with the fairway curving away to the left and deep dire trouble all along the left-hand edge.

The fourteenth is the last short hole and I suppose the most photographed of all for it sits in a lake with water almost all round and bunkers and trees protecting the fringes. It is downhill and a four-iron or even a five will get you there, so perhaps it's not as tough as it looks but it's nice to see your ball sitting on the green waiting for you to go down there to putt. This hole like others I think looks and therefore plays easier than thirty years ago before the trees grew up. Then the extent of water and sand at this hole used to be terrifying. It was at this hole my friend Stephen Potter, the noted gamesman, tried to putt out of a bunker whereupon the great John Brown, president of the club for close on forty years, told him that if he had succeeded the bunker would at once have been deepened.

The long long fifteenth hole, 603 yards off the back tee and gently uphill most of the way, requires you to drive over the lake, but the carry is not too far. The difficulty here is the sheer length of the hole for there is hardly a bunker on it but one of them, over the back of the green, destroyed your author's best, indeed I suppose only, chance to beat 80 at Pine Valley when my third shot went too far giving a lie in a footmark and a seven instead of the birdie hoped for when the ball was in the air. Another feature of this hole is that the farther you go up this seemingly unending fairway, the narrower it gets.

The sixteenth with a big carry off the tee, a good 200 yards on the best line, takes you downhill to an attractive green beside the lake, a fine hole and not at all easy for if you opt for a shorter carry off the tee you are beset by bunkers and rough between you and the pin and almost certainly have to settle for a five.

The seventeenth, uphill all the way with its green back to back with the tenth, plays much longer than its 332 yards, so if you drive well up the curving sweeping fairway you have a good punch over a big sand waste to make the small sloping green.

So to eighteen, one of the great finishing holes in golf, 410 yards with a big plateau green sitting above a range of bunkers and in front of that a pond. At least your drive is downhill; if you don't hit a corker you must play up short of the road and pond before you hit a six or seven-iron up to the pin. But if you hit a good drive you have the chance of one of the great shots in golf, a three- or four-wood or even a three-iron up and home over all the trouble in front. And if you bring it off, what a moment to remember.

The amateur record was set at 70 in almost the first tournament organised at Pine Valley, by George Rotan in 1922, and this stood until 1961 when George Rowbotham did a 67; this has never been beaten in competition by pro or amateur. In 1937 and some years afterwards a small group of professionals was invited to a tournament at Pine Valley to play with members. As the *Short History of Pine Valley* reports, 'In our 450 rounds of play by these professionals, par was only broken twice; in 1938 by Craig Wood with 69 and in 1939 by Ed Dudley with 68.'

The first of these 72 hole tournaments in 1937, Sam Snead and Jimmy Thomson tied at 302 or 22 over par. Next year Craig Wood won with 286, only six over par.

The National

The National Golf Links of America is a splendid course, and I say course advisedly; it was the brainchild of the late Charles Blair Macdonald, who was determined—and he was a very determined and opinionated man, highly articulate and partisan—to build in America a great golf links to stand comparison with the championship links of Scotland, where he had been educated. This then was the first *great* course in the United States and in the words of Herbert Warren Wind he 'revolutionised golf architecture in America. . . . In building the National, old Charlie Macdonald was out to show Americans what a first rate British course looked like.' This he did, in the dunes and scrub land near Southampton at the far end of Long Island over 100 miles from New York. His statue stands in the Big Room at the club to testify. Links, it just isn't quite. The rough is too pronounced, the fairways a shade too lush. But seaside golf at its best it is with pure white sand in the bunkers and scrapes and when in the mood it can savage you with a terrible north-west wind off Long Island Sound.

Bernard Darwin gave this description of his first sight of the course in 1913 when it was just completed:

'I shall never forget the moment of my first arriving at the National. It was well timed, for the sun was just setting; we drove along a lonely sandy road amid huckleberry bushes. Everything was seen in a half-light, fading and fantastic, and on the horizon was a broad strip of flame, while between it and the waters of Peconic Bay there ran a narrow strip of jet black that marked the curves beyond the Bay. Here, after stifling New York, was peace and coolness and seaside golf, and, indeed, further experience has convinced me that, taking all things into consideration—the golf, the company, the view, and the cooking—there is in the world no more delightful place in which to play than the National Golf Links of America.'

Characteristic of the National are big plateau greens and big deep bunkers. Many of these—too many some think—are invisible and are only shown by marker flags. But Macdonald believed in giving everybody a chance to enjoy the course, so there is nearly always a diagonal carry to help the shorter players and sometimes an easy though longer way round to the green. The diagonal carries off the tee are a constant nagging source of worry to the ageing golfer like myself who has to pick his spot to cross or lose a shot in the sand.

As a club it is small and extremely comfortable, the service is impeccable and in my view its plain delicious food is the best in America.

The National has never sought championships or publicity of any kind and its remoteness and exclusiveness keep it relatively unknown. The Walker Cup was played here in 1922 and that is about the only famous event. What is known about it is generally inaccurate, such as the myth that all the holes are copies of famous holes in Britain. Certain holes are supposed to resemble famous holes in Britain, but on the whole they bear so little resemblance that you wouldn't recognise them unless you were told. What's more, these holes in my opinion and the opinions of many are not the strongest in the layout.

The first hole is a drive and pitch of 310 hards or so to a plateau green, small and folded; the drive is not too tough though over bunkers, and bunkers beset the left side of the green. In all there are twenty-three on this hole!

The second is the 'Sahara', an even shorter par four of 252 yards, driving over a big bunker in a hill. It is longer than the 'Sahara' at Sandwich and really resembles it very little. The next is the 'Alps', possibly a better hole than the seventeenth at Prestwick, rather longer with more bunkers, and a bigger green for the blind shot. The fourth at 172 yards is the 'Redan' and a much better hole than the 'Redan' at North Berwick, for here you can see the whole hole, as it is not blanketed by that unnecessary hill.

Five, the 'Hog's Back', is a shortish par five and once again the carry from the tee causes anxieties for those whose length is waning. Then number six is a very short par three, but the green runs across the line so the shot is very tight and the bunkers are grasping.

The seventh, called 'St Andrews', is supposed to resemble the 'Road Hole' and while the green is a fairly faithful model, the rest of the hole is totally different and much inferior. No Stationmaster's Garden, only wild rough and bunkers and no road, only a deep trap.

The eighth, the 368-yard 'Bottle', is a beauty, a really fine hole with a stiff shot to hit home to a high plateau green which slopes away from you. So with a par five of 527 yards with a tough diagonal carry off the tee and water to catch a slice, and a second shot over a big bunker in the middle of the fairway rather like 'Hell', you are at the end of the course.

Turning now for home the golf stiffens perceptibly. As my friend Ike Grainger said, 'From now on in you've got a real golf course.' The tenth, 'Shinnecock', is a 412-yard two-shotter with bunkers up by the green perceived only from their marker flags—as I have said these hidden bunkers abound at the National, rather too many I think. Then towards the bay is another two-shotter of 405 yards with half the green in a shallow natural saucer and the left-hand side on a little plateau, a very pretty green. Then the 374-yard twelfth gives us a stiff shot to a domed plateau green; as one of my partners said, it's like pitching on to a bald man's head.

The short thirteenth of 162 yards over water is supposed to be like the 'High Hole In' at St Andrews. It resembles it in difficulty in no way, and is a very colourless attempt.

But the next, the 337 yard 'Cape' hole, makes up for it, a real splendid hole—a drive over water, a bumpy fairway, more water in front of and to the right of the green, and a plateau to pitch to. The next too, 'The Narrows', is another fine two-shotter, 370 yards to a green set up to take the shot. Sixteen is another great hole, the drive over water and a real good hit needed to clear the steep confronting hill, then a resolute shot over the guarding cross-bunkers, again just a little too invisible, into the shadow of the great windmill and on to a green that for once gathers the ball.

The seventeenth, 'Peconic', 338 yards downhill doesn't sound too formidable but you have a diagonal carry off the tee over a huge bunker which makes you scratch your head to judge how much to bite off, and a range of low sandhills in front of the green. After a mishit drive a five-wood off the hard sand in the big bunker which bored home straight over the protective range right to the stick, perfectly exemplified the extreme of pleasure which only golf can afford. The last hole is a long uphill slog past the club-house, with cross bunkers to carry with your second; it is the only par five in the second nine, and not a great favourite of mine though Bernard Darwin gave it high praise. It passes near enough to the club-house for a member to have hit on to the roof twice—and played off it once—in a tournament in two successive years. The second year the ball lodged in the lead flashing of the roof and can be seen stuck there to this day.

Shinnecock Hills

Next door to the National is Shinnecock Hills built in very similar country but rather further from the sea and therefore even more of a course and less of a links. It is older than the National, being built in 1892 and therefore one of the oldest in the United States and indeed it was used for one of the earliest American Championships. In those days it was short and mild and earned the slur of being 'ladylike'. Now rebuilt and toughened up it is said by those who know to be in fact harder than the National, but I didn't play it.

Links Club

Another course of Macdonald's is the Links Club on Long Island, less than an hour's run from New York. The holes have a great similarity to those at the National though the surrounding trees give a different overall impression. But the big plateau greens are there, the big bunkers too; there is an 'Alps' hole with a blind second shot over hill and bunker, a 'Redan' but running to the right instead of the left and a better likeness to the 'High Hole In' at St Andrews than the thirteenth at the National. There are some splendid two-shot holes in this rolling course of which I would pick the fifth of 383 yards with the green on a natural plateau framed by trees as the choicest. There is a very attractive short par five at the eleventh with the second shot over water but as always Macdonald offers a way round for the short and elderly. I thought the Links Club with its delightful small club-house made from an old farmhouse an uncommonly pleasant place to spend a mild October afternoon.

The Country Club

The Country Club at Brookline is historic turf indeed, but let us get the name out of the way before we go out to play this excellent and famous golf course. It is called just, *The* Country Club, not the Brookline Country Club

Golf in the shadow of the Rock of Gavea near Rio de Janeiro in Brazil
(*Carlos Taylor*)

ABOVE Golf at Crans-sur-Sierre in Switzerland, high in the Alps above the Rhône valley. The spotted dog is no relation of ours (*Swiss National Tourist Office*)

BELOW A French golf links. Playing amongst the dunes and pines at Le Touquet on the Channel coast (*French Government Tourist Office*)

ABOVE Golf in Hong Kong. The seaside course at Shek-O, a short and amusing layout on Hong Kong Island (*Golf Illustrated*)
BELOW The second green on the West Course of the Royal Melbourne Club where the Canada Cup was played in 1959. Tea-tree scrub, which is such a feature of Australian courses, is very prominent here (*Dr W. I. Whitton*)

ABOVE A new layout in the south of Spain at Sotogrande where Robert Trent Jones has created a new course among the cork trees. The player is making a pitch shot to the short par four 5th (*Sotogrande Club*)

RIGHT Golf at Pau on the French slopes of the Pyrenees. It is the oldest club outside the British Commonwealth, older indeed than any club in England except Blackheath and Old Manchester. It was founded by British visitors in 1856 (*Karquel by permission of French Government Tourist Office*) or by any other such title, simply because it was the first in America when it was formed in 1882. So there is no need for any qualifying additions; in this it is like the British postage stamps which, because they were the first, are the only ones in the world which don't carry their country's name.

Two U.S. Opens have been played here, including the most famous of all, four U.S. Amateurs, the Walker Cup, the Ladies' and lesser events.

I don't think anyone can dispute that the U.S. Open of 1913 was the most famous of all, for it marked one of the great climacterics of the game, the day when it could be proved that America could take on the best in the world and beat them. A day when the young White Hope came from behind to overtake two great British pros, until then the lions of golf, to force a tie for first place and then, on the next day, to shatter them in the play-off. No wonder Francis Ouimet's victory electrified all America and sent the popularity of the game bounding forward to the unheard of heights of today. It has justly been called the most famous round of golf ever played. What is more, no winner, and in 1913 he was no more than a boy of twenty, wore his laurels with more modesty and grace until his death, only a few days before I wrote this. Ouimet had a host of friends across the Atlantic; he is, so far, the only American to captain the Royal and Ancient and on playing himself in he committed a graceful illegality. The caddy who gathered his ball, and he had to be far far down the course, was rewarded by a five-dollar gold piece—instead of the traditional sovereign—which a U.S. citizen was not allowed to own.

Ouimet's play in 1913, in soaking rain on a sodden course, against Vardon and Ray has often been told, and never better than by Bernard Darwin, who was there. The bare facts are that he had a terrible 43 for the first nine of the last round and a five at the tenth which was then a short hole, so that in the end he had to do the last six holes in 22 shots, two under par, to tie. He holed a short mashie chip for a birdie three at the thirteenth, got a par five at the next and scrambled a par four at the fifteenth. That left the last three holes to be done in one under par. At the short sixteenth where he hoped for his second birdie, he had to hole a horrible eight-footer for his par. Then at the dog-leg seventeenth he holed a most difficult twelve yard putt downhill, right into the middle of the hole for a birdie three and then he was safe home with four at the last. Next day, when no one thought he stood a chance against the British giants, he just slaughtered them with a 72 against Vardon's 77 and Ray's 78.

Now for a round out there. The course is only about seven miles from the centre of Boston but in secluded grounds well covered with trees and scrub and rolling grass plentifully sprinkled with rock outcrops. The course is fairly but not inordinately long but gives you some run, and I would say that its characteristics are small greens with pronounced slopes, close

Golf in America – the East

bunkering, and for the U.S.A. a surprising number of shots where you can't see the bottom of the pin. There is also a surprising number of short par fours, excellent holes they are too, but it's unusual to find in a first-class championship course from the mid-tees lengths of 290 and 280 in the first half, both of them uphill though and a 330-yarder on this half too, with a 310-yard tenth. This with my decaying length suits me fine, especially as there are only three short holes. However, there are plenty of big par fours to stretch you out and one pretty big par five.

You start out innocently enough over the old polo ground inside the old race course which survives as an oval gravel road but even if you have all the world to drive into, your second has to be very long to get over the road and up to a small green if you want a par. Next you beat uphill at the 290-yard second and pitch to a small saucer of green very much beset by bunkers. The third is a beauty of 430 yards; you drive down into a narrowing valley with great banks concealing rock outcrops converging on the fairway from either side about 270 yards out. Over or between these you go to a small tightly trapped green with a lake behind it.

Four is only 330 yards but after crossing a deep ravine with your drive you seem to have the steam taken out of the shot by the swell of the fairway so that your pitch on to the green in a dell, over the cross-bunkers, can be a stiffer shot than you expect.

At the fifth you can but should not, slice out-of-bounds, though Ouimet did in the 1913 play-off and recovered with his second ball. This hole needs a fine second shot over bunkers to a small green sloping from the right, as it is 415 yards long—a difficult tough four. The 280-yard sixth uphill is bunkers, bunkers all the way and a tiny green when you get there—not easy.

The seventh is the first par three, a stiff iron or spoon shot of 190 yards to a plateau green with bunkers on the left and humps of rough grass all too near on the right. The rough indeed *is* rough at the Country Club, and no nonsense.

Eight is uphill and if you can't drive very far you can only see the top of the pin, though with beginner's luck I did get myself a birdie putt there. The 415-yard ninth is back parallel and again the shot in is blind over the crest of a hill. This brings you back near the club-house and is a change from the original order of the holes.

Ten is a drive and pitch back again with a big hill to carry in front of the green. After that we have a superb double curvature par five, driving up a valley, clearing a big shoulder on the second shot and a small ditch and then pitching up to a small plateau with three big spectacular bunkers in the plateau face. After that we have a minute par three of 130 yards downhill but the green is tiny and doesn't gather you at all; the bunkers do.

Thirteen is hard beating to get home in two over cross-bunkers in front of the small green. The fourteenth is a fine uphill par five of 515 yards which plays all its length, though Don Callaghan, the pro, was nearly home in two against me, and got a birdie easily.

At the fifteenth we come back to the club-house again with a 415-yard par four; we drive over a hill but again there are many traps round the small green with a good slope to it, just as thirteen had.

The short sixteenth is not too tough if you get over the guarding traps. Then comes 'Ouimet's hole', the seventeenth, a dog-leg left; now there is a beautiful plateau green beyond bunkers—several—but I believe in 1913 the hole was shorter, with the green more away to the left. Today at 360 yards it is a lovely hole and at the angle of the dog-leg there is still 'Vardon's Bunker' which can spoil your game today as it spoiled his in 1913, and Jacky Cupit's in the 1963 anniversary open. The last hole is like the first in that you drive over the racetrack and on to the vast polo field but you'd better hit a good one as the green is perched up above big bunkers right on the green's edge, so if it's only 390 yards, your last shot is all carry and farther than you feel it ought to be. That is the round on the original course, or, more properly, the modified original course; for the 1963 Open some holes were brought in from the new nine, three I think, but otherwise Old Faithful stood up to the modern battering rams, and very well too, for in windy weather only three scores beat 70 I believe in the whole tournament.

Philadelphia has long been a stronghold of cricket in the United States and has fathered one of the greatest fast-medium bowlers of all time, J. B. King, who, if he had had the opportunities of England or Australia, might have ranked with Maurice Tate or Bill O'Reilly—even Sydney Barnes possibly.

Merion

In 1865 the Merion Cricket Club was formed and continues to this day. The cricketers took to golf and built themselves a course about a mile from their cricket ground in 1896. By 1910 this was looking insufficient and the Merion Club broke new ground at Ardmore with an entirely new eighteen-hole course, the famous East Course, and followed it with a second eighteen a year or so later. Golf is now independent of the Cricket Club.

The East Course, which was opened for play in 1912, was the work of one of the members, Mr Hugh I. Wilson, and so indestructible has his design been that the course has been hardly altered to this day and still, in spite of its limited length, stands up to the assaults of today's great hitters. Only once has Merion been made to look small and that was in the Eisenhower Trophy team matches in 1960 when Jack Nicklaus while he was still an amateur carded 66, 67, 68 and 68 to set a record total of 269 and scatter the invaders to the four winds.

Many famous events have taken place here. The Amateur Championship of 1916 in which the infant Jones survived two rounds; the championship of 1924 in which young Jones won his first Amateur title and most famous of all the Amateur of 1930 in which the veteran Jones, all of twenty-eight years old now, won the last title of the Grand Slam, the greatest performance by the greatest golfer of all time. Quoting Bernard Darwin once more:

'He retired at the right time and could say with Charles Lamb "I have worked task work and have the rest of the day to myself." After Tom Cribb had beaten Molineaux for the second time in the great battle of Thistleton Gap it was decided that he need never fight again but should bear the title of Champion to the end of his days. I think that most golfers in their hearts grant the same privilege to Bobby Jones.'

The U.S. Open has been here twice, in 1934 and in 1950, the year in which Hogan made his first great comeback after his fearful motor smash of the year before. The U.S. Amateur returned in 1966 under stroke play rules—and more's the pity say I—and was notable for a foreign victory, only the third in the history of the Championship, by Gary Cowan of Canada.

The layout of the East Course, which is remarkably compact, is what we would call parkland, good grass and fine trees, with some strong natural features including two streams and a large disused quarry, of which more in a moment. The bunkering is severe and plentiful; the traps are close to the greens, deep and beautifully moulded.

We start with a heavily bunkered dog-leg four of moderate length and here we notice at once a Merion feature, the baskets on the flagsticks instead of flags, a thing I'd not seen for forty years. It is claimed here, and I don't doubt it's true, that these sticks and baskets are the lineal descendants of the shepherd's crooks and lunch baskets which used to mark the holes in Scotland years ago. Next we have a long long par five uphill, followed by an excellent 'reverse-Redan' hole of 175 yards or so with a plateau green and deep bunkering along the right flank. We then hit an even longer par five with an uphill drive but then mostly downhill with the third shot over a small stream.

This stream nags at us all the way along the fifth as it runs all along the left-hand side of the fairway whose natural slope draws the ball towards it. So does the green which has a pronounced slope, so that getting home in two here is a feat of both strength and accuracy. Six is another long par four, after which the course changes character, offering from the regular tees seven holes on end without exceeding 400 yards on any of them.

Of these the seventh is a beauty, hitting up to a plateau green heavily bunkered below and to the left, while the eighth is a devil, only 340 yards long but with a tiny green on a shelf and deep close bunkering to get over—and no way round.

The ninth is a one-shot over water, farther than it looks but not too tough, and the tenth, another dog-leg, is perhaps the least difficult on the course. So far so good, but now we come to number eleven with its plaque commemorating the hole where Jones beat Gene Homans by eight and seven in the final of the U.S. Amateur in 1930. This is a devil of a hole; you start with a nice drive downhill to a pleasant flat stance, then in front of you you see a small, tiny even, pear-shaped green with a bunker eating into the left side and Cobb's Creek, winding past the front entrance and swirling round in a curve to embrace the green to the right and rear. Well perhaps you have only a seven-iron to play or something like it but the penalties of failure are awe-inspiring. I thought I'd 'played it' but the ball slid off into the bunker and the shot out of that on to the minute green with the creek behind made the Road bunker shot at St Andrews at once come to mind. Well, we can comfort ourselves that Sarazen took seven here and so lost the 1934 Open.

The twelfth, a dog-leg uphill, is not too brutal but the thirteenth is a tricky little par three, with a small green and deep bunkers right alongside. Then come two longer par fours dog-leg left and dog-leg right with out-of-bounds on the 'leg side' to use a cricket term and then we must brace ourselves for a tremendous finish. At the sixteenth, 445 yards off the back tees, 425 from ours, we have to hit our second across the old quarry now grassed over but still a deep pit with three bunkers yawning at you in it and a lot of wild broom brushes; it's as tough a shot as the famous second to the eighteenth at Pine Valley. Even if you play short you still have to hit a stiff third shot, a five-iron or something like it to get up.

At seventeen you come back across the quarry with a long long one-shot hole beautifully bunkered and very much farther than it looks—a full belt with a driver for me.

The last hole over two ravines is another beautiful hole and the small crown-green a really hard one to find. The most celebrated stroke here was Hogan's 285th shot in the 1950 U.S. Open, a full-bore number one-iron second shot right up to the stick which secured him a tie while he was still in severe pain from his motor smash. He won the play-off easily.

Garden City

Garden City, about twenty miles from New York on Long Island, is another American championship course with a venerable history, the U.S. Amateur first being played here in 1900 and the U.S. Open for the first and

Golf in America – the East

only time in 1902. The Walker Cup match was held here in 1924. It was also the home green of that formidable competitor, Walter J. Travis, who won the British Amateur, against all the odds, at Sandwich in 1904—the first foreigner to do so—and the U.S. Amateur thrice.

It was here too in 1936 that the late Jack McLean did something to redeem our prestige after the disastrous Walker Cup match at Pine Valley at the end of which 'our score was as blank as our faces', to use a favourite quotation of Bernard Darwin's. McLean played beautifully in the U.S. Amateur and reached the final against Johnny Fischer; he was deprived of the thirty-fourth hole by a self-imposed stymie, halved the thirty-fifth in birdie fours and so reached the last hole one up and one to play. He was robbed of victory by a two from his opponent and lost to another birdie at the thirty-seventh hole—a cruel end. It was left to the late great Pam Barton—she was afterwards killed on active service in World War II—to bring home a win for Britain that year as she was not only British Champion but she also won the American Ladies' Championship, a rare victory. Since that year British golf successes in the United States have been conspicuous by their absence save for a gallantly halved match by our ladies in the Curtis Cup in 1958 and a halved game in the Walker Cup series in 1965, which surely ended with one of the blackest days in the history of British amateur golf.

Well I thought that Garden City was a pleasant contrast to a lot of ordinary run-of-mill golf in Canada and the U.S., much tougher, with carries from the tee, the rough really rough and deep testing bunkers. A grassland course, it has an unconventional layout for these days with only three short holes including the eighteenth over a lily pond and the holes go round in a single loop. They have also had the skill to make several short par fours both difficult and good. The first hole is one of these with a tight shot over a guarding bunker and the ninth (316 yards) also a difficult pitch. The only par three in the first nine is the second; here a narrow valley runs away from the tee and the green is located on top of the right-hand escarpment of this with a deep bunker in the valley bottom, so making a sort of 'Redan' hole. Some good two-shotters follow, notably the very attractive 405-yard eighth where you have to get home over a road and shallow cross-bunkers; this with a couple of par fives makes up the first nine holes. Coming in there are two notable short holes, the island green at the twelfth and the 151 yard eighteenth.

Ekwanok

I was very glad to see that Ekwanok at Manchester, Vermont, was numbered among the elect, having played very happily there with my friend

Rush in the autumn of 1967. It was host to the U.S. Amateur in 1914 when Francis Ouimet demonstrated that his winning the Open the year before was not a flash in the pan, and it still offers a very attractive test of golf even if it caters principally to holiday visitors. Located in a shallow valley with spurs of the Green Mountains to east and west and overlooked by Mount Equinox, 3,816 feet high, it is at its best when the autumn colours blaze among the millions of hardwoods which cover the mountain sides on either hand. The course which is in parkland is not inordinately long or outrageously difficult but it contains some outstanding holes which pluck at the memory, notably the par-four third of 343 yards guarded by water, and the immense 598-yard seventh where after an exhilarating long drive downhill you have to cross a big steep hill with your second to get a sight of the green for your third; a big hole in every sense of the word.

More attractive is the 328-yard eighth with a shot to a tightly-bunkered green, rather similar to the 323-yard fourteenth. There is also that rarity in American golf, a completely blind second shot to a guarded green, the 357-yard twelfth. The last four holes, all stiff par fours, give a no-nonsense finish, the sixteenth and eighteenth at 404 and 403 yards uphill especially.

Baltusrol

I am indebted to my friend Pat Ward Thomas for explaining the origin of the name of Baltusrol, the big championship course near Springfield, New Jersey, some twenty miles south-west of New York. It owes its name to the murder for gain of a Dutch farmer named Baltus Roll in 1823[1] who lived up in the woods nearby. The course now consists of two full-size eighteen-hole parkland circuits, of which the present championship layout, the Lower Course, has the forbidding finish of two par-five holes aggregating over 1,100 yards of which the seventeenth is said to be 623 yards off the back tee. It might be Moor Park only the golf is a good deal longer and harder. Earlier championships—and Baltusrol has had more than most courses—were either on the Upper Course or on the original first layout. In 1954 Ed Furgol, for all he had a withered left arm, won the U.S. Open here in a dramatic fashion. Dick Mayer, who won in a later year, blew his chances with an eight at the last hole and Littler missed a putt that would have tied; Furgol in trouble in the trees at the last played away on to the Upper Course, got home in three and won the title. In 1967 Jack Nicklaus gave the great long course a pasting though for a time the impossible seemed possible and Marty Fleckman, then still an amateur, led after three rounds.

My own experience of Baltusrol was in 1956 and memory is a bit hazy

[1] Dan Jenkins, however, prefers 1831.

though I see my card shows that the four short holes treated me well with three threes and a deuce. I also remember that our pleasure in the Lower Course was not sufficiently damped by soaking wet rain accompanying us on the inward nine to keep us from playing them. It was a pleasure too that day to meet some of the great in the pro shop, Johnny Farrell, U.S. Open Champion in 1928, whom I'd last seen at the Ryder Cup at Leeds in 1929 and now as grey, lean and handsome as the Shah of Persia. Even more, it was pleasing to meet the Cornishman Long Jim Barnes who had won the U.S. Open in 1921 and ours in 1925 still tall and straight as a ramrod at sixty-seven and see him poling out some shots to illustrate some point he was making to a young assistant.

Baltusrol's most famous hole is the short fourth on the Lower Course over a long stretch of water. The green is built above a low stone wall and slopes up from the brink to three bunkers at the back; if you're short it's death but if too far a return shot of the utmost delicacy is needed. Moreover the green is rather set across the line of play.

Olympia Fields

My recollection of the championship course, one of the five at Olympia Fields, outside Chicago, which I played in 1954 is equally dim in the mists of memory as I only recall one beautiful two-shot hole, the third, surrounded by trees, because I suppose I hit a fine shot up to the high green; I can see my three-iron now going straight for the flag. Then the mist comes down and all that I remember is sweltering searing heat.

Country Club of Detroit

We can do somewhat better with the Country Club of Detroit, as I played there in 1967 albeit on a bitter cold windy day in early May with the wind off Lake St Clair. Luckily Fred Kammer, the former U.S. Walker Cup player, who was in the party, had thoughtfully provided a flask of vodka for without some external source of warmth a ride in a golf cart was a distressing experience.

The course is on fairly flat parkland with the club-house on a small knoll which you play down from at the first and tenth and up to at the ninth and eighteenth. The elm trees in an area famous for them are a big feature of the course and it is a grievous pity that the Dutch elm disease seems to have their days numbered. The elms come into play at several holes notably the third where a group of them dominate the play for the whole 500 yards.

The course is considerably bunkered with some attractive moulding of the built-up green at holes like the short fifth and eighth and the two-shot sixth. As in so many American courses the second half is appreciably the longer of the two.

The Country Club of Detroit has been used twice for the U.S. Amateur Championship notably in 1954 when a young man called Arnold Palmer, unknown in Britain, beat Robert Sweeney, who was well known here, by a hole in the final. Palmer was promptly picked for the Walker Cup side of 1955 but turned pro instead of playing. He has been heard of since.

Oakland Hills

We will end this long chapter with a visit to Oakland Hills, fifteen miles or so outside Detroit, a pleasure enjoyed in May 1967. By this time the impossible 'Monster' that Trent Jones had created from a rather ordinary grassland course by Donald Ross for the 1951 Open Championship had been reviewed and restored to a more lenient layout. Hogan who won in 1951 is reported to have said, 'If I had to play that course every week, I'd get into another business.' Nevertheless the 'Hawk' cut the 'Monster' down to size with scores of 76, 73, 71 and 67, the last one of the greatest rounds in the history of the game.

Since then Oakland Hills has, as Dan Jenkins puts it, 'finally gotten into that sound category: tough but fair'. I must say that artificial as it is and must be on such land I found it a very fine course indeed, long, tough and very heavily bunkered, the greens small and with tiny entrances. If I hadn't had a nine-iron that was 'hot' that day I'd have had a very rough time of it. The short holes are in absolute minefields of bunkers, notably the thirteenth which is almost completely surrounded and the long uphill seventeenth which has huge and deep traps on all sides.

Several of the two-shot holes are formidably long, five of them over 410 yards and those that are shorter are suitably protected and difficult of access, like the splendid uphill sixth and eleventh. The most famous hole of all is the 389-405-yard sixteenth, the front of the green protected by a lake and the back by a group of four traps to discourage the safe long shot, especially the small pot just at the back of the green. Dan Jenkins, who makes this his sixteenth in 'the best eighteen golf holes in America', has this to say:

'The sixteenth hole is a perfect example of all that is excellent about the course. There would appear to be room for numerous blunders, but actually you cannot err and get a par unless you know, for example, how to hit a shot from a lake bottom. This hole, the Lake Hole, as it is called, was always dangerous, but gradual improvements have made it superb. Robert Trent Jones moved the green so that it protrudes into the water like a

Golf in America – the East

thumb. Behind it he inserted an array of bunkers, one of them a tiny pot trap that is a major factor in how the hole is played. The approach to the green, usually hit with a mid-iron, is a rugged challenge when the pin is set to the right, as it frequently is, because the shot must carry the water. Over 200 balls a month are swept from the lake bottom, which is telling you something you would as soon not know. Moreover the shot must bite hard on the narrow green and stop short of the bunkers after it has cleared the lake. The small pot bunker quells the itch to hit just a bit long on purpose, because an explosion shot out of it back toward the water is enough to make the short ribs twitch. Finally, the green has two levels, and if you are on the wrong one you are in bogey land. But the trouble actually begins back on the slightly elevated tee. A cluster of trees about 100 yards out, sitting just in the right-hand rough, is inconveniently tall and cleverly placed, making it much too risky to try to lop off part of the 405 yards of distance by going to the right.'

For my part I was glad to settle for an inglorious five.

11 Other foreign parts

Keeping to the rule laid down for this book that all the courses we visit are within the personal knowledge of the author makes this chapter even more of a ragbag than any of the others with so many notable omissions through lack of knowledge that I refuse to list them. Pains have been taken, too, to try to avoid making a 'look where I've been' catalogue of courses abroad, so I will try to limit the comment to places and courses of some special note.

Scandinavia

Starting in Europe with Scandinavia, the limitations of the author's knowledge are conspicuous for all Sweden which is now full of good golf is unfortunately a closed book save for one round at Lidingö near Stockholm; indeed I can only recall playing on two other courses in Scandinavia, Helsingør in Denmark, a pleasant parkland course, and Trondheim in central Norway which at one time had a distinction, as it claimed to be the most northerly golf course in the world, rather over 62 degrees north. This claim can no longer be sustained for there is a golf course in the southern extremity of Iceland which may well be farther north, and new construction in Sweden has put a course in Luleå away north of either, at about 66 degrees north; then Alaska may beat all of these but I've no check here. Certain it is that the claim for this distinction for Yellowknife, on the Great Slave Lake in the North-West Territory of Canada, must be rejected. I once had a game at Yellowknife, a strange experience on a course entirely built on sand. We played a match that lasted two days, i.e. from 11.45 p.m. on one day to 12.15 a.m. on the next in the midnight twilight of high summer beset by a cloud of mosquitoes like a fog, a bizarre game.

Other foreign parts

While on the subject of northness, we might just touch on southness though I can't claim to have played very far 'down' at all, not even as far south as Dunedin in New Zealand, but there is always some interest in such records. I had imagined that the most southerly course would be at Dunedin or perhaps Commodoro Rivadavia in the Argentine, but I had forgotten that the Falkland Islands, about 52 degrees south, had been settled by Scottish sheep farmers, but Punta Arenas in Chile even beats that with its club at 55 degrees south. Further south still, near Ushuaia at the south end of Tierro del Fuego there are three primitive holes at a resort hotel which may one day become a course.

We have now strayed away from Trondheim and its historic turf but it stays in my memory as a pleasant, nine-hole layout amid fir trees and birches; at mid-summer they play an all night tournament.

Moving south I have nothing to say of Germany though golf is now flourishing there, or about Belgium, and only one short comment on Holland where I have played the links at Wassenaar north of The Hague. I say links advisedly for this good natural course is laid out in a huge area of dunes and links-land that stretches for miles along the Dutch coast; you might be at Burnham or Birkdale.

Switzerland

Switzerland now has a magnificent course at Crans-sur-Sierre high above the Rhône Valley, which alas I have not played since 1925 when it was called Montana and the nine holes of golf was primitive in the extreme. Now you have the real thing there and in addition one of the finest views in Europe across the deep valley to the Pennine Alps with snow peaks like the huge Weisshorn, 14,800 feet, the Zinal Rothorn and the Dent Blanche most prominent. I have a soft spot for the little old course here, for on it, at an early age, I was put to play an 'International Match' with Dr Green and myself 'representing' England and the local pro A. Duplan and Dr Matthey for Switzerland; we got thrashed too, in front of a gallery of sixteen spectators.

France

Moving into France, where golf is growing fast and continuing its tradition of raising a first-class group of lady players, it would be appropriate to start in the south, for at Pau in the foothills of the Pyrenees is the first golf club on the Continent and after Calcutta and Bombay the oldest outside the British Isles. Unfortunately it is off my list, so there is nothing to say.

So let us move on to Chiberta a couple of miles up the coast from Biarritz where there is an excellent golf course, a little like Cypress Point in California, in that it is a mixture of sandy holes among the pine trees and links holes on the close-cropped turf along the shore. The links holes from two thru' eight as the Americans say and from eleven to fourteen are the real thing with natural plateaux like those at the second and sixth greens, humps, hollows and crisp turf. I thought this was a thoroughly enjoyable course and to be preferred to the venerable Biarritz golf course up by the lighthouse which is much older.

In this neighbourhood, a little further south are the two good inland courses of La Nivelle and Chantaco directed by M. René Lacoste whose distinction at lawn tennis barely exceeds that of his wife and daughter at golf. These courses are on either side of the Nivelle River a couple of miles inland from St Jean de Luz. I didn't play La Nivelle but found Chantaco very enjoyable, a heathland type of course, with pines and hard woods, hilly and attractive; the only weak spot is the finish, three holes on very flat land in a meadow down by the river. The scenery with the mountain of La Rhune is pleasant and so is the neighbouring village of Ascain where you can eat well and the local men play Pelota in the village square. There is another course just north of Biarritz on the coast at Hossegor. I don't know about the golf but the name attracts me for it is derived from the British Horse Guards who were encamped here in the winter of 1813–14 after Wellington and the allied troops had driven the French out of Spain and invaded France.

This area of France has produced some fine golfers besides the distinguished ladies, notably Arnaud Massy who came from Biarritz and was the first foreigner ever to win the British Open Championship which he carried off at Hoylake in 1907; he nearly did it again in 1911 at Sandwich when he tied for first but lost on the play-off to Vardon. Another notable is Jean Baptiste Ado who hits the ball a country mile, one of the longest hitters in the game.

There is a fine stretch of dune country near the mouth of the Somme and several golf links could be put here with room for many more. Two have been built at Le Touquet with a short nine as well. The old course is largely among trees but the new has a more open layout. One pleasing characteristic is the presence of wild Evening Primroses, with their lemon-yellow flowers, in the rough. I made a special pilgrimage to Le Touquet to play these courses but a full gale blew up in the Channel with a great soak of rain so that is a pleasure deferred.

Spain

Golf is rising fast in Spain and new courses are springing up on all the holiday coasts. Moreover it has one of the leading golf architects in Europe at the present time in the person of Javier Arana. He made his name with the big sweeping hilly course, the Club de Campo, on the outskirts of Madrid which is big in all senses of the word, indeed a little too big for me with its hills and dales. Subsequently Arana laid out a fine course at Bilbao on the north coast which I don't know and another, Guadalmina, on the Costa del Sol, which I do, in sight of the Rock of Gibraltar; this course runs up a river valley inland from the coast, after a short first hole parallel to the shore, so is in no sense a links, but it offers some attractive golf, quite long enough for a holiday coast and some plateau greens in a mild ridge which runs up one side of the valley. The country round Guadalmina is charming with a range of craggy hills close to the coast. Without a doubt Arana's best-known and most famous course is El Prat, near the Barcelona Airport, on land very close to the Mediterranean. This ground is virtually links-land, hard spare turf and sandy subsoil with liberal groves of umbrella pines and palm trees; a salt lagoon also helps to make life difficult. These pines make an exceeding tight shot at the 140-metre third hole for example while an odd hazard, or rather interruption, at the short eleventh is an airport marker light. Although the ground is pretty flat some judicious building up and moulding of greens has been done and the flatness never becomes dullness. An excellent course.

Returning to Madrid I must make a short reference to the oldest club there, the Real Club de Puerta de Hierro, for I have played there so often and once and only once in an Open Championship; I entered the Spanish Open in 1958 as a joke and nobody said me nay so I played though did not make 'the Cut'. Peter Alliss, with whom I could possibly have been confused, in fact won, with a ridiculously low score; in his last round I saw him reach the eighteenth green from the tee, a distance of 385 metres, downhill, with his fifty-ninth stroke. It is true that the Puerta de Hierro course, or rather courses—for there are twenty-seven holes—are rather short and on the main course there are six par-three holes, four in the first half, including a formidable first hole across a deep cleft in front of the tee to catch an early morning top. These deep ravines, so deep as to be crossed by bridges, are a feature of the course. There are however plenty of good two-shot holes, notably the twelfth and thirteenth with the drive at each into a deep valley to be followed by a punch with an iron up to the green. Of the short holes, the third, to a small plateau green is the pick I think.

The most famous Spanish golfers to date, the Miguel brothers, are attached to Puerta de Hierro, where indeed they started life as caddies; the best of these, Angel, won the individual prize in the Canada Cup competition at Mexico City in 1958, the year that Ireland won the Cup, after a tie with Harry Bradshaw; it is hard to imagine two players less alike than these two must have looked in playing the tie.

In many ways my favourite course in Spain is at Pedreña on the north coast across the great harbour of Santander. This course produced that fine professional Ramón Sota. You embark in a small ferry called 'Caddi II' and chug across the harbour to land at the club steps and there you are. It is not great golf and there are no tremendous holes on it but it is a beautiful place to play golf and on fine days the view up and down the coast is one of sea and of row behind row of mountains, the whole chain of the Cantabric mountains, crowned by the snow-clad Picos de Europa to the westward. It is all good fun and you ought to have a score under 80 without bursting your boilers. There are some attractive trees on the course, otherwise it is heavily rolling hilly grassland with some delightful wild flowers including the vivid blue Lithospermum Heavenly Blue in the rough at the top of the course by the tenth green. Pedreña is strongly recommended and so at the end of the day is a visit to the Bar del Puerto in Santander for some fresh sardines grilled for supper or other seafood, perhaps a lobster.

To finish Spain we should without doubt take a look at Sotogrande on the Mediterranean coast a few miles from La Linea the Spanish town which lies opposite Gibraltar. Here a big land development has been launched with American money—you can get an acre of land and a fine house for about $100,000—and already a splendid estate is taking shape; several houses have been built and a full length golf course laid out. The course was designed by Robert Trent Jones and bears all his characteristic features, huge long tees, big greens or special shapes for alternative pin positions, some fierce, almost freakish, slopes in the greens and a wide, too wide perhaps, use of water as a hazard. Two lakes of some size have been created and another natural one enlarged.

The course runs inland from the sea, over some flat ground first and then works towards a slope and hill well clad with cork oaks; the first nine holes among the trees have their attractions especially the two-shot seventh with a downhill drive and then a short or fairly short iron shot to a green protected on the right by a small stone-banked lake. Some fierce slopes there are on this green and also on the short par-fourth fifth, such that your ball can run back off the green if not 'up'. The third, another short par four, has a strange green shaped like a four-bladed propeller or a four-leafed clover, protected by bunkers which permits some fantastic pin placings. The course indeed might almost be part of the Royal Montreal layout and I am sorry to say that I don't care for it very much.

South America

We must now take off on a far flight and just have a brief look at a few courses of merit which I have met in South America.

Other foreign parts

The first of these is Gavea in Brazil on the coast south of Rio de Janeiro beyond Copacabana and Ipanema Beaches. The location of Gavea—which Herbert Warren Wind tells us means Crow's Nest—is spectacular in the extreme as it is dominated by the huge monolithic Rock of Gavea which hangs 2,000 feet over the course like a great monster. The course is divided sharply between the holes among the hills—the whole of the first nine and last four—and the five holes down on the flat sandy land near the beach, a belt of something like links-land though shaded with palm trees.

The first nine holes are hilly in the extreme and rather a strain on tired old legs but there are four par threes to help you along, two, the third and sixth, a hard punch up to a plateau green and one, the eighth, a great sweeping iron or five-wood from the top of the course to a green protected by water, eighty-five feet below. The pick of the two-shot holes is undoubtedly the beautiful downhill fourth over a stream. The second half is much longer, and less picturesque.

I would regard a game at 'Gavea' as a must in spite of a virulent attack made on my ankles by some species of stinging ant at the ninth which burned like fire for some minutes, longer indeed, and was only assuaged by an ice-charged gin and tonic, two in fact, as the recommended remedy.

In the Argentine, the country round the estuary of the River Plate, the Camp, is as flat as a pancake and all round the great city of Buenos Aires the construction of golf courses—and there are many of them—has had to recognise this awkward fact. The course of the Jockey Club, the most famous, has therefore presented a problem to its architect, Dr Mackenzie. It has been met by a number of ingenious scrapings and shifting of earth in the moulding and shaping of swales, mounds and plateaux on which greens and their approaches have been set; for the rest, trees dictate the play to the holes. The result will give us a good test of golf, as good as any in the Argentine, but the stigma of artificiality cannot be escaped.

The Canada Cup was played here in 1962 and Sam Snead and Arnold Palmer beat de Vicenzo and de Luca for the first prize and de Vicenzo won the individual prize with a score of 276. De Vincenzo is, and over many years has been, the greatest of the many fine Argentine professionals; he set the seal on his career in 1967 when at the eleventh hour he won the British Open Championship at Hoylake to everyone's delight. And, of course, but for a clerical error would have tied for the Masters' in 1968.

At La Paz in Bolivia, the highest capital in the world, there is a golf course at the southern end of the city which I visited in 1967, and there is another in the city too, I believe. What we saw lay under the great snow-covered volcano of Illimani which is 21,000 feet high, and was a pleasant grassy course. This may well be the highest golf course in the world though I am not sure but it certainly lies at about 11,000 feet. I have not been able to find out how it compares with Oruro also in Bolivia in this respect or with anything on the altiplano of Peru. The lowest course is I suppose one which I have been told is to be found at the Dead Sea, while there is another below sea level at Stovepipe Wells in Death Valley in the desert of California.

Pacific

Our last area is the huge Pacific and little enough to comment on I fear. Nevertheless on the way there it would be enjoyable to stop briefly in Hong Kong—it always is—and if we can't find time to play up at the big courses at Fan Ling near the Chinese frontier, it is fun to have a round on the short Shek-O course on Hong Kong Island. This course lies along the edge of the ocean, where there is a fine rocky coast, on which the seas burst robustly, with a few holes on the landward side. Shek-O is not particularly long or hard, under 5,000 yards, but I've always enjoyed a round there. I was to have played on the short course of the Royal Hong Kong at Deep Water Bay, also on the Island, last time I was there, but the tail end of a typhoon passed by and we had nineteen inches of rain in twenty-four hours and that was that. In Hong Kong the caddies are usually women, and pretty mature matrons at that. I wonder what the devil they think we are trying to do.

Australia

So to Australia for the last review. When I am in Sydney my friend Buckley always takes me to the Australian Golf Club in Kensington and an excellent course it is. It lies on crisp dry sandy soil with few trees which gives almost links-land turf though the urban surroundings tend to repel the idea. I like its plain assertive name too, The Australian Golf Club, with no geographical additions, like The Country Club near Boston. Down to Melbourne and we can find excellent golf again especially on the courses on the Sand Belt which lies to the south-east of the city near Port Philip Bay; this is a band of pure white sand on which excellent golfing turf can be grown. The oldest and most famous club here is Royal Melbourne which has two fine full-length courses. The considerable bunkering at Royal Melbourne attracted the comment of Herbert Warren Wind, the American writer and critic, who praised the courses highly.

What especially caught my eye was the characteristic Australian rough reinforced by thickets of tea-tree and mimosa, wattle in the 'strian vocabulary, which make it so unlike anything else in the world. Another peculiarity of Australian golf is the number of left-handed players which I

Other foreign parts

believe may be as high as 25 per cent of the total, far higher than elsewhere in the golfing world; certain it is that one four-ball game which I saw at Royal Melbourne was made up of four left-handers, a thing I have never seen anywhere before or since. Whether this has anything to do with the Australian fondness for cricket where left-handers are welcome I don't know, or is it related to being 'down under', a situation which is alleged to send the bath water swirling out of the plug hole in the opposite direction to the prevailing direction up here? The West Course at Royal Melbourne, which is usually regarded as the Championship circuit, has housed the Canada Cup, in 1959, which the Australians Peter Thomson and Kel Nagle appropriately won, although the Canadian Stan Leonard beat Peter Thomson in a sudden death play-off for the individual title at 275.

Lastly in Australia and lastly in this book let us if we possibly can get down from Melbourne to Barwon Heads, beyond Geelong, right at the narrow mouth of Port Philip Bay, for here is a true golf links, fairways, greens, rough and atmosphere all correct and a most refreshing and enjoyable place to play golf. With these rolling fairways, piled up dunes, sandhills, plateaux and dells and the colour and pace of the grass you might be at Dornoch except that the golf is not so tough, or to be truthful, not so good. Barwon Heads is fun, it's good golf and there are some splendid holes but it could be moulded just a little with advantage; and being right on the coast it can certainly feel the wind and it can be cold if you get a blow from the south.

Barwon Heads to Dornoch is a far cry and in between these two links is every conceivable type of golf course, some in the most improbable places and unsuitable ground. The inventors of the game as we know it, a hundred years or so ago would have been astonished at the places where the game is now played but golf has been adaptable enough to survive layouts in tropical jungles or where no blade of grass can grow. That is fine but to my taste the links-land, wherever it may be, is the best place to play the best of all games.

Acknowledgements

First of all I would like to thank my wife for the idea of the book, for giving it a name and for suggesting the dedication. I would like also to thank two old friends, Fred Taylor of Oxford and Jim Fisher, for reading the manuscript and making many helpful suggestions; also my two secretaries, Pat Brown and Penny Cloney, for endless hours of spare-time typing.

There have been many kind helpers with photographs, but I would like to single out Tom Scott, the editor of *Golf Illustrated*, Percy Huggins, the editor of *Golf Monthly*, and Keith Mackie, the editor of *Golf World*, for their interest and useful suggestions. The United States Golfing Association has also been most helpful, as have the Canadian Pacific and Canadian National Railways, the Sea Island Company in Georgia, Pinehurst Incorporated in North Carolina, and the tourist organisations of Bermuda, Eire, Northern Ireland, France and Switzerland.

I would like to thank Mr Warner Shelly of Pine Valley for the trouble he has gone to to provide pictures of that famous course. Mr George Adams of Vancouver, too, was very helpful in providing some pictures of Capilano and Oak Bay. I would like also to single out Mr Douglas Converse for his help on some Canadian matters, Mr Ronnie Martin of Buenos Aires, Mr Gordon Lindley and Mr Morris Kantor of São Paulo, and the Golf Clubs Association for their kind help. Finally, a word of thanks to Mr P. R. Beddy of Shell-Mex, Mr Frank Hole of British Transport Hotels and all the secretaries of the golf clubs of St Enodoc, Felixstowe Ferry, Royal Worlington and Newmarket, Burnham and Berrow, Southport and Ainsdale, Royal Lytham and St Annes, and Hayling, as well as many professional photographers who have been exceptionally helpful.

There are many quotations in this book and I would like to make grateful acknowledgement to the many authors and publishers who have

Acknowledgements

allowed me to quote most of them most generously free of charge. These are as follows:

1. *The Golfer's Handbook*, Glasgow, for permission to quote in Chapter 1 (p. 1) Lord Balfour's views on golf, in Chapter 2 (p. 21) the story of Old Willie Park and in Chapter 4 (p. 57) the reference to the funeral of Vardon.

2. Henry Longhurst for permission to quote his general views on British (Chapter 1, p. 1) and Irish (Chapter 6, p. 67) golf courses; and also to quote from 'It Was Good While It Lasted' from Herbert Warren Wind's anthology *The Complete Golfer* in Chapter 2 (p. 26) on the Walker Cup in 1936.

3. Bernard Darwin has been freely drawn upon and I am grateful to Messrs Jonathan Cape Ltd for permission to quote from *The Golf Courses of Great Britain* on St Andrews in Chapter 2 (pp. 12–13), on Muirfield also in Chapter 2 (p. 22) and on Aberdovery in Chapter 5 (p. 65). Bernard Darwin's description of the National Golf Links of America in Chapter 10 (p. 138) is quoted from *Green Memories* by the kind permission of Sir Robin Darwin, C.B.E., Messrs Hodder & Stoughton Ltd, the publishers, and Mr Darwin's literary executors. Mr Darwin's opinions of Prince's and Deal in the booklet issued by Prince's Golf Club are quoted with the club's permission.

    Messrs Chatto & Windus Ltd, the publishers of *Golf Between Two Wars*, Mr Darwin's literary executors and Sir Robin Darwin, C.B.E., have allowed me to quote two passages, the first on the Open Championship of 1921 in Chapter 2 (pp. 16–17) and the second on Bobby Jones in 1903 in Chapter 10 (p. 144).

4. Messrs Laurence Pollinger Ltd, authors' agents, have given permission to use quotations from *The Walter Hagen Story* by Walter Hagen in Chapter 1 (pp. 3, 4 and 7) on his championship days in Britain, and in Chapter 4 (pp. 56–57) on his first meeting with Vardon. The proprietors of this book, which was originally published by the Windmill Press, are Messrs Simon & Schuster Inc.

5. Messrs J. M. Dent & Sons Ltd, the publishers of Robert Browning's *History of Golf*, have allowed the use of a quotation in Chapter 1 (p. 8) from Catherine of Aragon and of a list of historic clubs in Chapter 8 (p. 91); I have also been allowed to quote from the same source in Chapter 10 (p. 130) on the history of golf in Canada.

6. Robert Trent Jones has given permission to quote his views on the Old

Acknowledgements

Course at St Andrews in Chapter 2 (p. 13) from Herbert Warren Wind's anthology *The Complete Golfer*.

7 The quotations in Chapter 2 (p. 13) on St Andrews, in Chapter 4 (pp. 55–56) on the Great Triumvirate and in Chapter 9 (p. 111) on Augusta are taken from *Golf Is My Game* by Robert Tyre Jones, Jr, Copyright (c) 1959, 1960 by Robert Tyre Jones, Jr. Reprinted by permission of the author and Messrs Doubleday & Company, Inc., and also of Messrs Chatto & Windus Ltd, who hold the British rights.

8 Messrs Macmillan & Co. Ltd, the publishers of *The Story of the Royal and Ancient* by J. B. Salmond, have allowed me to quote from it the famous story of Admiral Maitland Dougall in Chaper 2 (pp. 19–20).

9 *The New Yorker* and the author have allowed me to quote from articles by Herbert Warren Wind in the pages of *The New Yorker*:
    (a) on Muirfield in Chapter 2 (pp. 23–24) from its issue of August 13th, 1966;
    (b) two passages on Dornoch in Chapter 3 (pp. 31–32 and p. 34) from its issue of June 6th, 1964.

10 The Honourable Company of Edinburgh Golfers who issued the Open Championship programme of 1966 has permitted a quotation from Sam McKinlay on Muirfield in Chapter 2 (p. 24).

11 Frank Pennink's invaluable *Golfer's Companion* has been freely consulted and its publishers, Messrs Cassell & Co. Ltd, have permitted a quotation on the links at Westward Ho! in Chapter 5 (p. 62) and a reference to Liphook in Chapter 8 (p. 105). In addition, Pat Ward Thomas has allowed me to use in Chapter 6 (p. 68) his quotation on Killarney, also from the *Golfer's Companion*, subject to his slight amendment.

12 Patric Dickinson's delightful *A Round of Golf Courses*, published by Messrs Evans Brothers Ltd, has also been much consulted and Mr Dickinson has permitted quotations in Chapter 2 (p. 12) on St Andrews, in Chapter 5 (p. 62) on Westward Ho! and (p. 65) on Aberdovey, and in Chapter 8 (p. 100) on Walton Heath.

13 The Kirk Session Records of Perth are quoted in Chapter 3 (p. 30) on the evils of Sunday play.

14 Messrs Charles Scribner's Sons, the publishers of Robert Hunter's *The Links*, have allowed me to make a quotation in Chapter 7 (p. 79) on Hoylake.

Acknowledgements

15 The Secretary of the Royal West Norfolk Golf Club has permitted a quotation in Chapter 8 (p. 97) by Tom Scott on Brancaster links taken from the club booklet.

16 A quotation in Chapter 10 (pp. 149–150) is reprinted from *Sports Illustrated*'s 'The Best 18 Golf Holes in America' by Dan Jenkins. Copyright (c) 1966 by Time Inc. and used by permission of the publisher, Delacorte Press, and Time Inc.

17 The Secretary of the Royal Cinque Ports Golf Club has given me permission to quote in Chapter 4 (pp. 48–49) some of the opinions of famous players on the links which hang in the club's bar.

18 Herbert Warren Wind has given us permission to make another quotation from his anthology *The Complete Golfer* in Chapter 10 (p. 137) on the National Golf Links of America.

19 Finally I would like to thank Messrs Allen & Unwin for allowing me to quote freely from *The Curve of Earth's Shoulder* in Chapter 9 (pp. 111–113) on the Masters' Tournament at Augusta.

Bibliography

The Golfer's Handbook 1967, Golf Monthly, Glasgow
Frank Pennink's Golfer's Companion, Cassell & Co., London
A Round of Golf Courses, Patric Dickinson, Evans Brothers, London
Golf in Europe, Saul Galin, Hawthorn
The Links, Robert Hunter, Charles Scribner's Sons, N.Y.
A History of Golf, Robert Browning, J. M. Dent & Sons, London
The Golf Courses of the British Isles, Bernard Darwin, Duckworth
The Golf Courses of Great Britain, Bernard Darwin, Jonathan Cape, London
Green Memories, Bernard Darwin, Hodder & Stoughton, London
Golf Between Two Wars, Bernard Darwin, Chatto & Windus, London
Golf, Bernard Darwin, Burke, London
Life Is Sweet Brother, Bernard Darwin, Collins, London
The World That Fred Made, Bernard Darwin, Chatto & Windus, London
Every Idle Dream, Bernard Darwin, Collins, London
Out of the Rough, Bernard Darwin, Chapman & Hall, London
Playing the Like, Bernard Darwin, Chapman & Hall, London
The Bobby Jones Story, O. B. Keeler and Grantland Rice, Tupper & Love
Golf My Life's Work, J. H. Taylor, Jonathan Cape, London
The Badminton Book of Golf, Horace Hutchinson, Longmans
Fifty Years of Golf, Horace Hutchinson, Country Life
My Game and Yours, Arnold Palmer, Hodder & Stoughton, London
Professional Golfer, Arnold Palmer, Pelham, London
Arnold Palmer, Mark McCormack, Cassell & Co., London
The Walter Hagen Story, Hagen and Margaret Heck, Heinemann, London
The Complete Golfer, Herbert Warren Wind, Heinemann, London

Bibliography

Go Golfing in Britain, L. Claughton Darbyshire, Sunday Times, London
Golf Is My Game, Robert Tyre (Bobby) Jones, Doubleday & Co., N.Y.
Bobby Jones on Golf, Robert Tyre (Bobby) Jones, Doubleday & Co., N.Y.
The Story of the R. and A., J. B. Salmond, Macmillan & Co., London
The Book of the Links, Martin H. F. Sutton, W. H. Smith & Son, London
Scotland's Gift—Golf, C. B. Macdonald, Charles Scribner's Sons, N.Y.
The World of Golf, Charles Price, Cassell & Co., London
Short History of Pine Valley, John Arthur Brown
My Golfing Album, Henry Cotton, Country Life
St Andrews—Home of Golf, J. K. Robertson, Innes
Golf Addict Among the Scots, George Houghton, Country Life
Dai Rees on Golf, Dai Rees, Duckworth
It Was Good While It Lasted, Henry Longhurst, J. M. Dent & Sons, London
You Never Know Till You Get There, Henry Longhurst, J. M. Dent & Sons, London
Only on Sundays, Henry Longhurst, Cassell & Co., London
Sheridan of Sunningdale, James Sheridan, Country Life
Golfing America, E. A. Hamilton and C. Preston, Doubleday & Co., N.Y.
The Best 18 Golf Holes in America, Dan Jenkins, Sports Illustrated, Delacorte Press, N.Y.
The Book of Golf, Louis T. Stanley, Max Parrish, London
Golf Architecture in America, George C. Thomas Jr, The Times-Mirror Press, Los Angeles
The Curve of Earth's Shoulder, Peter and Consuelo Allen, George Allen & Unwin, London